SOCIAL COGNITION
AND
CONSUMER BEHAVIOR

M. Joseph Sirgy

PRAEGER SPECIAL STUDIES • PRAEGER SCIENTIFIC

Library of Congress Cataloging in Publication Data

Sirgy, M. Joseph.
   Social cognition and consumer behavior.

   Bibliography: p.
   Includes index.
   1. Consumers 2. Social perception. 3. Cognition.
4. Marketing research. I. Title.
HF5415.3.S57 1983   658.8'342   82-24534
ISBN 0-03-062462-2

Published in 1983 by Praeger Publishers
CBS Educational and Professional Publishing
a Division of CBS Inc.
521 Fifth Avenue, New York, New York 10175, USA

© 1983 by Praeger Publishers

3456789 052 987654321

Printed in the United States of America
on acid-free paper

I dedicate this book to world peace and prosperity and
to the enhancement of humanity through science and technology.

Preface

This book contains an integrated theory of social cognition. It is an "integrated theory" because it serves as a theoretical perspective that unifies the many micro social cognition theories into an integrated whole. I realize that the term "theory" and especially "integrated theory" is quite "loaded." Not too many of us psychologists are in the business of developing theories. When we develop a theory, we tend to be quite cynical at the beginning. We automatically erect our critical defenses, ready to "shoot down" the so-called theory.

I have often heard the statement "It's much easier to criticize a theory than to develop one." Not only have I often heard this statement, I admit having uttered it many times over. I fully realize that many psychologists and social scientists will expose themselves to the theory developed in this book quite reluctantly and possibly use their sophisticated "schemas" to counterargue every idea, every sentence, and possibly every word.

I have searched my soul many times over, asking whether the ideas developed in this book constitute a theory, or a theoretical framework, or an approach or orientation, or only a model, or anything at all. I have to say after a great deal of thought that I believe that I have developed a theory in this book. It is a theory because its propositions are internally consistent. It is a theory because it goes beyond describing psychological relationships—it explains these relationships. It is a theory because it is parsimonious in its constructs, extensive in explanation, and empirically testable. Of course, the final say as to whether it is theory rests with the philosophers of science. And whether the theory is valid is another question that is yet to be answered. In the consumer-behavior application part of the book, I present some evidence supporting some of the models derived from the proposed theory. However, much more testing is needed, and it is hoped that those researchers who decide that this is a viable theory will contribute to the testing of the theory's propositions and models.

The theory presented here serves to integrate motivational phenomena with information processing principles. This is done within a social cognition perspective. Furthermore, a serious attempt is made to relate the proposed integrated theory to various psychological theories, addressing motivation, emotion, perception, learning, belief change, and attitude, among others.

This theory is the result of at least seven years of fruitful and laborious thought. Ever since I began graduate school in psychology, I was constantly bewildered by the fragmentation and overspecialization of our discipline. Personality psychologists, social psychologists, cognitive psychologists, developmental psychologists, psychophysicists, not to mention all the other applied psychologists, have been into their own "niche" quite removed from macro or general psychology. This situation has caused much frustration for people like me who are more interested in the macro picture and who try to fit the micro elements under the overall macro umbrella. Thus, I have tried to relate the micro theories to one another using a systems approach or some kind of "gestalt." The result, I believe, is the synergistic view presented in this book.

Who should read this book? This book is written for two primary audiences: consumer psychologists and social/personality psychologists. However, this is not to say that other professionals would not be interested in the ideas presented in this book. On the contrary, I see this book reaching out to general psychologists, market researchers, economic psychologists, cognitive psychologists, communication specialists, general systems theorists, artificial intelligence specialists, and other applied behavioral researchers. The ideas presented here are directly and indirectly relevant to all these professionals.

Can this book be used as a textbook? This book is written to all audiences who have a basic and fundamental understanding of psychological theory and especially of social psychological theory. Without this prerequisite background, the reader would have a hard time understanding, much less appreciating, the theory. Consequently, the use of this book in undergraduate psychology and/or marketing courses may be inappropriate. However, the adoption of this book in graduate level psychology and/or marketing courses (especially in a graduate course in consumer behavior) is highly encouraged. It becomes even more effective at the doctoral level.

In a consumer behavior graduate course, this book can be viewed as a competing theory to Bettman's theory on information processing applied to consumer choice. His book provides an integrated information processing theory whereas this book introduces an integrated social cognition theory, both applied to consumer behavior. These two books can be used conjunctively to present two major psychological approaches to understanding consumer-behavior phenomena.

Acknowledgments

I would like to express my special thanks to a number of people who helped me directly and indirectly in writing this book. Credit is first due to those who inspired me and provoked my thoughts toward integration, gestalt, and synergism. These are the general system theorists such as, Von Bertalanffy, Boulding, Simon, and Miller, to name a few. I was influenced by my interaction with my mentors, Seymour Epstein, Ervin Staub, and James Averill at the University of Massachusetts, who have indirectly provoked my thinking in the underlying cognitive dynamics of motivation and emotion. My thanks also extend to all the psychologists and social scientists who have interacted with me in one way or another and stimulated my thoughts.

I thank all my students who have labored with me in conducting research related to this theory. These include Lisa Kassem, Kristin Wallace, Anne Gilbert, and Steve Labassi. My special thanks goes to Lisa Kassem who helped me see things in a different light.

For all those who labored typing and retyping one version or another of this book, I extend my gratitude. Above all my special thanks goes to my wife Karen and my daughter Melissa who in many ways gave me the space, freedom, and emotional support to undertake this project. Karen also helped with many of the clerical aspects of the book. Without her help I would have been unable to meet the publisher's deadline. I owe her additional thanks.

Contents

Chapter   Page

LIST OF TABLES AND FIGURES

TABLES

FIGURES

Introduction

Consumer behavior has been addressed from a number of theoretical perspectives. For example, Howard and Sheth (1969) have used learning theory to explain, describe, and predict consumer-behavior phenomena, whereas cognitive theory was used by Markin (1974) and Bettman (1979).

In the last decade social psychologists have developed many theories that explain social behavior using cognitive constructs. This cognitive orientation in social psychology has been coined social cognition. Social cognition in social psychology is now rapidly maturing. It has taken a form of a research paradigm or a macro theory in psychological investigation (Carroll and Payne 1976).

In Part 1 at least three tasks will be accomplished. First, social cognition in psychology will be introduced to the reader. Second, consumer behavior as a social science will be defined using a developmental or growth model, and an organizational schema will be introduced to identify and classify traditional concepts in consumer behavior. And third, an attempt will be made to show how social cognition theory is used within the scope of the consumer-behavior discipline.

In Part 2 the integrated social cognition theory will be introduced and its proposition delineated. The various structures and processes of social cognition will be elaborated. The processes of perception, evaluation, and behavior will be explained in terms of the activation and operation of the needs for cognitive enhancement, consistency, and differentiation. These processes involve perceptual and evaluative congruity, affect, decision making, and labeling.

Part 3 will provide a detailed treatment of the various components of the consumer-decision cycle and treat them in terms of the theoretical propositions introduced by the integrated social cognition theory. Furthermore, traditional consumer-behavior theories (mostly borrowed from the psychological literature) will be reinterpreted in light of the proposed theory.

PART I
Social Cognition
And
Consumer Behavior

CHAPTER 1
Social Cognition In Psychology

The essence of the study of social cognition involves the study of inferences, decisions, responses, and/or behaviors of individuals in a social context. Social cognition as an emerging discipline in psychology is cognitive psychology outside the laboratory, figuratively speaking. But that is not to say that social cognition borrows heavily from cognitive psychology as most applied disciplines do. On the contrary, social cognition has its history and roots in social psychology. It has developed from a number of theories in social psychology that had one common element—a cognitive orientation. These social psychological theories that are construed to be responsible for the development of social cognition as a scientific paradigm in psychology are presented briefly in the following sections.

EXPECTANCY-VALUE THEORY

Many social scientists have been implicitly and explicitly concerned with the prediction of behavior or disposition to engage in behavior (overt behavior). Various models have been developed that predict behavior based on the cognitive components of expectancies and values. This trend of expectancy-value models has been initiated by Tolman's (1932) work. Tolman introduced the notion that behavior is a function of the demands of the organism, the values or goals available in the environment, and the expectancy of goal attainment.

During the last several decades there have been a considerable number of theorists who have worked on expanding the logic

of expectancy-value theory. In all of this work the basic position
has been to argue that behavior is a function of the expectancy
of value attainment and the actual degree of value or incentive
that is available. Table 1.1 shows a summary of expectancy-
value models.

SOCIAL COMPARISON THEORY

Social comparison theory (Festinger 1966) and research
(Latane' 1966) have been concerned with the tendency for
individuals to infer information about themselves by comparing
themselves with others. Other research and theory, such as
comparison level theory (Thibaut and Kelley 1959), assimilation-
contrast theory (Sherif and Hovland 1961), and reference scale
formulations (Upshaw 1969), all have a common element—that of
comparing a perception (self or other) with a referent or comparative set.

ATTRIBUTION THEORY

Attribution theory and research have been concerned with
how actors make attributions about the causes of their behavior
(self-perception) and others' behaviors (person perception).
Research on attribution phenomena has taken several forms.
Heider's (1958) work in "naive psychology" has been the primary
force in attribution research. This work has been followed by
Bem's (1967, 1972) self-perception theory, Jones and Davis'
(1965) correspondent inference theory, Kelley's (1967, 1973)
attribution theory, Weiner's et al. (1972) cognitive theory of
achievement motivation, and more recently Nisbett and Ross'
(1981) misattribution theory. The element that ties these theories
together is the umbrella of attribution theory that explains social
inference in terms of cognitive rules or implications.

IMPLICIT PERSONALITY THEORY

This theory refers to the tendency of an actor to infer
other personality traits of an observer given one or more traits
(Bruner and Taguiri 1954). It is a set of expectations about
which personality traits are mutually associated in the perceiver's
mind. It is included under umbrella of social cognition because
of its cognitive orientation in modelling the social inference

TABLE 1.1 Summary Table of Expectancy-Value Theories

Theorist	Major Theoretical Constructs					Response
Tolman (1932)	Expectation of achieving desired outcome	×	Demand Level for given outcome	×	Level of given outcome	→ Performance vector
Lewin et al. (1944)	Subjective probability of achieving desired outcome	×	Value of desired outcome			→ Force
Rotter (1954)	Expectancy of achieving desired reinforcement	×	Value of reinforcement			→ Behavior potential
Edwards (1954)	Subjective probability of achieving desired outcome	×	Utility of desired outcome			→ Behavior choice
Rosenberg (1956)	Degree of instrumentality for goal or value attainment	×	Degree of satisfaction anticipated as a result of value attainment			→ Attitude
Dulany (1967)	{ Hypothesis of the distribution of reinforcement	×	Subjective value of reinforcer } + { Behavioral hypothesis	×	Motivation to comply }	→ Behavioral intention
Fishbein (1963)	Subjective probability that a specific object is related to a specific attribute	×	Evaluation of that attribute			→ Attitude
Fishbein (1967)	{ Belief that a specific behavior leads to specific outcome	×	Evaluation of that outcome } + { Belief that he should or should not perform that behavior	×	Motivation to comply with reference group }	→ Behavior intention

process and determining its causal conditions. For example, Cantor and Mischell (1979) suggested that our impressions of others can be organized into structured hierarchies or what are specifically called prototypes—central, clear exemplars of kinds of persons. These hierarchically organized prototypes, like other cognitive schemata, direct the perceivers' use of social information.

INFORMATION INTEGRATION THEORY

The work done in this area is primarily due to Norman Anderson and his associates (Anderson 1965, 1968, 1974; Anderson and Barrios 1961; Kaplan 1975; Kaplan and Anderson 1973). This theory describes how cognitive relations might be integrated into an overall impression. The theory specifically addresses the precise cognitive algebra involved in social inference.

CATEGORIZATION THEORY

This theory deals with concept formation, pattern recognition, stimulus identification, and stereotyping processes. These processes all involve the categorization of the perceived person or object using an internally evoked cognitive schema—a relatively specific cognitive structure, modifiable by experience, that acts as a pattern or template for perceptual experience. Some of the early work in this area has been credited to Bruner and his associates (Bruner 1957; Bruner and Goodman 1947; Bruner and Postman 1948; Bruner, Shapiro, and Taguiri 1958; Bruner and Taguiri 1954). The more recent work in this area has been done by Taylor and her associates (Taylor et al. 1978; Langer et al. 1972; Hamilton, 1979).

CONSISTENCY THEORY

Like information integration theory, this theory is concerned with cognitive interaction. This theory argues that significant discrepancies between interacting cognitions may create an imbalanced state that motivates the individual to act to resolve this "dissonance." At least four micro theories have been developed under the umbrella of consistency theory. These are Heider's (1946) balance theory, Osgood and Tannenbaum's (1955) congruity theory, Festinger's (1957) cognitive dissonance theory, and Rokeach's (1972) principle of belief congruence.

BELIEF CENTRALITY THEORY

This theory describes beliefs according to their degree of interrelatedness with other beliefs and addresses their implications on cognitive processes and social behavior. The most salient work in this area was done by Rokeach (1960, 1972). Epstein's (1973) theory of self-theory addressed the importance of the central-peripheral belief dimension in the maintenance of self-esteem, balance between pleasure and pain, and assimilating the data of reality. Jourard's (1964, 1971) theory of self-disclosure talked about the depth and breadth of information as it is related to the self.

SUMMARY

From the preceding discussion of these social psychological theories, the argument is made that these theories are responsible for the creation of social cognition as a macro psychological theory, a psychological paradigm, a scientific approach or mode of thinking, and so on. In essence social cognition can be described as a psychological discipline that concerns itself with the study of how individuals categorize social stimuli, make inferences about themselves and the objects and persons around them, and respond to their social environment.

CHAPTER 2
A Developmental Analysis Of The Consumer-Behavior Discipline

Seven different developmental levels of the consumer-behavior discipline are identified. These levels reflect the maturation process of the discipline.

LEVEL 1

When consumer behavior as a scientific discipline was originally founded, it was closely tied to the marketing concept.* Consumer behavior as studied at its birth stage can therefore be defined as the scientific study of the psychological structural and process dynamics, of individuals who consume an economic good, which is exchanged by a business organization for a profit, in one or more settings and in one or more time periods, for the purpose of satisfying consumers at a maximal profit.

---

*This section is mostly borrowed from Sirgy (1981, 1982). The marketing concept refers to the development and distribution of products and services that satisfy consumer wants and needs. The marketing concept has also been referred to as the marketing orientation. This type of business orientation is to be contrasted with the past production and sales orientations. The production orientation refers to the business practice that emphasizes product engineering or product innovation with little regard to finding out whether there is a consumer demand for those innovations. The sales orientation is not very different from the

Consumer behavior as a "scientific discipline" adheres to scientific principles and conduct. A consumer behaviorist, as any other scientist, develops and tests hypotheses about the nature of the consumption world. This is usually accomplished through the process of theorization, observation, testing, replication, cumulation, and closure. This effort goes toward the building of consumer-behavior theories that attempt to explain, describe, model, predict, and control consumer behavior.

The "psychological structural and process dynamics" inherent in the definition of Level I consumer behavior refers to those mediating psychological structures and processes involved in perceiving, interpreting, and acting upon product-related stimuli. Mediating structures may be exemplified by personality factors, self-concept factors, life-style factors, role factors, attitude factors, and so on. Mediating processes may include perception, motivation, emotion, learning, decision making, and attitude change. These phenomena fall under the auspices of psychology and social psychology domains. In other words the study of consumer behavior is partly the study of psychology and social psychology.

"Consume an economic good which is exchanged by a business organization for a profit" refers to the monetary transaction between the consumer and the business organization selling the product or rendering the service. The study of these monetary transactions incorporates the field of economics and therefore is partly construed as the study of economics.

"One or more settings and in one or more time periods" refers to either micro or macro approaches to the study of consumer settings and consumption time elements. In the micro sense the study of human behavior in different social settings falls within the domain of social psychology. In the macro sense we can talk about cultural or societal settings. Differences in macro settings fall in the realm of cultural sociology. Similarly, the study of time on human behavior is usually treated by social

---

production orientation with the minor exception that the emphasis is placed on selling what is manufactured irrespective of consumer demand. The marketing orientation starts with the consumer. Consumer needs and wants are studied and accordingly products are developed and distributed to meet consumer demand. More recently, the marketing orientation is being replaced with the societal marketing orientation in which the emphasis is not only placed within the consumer but also with the society at large (Kotler 1980).

psychology at the micro level and in anthropology at the macro level. Consequently, based on this perspective the study of consumer behavior is construed as partly the study of social psychology, social anthropology, and cultural sociology.

"For the purpose of satisfying consumers at a maximal profit" makes explicit that the study of consumer behavior has a primary function of maximizing business profits in exchange for consumer satisfaction.

The study of maximizing profits is linked not only with economics, but also with management science. Therefore, one can argue that management science has a role in the study of consumer behavior, and conversely, consumer behavior can be partly construed as the study of management science.

Based on this definition of consumer behavior, it can be seen that the study of consumer behavior was born as a multi-disciplinary scientific discipline having certain loyalties to psychology, social psychology, sociology, economics, anthropology, and management science.

LEVEL II

However, following the consumerism movement, consumer behavior diverted its attention to the study of public policy issues related to consumer protection and consumer satisfaction/dissatisfaction. This historical development provided an opportunity for consumer behavior to grow to the next developmental level (Level II).

At the second level of the maturation process, consumer behavior is therefore defined as the scientific study of the psychological structural and process dynamics, of individuals who consume an economic good, which is exchanged by a business organization for a profit, in one or more settings and in one or more time periods, for the purpose of satisfying consumers at a maximal profit and <u>protecting and educating consumers in the marketplace</u>.

At this developmental level, the goal of consumer-behavior studies has become twofold: one goal was (is) directed to maximizing business profits for the business organization in exchange for consumer satisfaction, and the second goal was (is) directed to protecting and educating consumers in the marketplace to offset business abuses inflicted on the mass consumers. This level of analysis of the study of consumer behavior has infiltrated the public policy domain and as such contributes to its knowledge bank (for example, Capon and Lutz 1979).

In many ways current consumer-behavior studies are "fixated" in the second level of the developmental continuum.

LEVEL III

This level of consumer-behavior study corresponds to the broadening of marketing activity to the nonprofit and public sectors. Consumer-behavior studies are becoming more and more directed by nonprofit organizations such as universities, hospitals, and other nonprofit services. Therefore, consumer behavior is defined at the third level of the developmental process as the scientific study of the psychological structural and process dynamics, of individuals who consume an economic good, which is exchanged by a profit or nonprofit organization, in one or more time periods and in one or more settings, for the purpose of satisfying consumers at a maximal profit, protecting and educating consumers in the marketplace, and satisfying consumers at a minimal cost to them.

This definition of consumer behavior incorporates nonprofit organizations with the additional goal of satisfying consumers at a minimal cost to them.

At this level consumer behavior as a scientific discipline contributes knowledge to those disciplines involved in nonprofit organizations such as educational administration, health administration, and so on (Kotler 1975).

LEVEL IV

However, many nonprofit organizations render goods and services that do not have precisely a monetary value, namely noneconomic goods. These may be exemplified in terms of religious services, political candidates, social ideas, and so on. Consumer-behavior studies can be (and are) conducted to study voting behavior, litter control, energy conservation, and so forth. These studies involve noneconomic goods and place consumer behavior at a higher level of the maturation cycle.

Based on this perspective, consumer behavior is defined as the scientific study of the psychological structural and process dynamics, of individuals who consume an economic or noneconomic good, which is exchanged by a profit or nonprofit organization, in one or more settings and in one or more time periods, for the purpose of satisfying consumers at a maximal profit, protecting and educating consumers in the marketplace, satisfying consumers at a minimal cost to them, and eliciting a social response.

This definition of consumer behavior is broadened to incorporate noneconomic goods such as social values for the purpose of eliciting a social response. In this case consumer behavior is said to study those social phenomena which concern political science, public administration, and community psychology, among others (for example, Cooper, Kehoe, and Murphy 1978; Lazer and Kelley 1973).

LEVEL V

But why do consumer behaviorists have to restrict themselves to the psychological world? Can they include the physical and biological structural and process dynamics of the individual consumer?

The key point here is that consumer behaviorists are no more restricting themselves to investigating those psychological structural and process dynamics of the target consumer but also are studying related physical and biological structures and processes. For example, consumer behaviorists are beginning to seriously look into left-right brain hemispheric functions (for example, Krugman 1977). They are in the process of developing sophisticated physiological measures for the specific purpose of investigating consumer response variables (for example, Watson and Gatchel 1979).

Therefore, at this level consumer behavior can be defined as the scientific study of the <u>psychological, physical, and/or biological structural and process dynamics</u>, of individuals who consume an economic or noneconomic good, which is exchanged by a profit or nonprofit organization, in one or more settings and in one or more time periods, for the purpose of satisfying consumers at a maximal profit, protecting and educating consumers in the marketplace, satisfying consumers at a minimal cost to them, and eliciting a social response.

This definition incorporates the study of physical and biological structural and process dynamics of the individual consumer. From this perspective consumer behavior overlaps with the natural sciences of biology, physics, chemistry, and so on and accordingly can contribute to these natural science disciplines in knowledge production and utilization.

LEVEL VI

The next level of the maturation of the consumer-behavior discipline is the release of the restriction placed on organizational marketing. Can marketing activity be conducted with or without an organization? Can two persons engage in marketing? Can two societies engage in marketing? Can we talk about marketing between or among social entities? (Bagozzi 1975).

It is argued here that economic or noneconomic goods can be exchanged by a social entity (that is, person, group, organization, or society) with another social entity. However, one needs to maintain the distinction between the marketing agent and the consumer, since the study of consumer behavior focuses on the recipient or consumer and not on the marketing agent or both.

Keeping this in mind, consumer behavior can be construed then as the scientific study of psychological, physical, and/or biological structural and process dynamics, of a social entity, which consumes an economic or noneconomic good, exchanged by another social entity, in one or more settings and in one or more time periods, for the purpose of accomplishing a specified goal.

Note that at this level the precise goals cannot be easily specified unless one specifies the specific level of analysis.

Here the study of consumer behavior is not restricted to the individual consumer but is allowed to investigate behavioral phenomena traditionally restricted to the fields of organizational buying behavior (for example, Johnson 1981), social psychology of family dynamics (for example, Davis 1976), group dynamics (for example, Moschis 1981), international marketing (for example, Cavusgil and Nevin 1981), quality of life (for example, Sirgy, Samli, and Meadow 1982).

LEVEL VII

At a much higher level we can talk about any kind of physical, biological, or social system exchanging matter, energy, and/or information with other physical, biological, or social systems. This would involve the science of general systems theory and research (Miller 1978; Berrien 1968; Kuhn 1975; von Bertalanffy 1968; Sutherland 1973; Boulding 1981; Laszlo 1972) that has been touched upon in the marketing and consumer-behavior disciplines (Samli and Sirgy 1982; Hunt, Muncy, and Ray 1981).

Consumer behavior is therefore at this level of maturity defined as the scientific study of a system's structural and process dynamics which exchanges values with another system for the purpose of accomplishing some specified goal.

TABLE 2.1 Developmental Levels in Consumer–Behavior Research

Level	Structures and Processes	Consumer	Product	Marketing Agent	Goal(s)
I.	Psychological	Individuals	Economic good	Profit organization	Satisfy consumers at a maximal profit
II.	Psychological	Individuals	Economic good	Profit organization	And/or protect and educate consumers
III.	Psychological	Individuals	Economic good	Profit or nonprofit organization	And/or satisfy consumers at a minimal cost to them
IV.	Psychological	Individuals	Economic or noneconomic good	Profit or nonprofit organization	And/or elicit a social response
V.	Psychological, physical, or biological	Individuals	Economic or noneconomic good	Profit or nonprofit organization	Any of the above goals
VI.	Psychological, physical, or biological	Social entity	Economic or noneconomic good	Social entity	Some specified goal
VII.	Psychological, physical, or biological	System	Value or utility	System	Some specified goal

14

SUMMARY

Consumer behavior is going through a developmental process. At least seven levels have been identified. In its infancy stage (Level I), the study of consumer behavior is referred to as the scientific study of psychological structural and process dynamics of individuals who consume an economic good exchanged by a business organization for the purpose of satisfying consumers at a maximal profit. Consumer behavior in Level II has grown to a stage in which its purpose is directed to both business and consumers for the purpose of satisfying consumers at a maximal profit and protecting and educating consumers in the marketplace. Level III extends consumer behavior to the nonprofit sector through which a nonprofit organization attempts to satisfy consumers at a minimal cost to them. Level IV takes consumer behavior into the sector of noneconomic goods. These profit or nonprofit organizations may attempt to elicit a social response from their public. Level V extends the study of consumer behavior into those physical and biological structures and processes of the individual consumer. This type of analysis goes beyond the traditional psychological study of consumer behavior. Level VI generalizes the study of consumer behavior across different social entities (that is, individuals, groups, organizations, and societies). Finally, Level VII deals with physical, biological, or social systems exchanging matter, energy, and/or information with other systems. Consumer behavior, therefore, is defined as the study of the physical, biological, and/or psychological structures and processes of a system that consumes value or utility exchanged by another system for the purpose of accomplishing some specified goal.

CHAPTER 3
A Classification Schema For
Consumer-Behavior Research Topics

Most consumer-behavior textbooks (Engel, Blackwell, and
Kollat 1978; Hawkins, Coney, Best 1980; Block and Roering 1979;
Loudon and Della Bitta 1978) organize consumer-behavior topics
using a conceptual schema that treats psychological and sociological influences on consumer-decision processes. Those psychological influences include information processing, learning,
perception, motivation, personality, attitudes, and life-style
factors. Those sociological influences usually include culture,
subculture, social class, group dynamics, socialization, reference
groups, and family influences. Consumer-decision processes
usually refer to problem recognition, information search, alternative evaluation, and choice and outcome evaluation.

There are many problems associated with this classification
schema of consumer-behavior topics.

First, consumer-behavior topics such as consumer public
policy, consumer education, consumer leisure, consumer quality
of life, diffusion of innovation, brand loyalty, store loyalty,
opinion leadership, communication, and market segmentation,
are all treated as special topics that do not seem to fit the overall conceptual framework.

Second, although internal (psychological) and external
(sociological) influences are conceptually positioned as structural
or determinant factors affecting consumer-decision processes,
they are never treated as such.* Most of the consumer-behavior

---

*Internal (psychological) factors such as self-concept
factors, personality factors, and life-style factors and external

books treat some of those factors as processes worthwhile of study independent of the consumer-decision cycle. For example perception is treated from a process orientation—how do consumers perceive products and services, how and under what circumstances do consumers perceive risk in the purchase of products and services, what are the functional and symbolic image characteristics that consumers perceive in various products and services, and so on. This general presentation of perception in consumer-behavior textbooks is that of an independent consumer process worthy of studying. But how consumer perception, as an internal psychological factor, influences consumer-decision processes (for example, problem recognition and information search) is not treated in any way or form. So how can perception be an internal psychological factor that influences consumer-decision processes according to the traditional classification schema of consumer-behavior topics? Similar problems exist with topics such as motivation, personality, learning, information processing, family decision making, and so on. These are not topics of internal and external influences. These, as they are treated in most consumer-behavior textbooks, are also consumer-decision processes varying across process and unit levels. Dimensions will be elaborated in a following section. Although some internal/external influences are treated correctly and properly as determinants of consumer-behavior or consumer-decision processes (for example, social class, subcultural influences, personality factors, self-concept factors, life-style factors, and so on), others should also be construed as independent consumer processes and not determinants of other processes. These include motivation, attitude formation and change, perception, learning, and family decision making, among others.

Third, as previously pointed out, learning, perception, attitude change, information processing, motivation, personality dynamics, socialization, problem recognition, information search, alternative evaluation, outcome evaluation, brand loyalty behavior, diffusion of innovation, and consumption over extended

---

(sociological) factors such as social class, subcultural influences, and family influences are allegedly treated as determinants of consumer decision making, and rightly so. It makes perfect sense that a consumer behaviorist would be interested in these phenomena only as they are related to consumption processes and not for the sake of studying these phenomena per se.

periods of time, are all consumer-decision processes. What makes one process different from another? The traditional classification system treats some as the only legitimate consumer-decision processes, while all others are considered as influences, and still others as special topics. It is evident from the mere inspection of these topics that what is needed is a level-of-analysis dimension classifying some consumer processes at the micro level (for example, sensation and perception, physiological arousal), some processes at the micro/macro level (for example, problem recognition, information search, alternative evaluation, and outcome evaluation), and still other processes at a macro level (for example, repeat purchase behavior, diffusion of innovation).

Fourth, if family decision making is treated as a consumer-decision process, then how would it be distinguished from individual decision making? Can consumer behaviorists address organizational decision making?* Is organizational decision making a legitimate consumer-behavior topic? A number of consumer behaviorists and consumer-behavior textbook writers (for example, Zaltman and Wallendorf 1979) argue for the inclusion of organizational buying behavior as a legitimate consumer-behavior research and education topic. Also, the preceding developmental analysis of the consumer-behavior discipline has shown that there is a movement in the direction of incorporating industrial buying with the study of consumer behavior.

How about societal decision making regarding consumption issues—issues of import decisions?† Why should this topic not be included in the study of consumer behavior. An argument regarding the inclusion of importing decision making at the societal level has already been made earlier.

---

*Organizational decision making, in a consumer-behavior context, refers to those psychological process dynamics occurring within the group of people who are responsible for purchasing of raw material, energy resources, and other supplies needed by the organization.

†Societal decision making, in the context of the study of consumer behavior, refers to those process psychological and sociological dynamics involved with those individuals or organizations responsible for making decisions regarding imports of matter-energy and/or information from trading countries in exchange of other forms of matter-energy and/or information.

These decision processes can be classified in the consumer-behavior discipline using a unit-of-analysis dimension varying from individual consumer decision making, family decision making, organizational decision making, to societal decision making.

Finally, what separates consumer-behavior topics such as consumer information search or diffusion of innovation from consumer education, market segmentation, and public policy issues? Of course, the former topics are descriptive/behavioral while the latter topics are prescriptive/normative.* Such a behavioral-normative dimension is needed to further classify consumer-behavior topics to help educators, researchers, and practitioners make sense of these topics as well as to provide a theoretical framework to evaluate and conduct consumer research.

A SYSTEM'S CLASSIFICATION SCHEMA

Today more than ever, scientists tend to think in terms of systems, and our characteristic models and simulations deal with a system or a component of one (McLeod 1974). From systems theory many concepts that are generalizable across scientific disciplines were learned. Some of the most popular systems constructs include the concepts of space, time, matter and energy, information, systems, subsystems, suprasystems, open systems, closed systems, conceptual systems, living and nonliving systems, structures, processes, types, levels, echelons, inputs, throughputs, outputs, and so on (Van Gigch 1974). From the vast repertoire of systems nomenclature, a selected number of systems constructs are borrowed in an attempt to develop a classification system for consumer-behavior topics. These are:

---

*Descriptive/behavioral phenomena refer to the value-free characterization and/or explanation of a process and/or structure involved with some entity, physical, biological, or social. Prescriptive/normative phenomena, on the other hand, refer to the value-laden characterization of a process and/or structure involved with a physical, biological, or social entity. It is value laden in the sense that it prescribes an optimal state of affairs, be it a process and/or structure. It points in the direction of what should be done, in contrast to what is out there and how it can be described and explained.

•unit levels
•process levels
•processes versus structures
•normativeness versus descriptiveness

In addition to these systems constructs, three marketing-related dimensions are employed to further classify consumer-behavior research areas. These are:

•marketing mix elements
•product type
•product level

Each of these dimensions is treated in some depth in the following sections.

Consumer Unit Levels

The universe contains a hierarchy of systems. Atoms are composed of particles; molecules, of atoms; crystals and organelles, of molecules; cells are composed of atoms, molecules, and multimolecular organelles; organs are composed of cells aggregated into tissues; organisms, of organs; groups, of organisms; organizations, of groups; societies, of organizations, groups, and individuals, and so forth (Miller 1978).

Consumer behaviorists are concerned with different unit levels varying from the individual, the family, the organization, and the society. Each of those units treated at different levels is construed to be a consumption unit that engages in a consumption-related activity.

Consumer behaviorists study individual decision making, family decision making, and organizational decision making, all with respect to buying products. Also, societal consumption decision processes, although not frequently studied as a consumer-behavior topic, may eventually be treated in the consumer-behavior discipline (Sirgy 1981a, 1982a).

Consumer Process Levels

Consumer-behavior phenomena are studied using different process frames. At the individual unit level, consumer-decision processes vary from a micro level to a macro level.

At the micro process level, psychophysiological consumer responses are usually examined. These may include topics such as product sensory characteristics, sensory stimulation of an advertising copy, right-left brain hemispherical roles in communications, and so on (Krugman 1977).

At the micro/macro level, individual consumer-decision processes are typified by those processes presented by the hierarchy-of-effects model (Lavidge and Steiner 1961). These are broadly classified into cognitive (perceptual), affective (evaluative), and conative (behavioral).

For example, with respect to a product category, consumer responses may be that of brand perception, brand preference, and brand choice. These consumer processes follow a cognitive, affective, and behavioral sequence.

With respect to price, consumer responses may take on a similar variation. For instance we usually investigate price perception, price preference, and price acceptance. These follow the triadic cognitive, affective, and behavioral sequence of attitude formation and change.

Furthermore, a macro level involves those individual consumer processes occurring across a larger time frame. These may include brand choice patterns over time (Jacoby and Kyner 1973), store choice patterns (Samli and Sirgy 1981), and diffusion of innovation (Rogers 1978). Historical analysis of economic behavior such as savings and spendings, product consumption, and use of special services are other examples of a macro process type of phenomenon.

Consumer Processes Versus Structures

General system theorists usually use the term process to mean change over time of matter-energy or information in a system (Miller 1978). In consumer behavior consumer-decision processes vary depending on the unit and process level. At the individual unit level and micro/macro process level, consumer-behavior process variables involve psychological processes classified along the cognitive-affective-conative dimension (Lavidge and Steiner 1961). At the family unit level and micro process level, consumer behaviorists examine such processes as syncratic family decision making, autonomous family decision making, husband-dominated family decision making, and wife-dominated family decision making (Davis 1976; Brown 1979).

General system theorists also concede that structure usually means generalized patterning. They recognize that patterning among conceptual or temporal variables is comparable to patterning among spatial variables. This term is used to mean stability or generalized patterning among any set of variables.

Consumer behaviorists study consumer structures of different types. The most accepted structural categories used in consumer behavior involve: life-style structures, personality structures, self-concept structures, demographic structures, sociocultural structures, geographic structures, product-related structures, and marketing effort structures. In each of these categories, those structural variables are usually related to process variables with the assumption that one or more structural variables or antecedent factors are affecting, influencing, or determining those consumer processes. For example classifying consumers as being of high or low socioeconomic status involves a sociocultural patterning. This structural variable in turn may be related to product preference as a process variable to examine the effects of socioeconomic status on search behavior. However, the attention devoted to the study of consumer structures is not independent of the study of consumer processes. We study consumer structures to examine structural effects on consumer processes. These consumer structures remain static or constant at every unit and process level and can be applied in direct relation to any consumer process.

Therefore, any given consumer study usually focuses on either a process variable (s) or a structural variable (s) but usually not on both. For example self-concept segmentation usually involves segmenting the market based on the consumer's self-concept. The focus of this consumer-behavior study, of course, is a structural one. But although there is a structural focus, we have to acknowledge that this study would be utterly meaningless without relating it to some process variable such as product preference, product usage, and so on. In other words we can perform a self-concept segmentation by breaking the market into several segments, each having a unique and identifiable self-concept profile along a preference dimension. That is, each one of these unique segments (identified by a special self-concept profile) may have similar or different preference for that product.

On the other hand, if preference segmentation is performed, the focus then is transformed to a process variable. Self-concept can be used also as a structural variable in the same context. The difference between this process orientation and the structural orientation involving self-concept segmentation is an important one. In the latter case (preference segmentation) the market is divided into several segments, each having a unique and identifiable preference profile along a self-concept dimension(s). That is, each segment identified as a high-preference segment, moderate-preference segment, or a low-preference segment can have similar or different self-concept scores on the designated self-concept dimensions.

Normativeness versus Descriptiveness

The distinction between normative/prescriptive and behavioral/descriptive consumer-behavior topics is essential since consumer-behavior research has infiltrated the public policy domain. One has to realize that normative consumer-behavior phenomena can be classified within the three-dimensional schema discussed previously (process levels × unit levels × process vs. structure). For example in the public policy domain, decision models have been formulated to identify consumer optimal decision making (normative). Optimal decision making models may fall under the individual unit level and micro/macro level category, with the exception that they are classified under the normative rather than descriptive dimension.

Marketing Mix Elements

As stated previously, the study of consumer behavior was founded as a research discipline under the auspices of marketing, and in many ways it remains loyal to its parent discipline. The objective of consumer-behavior study usually focuses on examining the relationships between those marketing mix variables (controllable marketing effort variables) and consumer/market response variables. Marketing mix variables involve price, promotion, product, and place decisions. Consumer-response variables are usually related to the corresponding marketing mix variables. For example consumer-behavior research delves heavily into investigating those consumer processes related to product decisions (a market mix variable). These processes may include product image, product need recognition, brand preference, brand purchase, brand usage, brand satisfaction, and brand loyalty. Understanding the psychological mechanisms of these consumer-response variables and establishing their determinants and consequent conditions are extremely important in ascertaining those variables that can be used by the marketing manager in influencing consumer and market responses in a favorable direction. For an illustrative listing of those consumer-response variables generally investigated by consumer behaviorists, see Table 3.1.

Table 3.1 Examples of Consumer Response Variables Broken Down by Marketing Mix Elements

Marketing Mix Element	Consumer Response Variables
Product decisions	Problem recognition
	Product image
	Product preference
	Product choice
	Product usage
	Product satisfaction
	Product loyalty
Pricing decisions	Price perception
	Price preference
	Price acceptance
Place decisions	Store image
	Store preference
	Store patronage
Promotion decisions	Information acquisition
	Media image
	Media preference
	Media choice
	Message awareness
	Message comprehension
	Message interest
	Message belief
	Message persuasion
Target market decisions	Life-style segmentation
	Personality segmentation
	Self-concept segmentation
	Demographic segmentation
	Geographic segmentation
	Benefit segmentation

Product Types

Since the argument was established that consumer behavior is partly the study of consumer-response variables associated with the marketing mix elements (price, product, place, and promotion), a follow-up question has to be posited: "marketing what?" Kotler and Levy (1969) classified marketing products as tangible products, services, organizations, persons, and social ideas.

Consumer-behavior study is therefore not a study of consumers per se. It is the study of consumer behavior as it is directly associated with a given product, be it a tangible product, a service, organization, persons, or a social idea. Of course, consumer behaviorists do not go about studying consumer-response variables with respect to one particular product; attempts are made at classifying products along dimensions such as: perceived risk (Bettman 1973), product familiarity (Sirgy 1981d), product conspicuousness (Ross 1971), product personalization (Sirgy 1982b), product types (Kotler and Levy 1969), and so on.

The point is not to argue for generalizability across product categories but to get a feel for the scope of different products to which the study of consumer behavior is applied.

Product Levels

One final classification dimension that might be of some interest is the fact that consumer behaviorists sometimes focus their attention on studying brand-related responses (for example, brand image, brand preference, brand satisfaction) and at other times product-related responses (for example, product image, product need recognition).

In marketing decision making it is customary to gather data at both the primary demand and selective demand levels (product and brand levels, respectively). Therefore, consumer-behavior principles linking response variables to specific marketing effort variables become more salient by specifying the product-specificity level of the principle at hand.

SUMMARY

Based on the present classification schema, consumer-behavior research topics can be classified into unit levels,

Table 3.2 A Summary Statement of the Seven Classification
Dimensions Used to Classify Consumer-Behavior
Research Studies

I. Unit Levels
   Study related to individual consumer behavior
   Study related to family consumer behavior
   Study related to organizational consumer behavior
   Study related to large group consumer behavior
   Study related to societal consumer behavior
II. Product Types
   Study related to tangible products
   Study related to services
   Study related to organizations
   Study related to persons
   Study related to social issues
III. Process Levels
   Study related to micro consumer processes (physiological)
   Study related to micro/macro consumer processes (psy-
     chological)
   Study related to macro consumer processes (behavioral)
IV. Process-Orientation versus Structure-Orientation
   Study related to a consumer process (problem recognition)
   Study related to a consumer structure (self-concept)
V. Normativeness versus Descriptiveness
   Study related to prescriptive consumer-behavior phenomena
     (optimal decision making)
   Study related to descriptive consumer-behavior phenomena
     (actual decision making)
VI. Marketing Mix Elements
   Study related to consumer responses to product stimuli
   Study related to consumer responses to price stimuli
   Study related to consumer responses to promotion stimuli
   Study related to consumer responses to place stimuli
VII. Product Levels
   Study related to brand level (selective demand)
   Study related to product level (primary demand)

---

varying from the individual to the societal unit. Within each consumption unit, a consumer-behavior phenomenon can be subclassified further into either micro, micro/macro, or macro processes. Within a specific process perspective, the same consumer-behavior phenomenon can be either process or structure oriented. Furthermore, reference can be made to whether the phenomenon is normative or descriptive. It can be subclassified further by product type (that is, product, service, organization, person, or idea), by product level (that is, individual brand versus generic product level), and by marketing mix elements (that is, price, product, place, and promotion).

CHAPTER 4
How Does Social Cognition Theory
Fit Within The Scope And Boundary
Of The Consumer-Behavior Discipline

Based upon the developmental model described here, the theoretical treatment of social cognition in consumer behavior is said to be limited to Level IV of the developmental dimension. That is, consumer behavior as treated by social cognition theory is defined as the scientific study of the psychological structures and processes of individuals who consume an economic or non-economic good, which is exchanged by a profit or nonprofit organization, for the purpose of satisfying consumers at a maximal profit, protecting and educating consumers in the marketplace, satisfying consumers at a minimal cost to them, and/or eliciting a social response.

Using the classification schema described previously, social cognition theory is positioned within the individual unit level, describing micro/macro consumer processes with direct relevance to the marketing mix elements. Although the focal point has been in relation to tangible products, social cognition theory is equally applicable to services, organizations, persons, and ideas. Social cognition theory is applied also to both product levels (that is, brand and generic levels).

Therefore, the reader should be cautioned about the limited focus of social cognition theory. It does not directly apply to family consumption, organization consumption, or societal consumption. The theory is positioned treating psychological processes varying along the cognitive (perceptual)—affective (evaluative)—conative (behavioral) dimension, that is, micro/macro individual consumer processes. It does not attempt to address micro psychophysiological structures or processes, nor does it tangle with macro structures or processes of aggregate units across time. Social cognition theory, as applied to consumer behavior, also attempts to describe, not prescribe, consumer social inference and consumption-related psychological processes.

Having positioned social cognition theory under the umbrella of the consumer-behavior discipline, the next step is to make an attempt to specify those consumer psychological processes which can be treated by social cognition theory.

The traditional classification of consumer psychological processes involving problem recognition, information search, alternative evaluation, and outcome evaluation will be abandoned and replaced by a more comprehensive model. The traditional consumer-decision cycle model is argued to fall very short in describing many other salient consumer processes that marketers seriously consider in making marketing mix decisions. For example, how do the components of the hierarchy-of-effects model used by advertising psychologists fit within the overall consumer-decision cycle? What about consumer decisions regarding store preference and patronage? How do these processes fit in the traditional problem recognition decision cycle? How about media preference and usage, or how about message persuasion?

Since consumer-behavior study usually provides consumer information to marketing managers, an attempt is made here to develop a consumer-decision model representative of those cognitive/affective/behavioral processes directly related to product, price, place, and promotion decisions. Consumer-behavior study should provide consumer information to the marketing manager that can be directly translated into marketing mix decisions.

A SOCIAL COGNITION CONSUMER-DECISION CYCLE

Based on this perspective, seven consumer-process stages are identified. Each stage involves consumer processes described along the cognitive-affective-conative dimension (see Figure 4.1).

Although stages are specified denoting a designated sequence of behaviors that consumers usually follow, it should be noted that one, two, or more stages can be skipped under routinized purchase conditions.* Also there may be feedback loops within

---

*Howard and Sheth (1969) referred to three types of consumer decision making: routinized decisions, limited problem solving, and extensive problem solving. The model presented here depicts the limited or extensive problem solving process.

Figure 4.1 A Proposed Social Cognition Consumer Decision Cycle

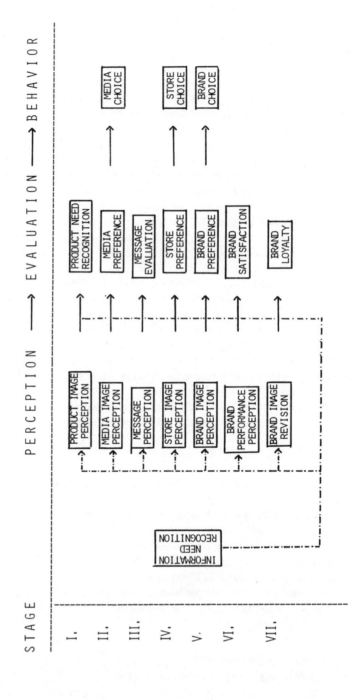

the decision cycle that are not shown in the overall model. The seven stages may be construed as representing the consumer-decision cycle under problem solving conditions.

Stage 1

The first stage of the consumer-decision cycle shows a perceptual process termed product image perception benefits and an affective process known as product need recognition. Product need recognition, as has been traditionally construed in the consumer-behavior literature, is a dissatisfaction state. That is, product need recognition is an affective state determined by the perception of current product benefits as directly compared with the individual desired product benefits. Significant discrepancies between these two psychological states are said to be responsible in triggering product need recognition, or the motivation to purchase a new product.

Stage II

The consumer perceives the alternative information sources available for him and their various attributes (media image perception) and benefits of these alternative information media sources between or among themselves or between an alternative and ideal standard evoked from the cognitive structures. The result of this comparison leads to the formation of media preference (affective) regarding the alternative information sources. This, under the proper conditions, is usually translated into information acquisition behavior or media choice (conative).

Stage III

In this stage the consumer receives information from one or more alternative information sources. This, of course, is message perception. The message attributes are compared with internally evoked beliefs about what the message attributes should be or some other form of attribute criteria, and the result of this comparison becomes message acceptance or rejection, message evaluation, or message persuasion. Based on this information, the consumer is now ready to go out there and shop for the desired product.

Stage IV

This stage involves the perception of the alternative stores available (and their image characteristics) from which the consumer can purchase the desired product (store image perception). This perception involves comparing the attributes of one store against another or against one's ideal set of attributes. The result of this comparison leads to store preference decisions, which in turn are usually translated conatively in terms of store choice or store patronage.

Stage V

Once in the store the consumer perceives the various alternative brands (brand image perception). He/She compares the attributes of one against the other or against criterion attributes evoked from his/her memory structures. The resulting decision is one of brand preference. This is usually transformed into brand choice.

Stages VI and VII

After purchase the consumer is usually cognizant of the brand performance and other related attributes (brand performance perception). The perception of brand performance attributes is compared with evoked beliefs and the resultant state is construed in terms of an affective disposition reflective of consumer satisfaction/dissatisfaction with that brand (brand satisfaction). This, in turn, motivates the consumer to reevaluate the brand image characteristics in light of his/her current experience with that brand (brand image revision). This reevaluation of the brand image revises his/her overall preference toward that brand. This determines his/her future disposition to repurchase the same brand when the need arises. This is what has been known in the consumer-behavior literature as brand loyalty.

With respect to information need recognition, it is argued that this process can occur simultaneously with any of the perceptual or evaluative processes at any stage of the consumer-decision cycle. The essence of information need recognition can be described as a heightened awareness of the need to acquire consumer information to help perceive and/or evaluate product, brand, media, or store-related stimuli.

This model is argued to be more representative of the consumer-decision cycle compared to the traditional cycle mainly because it describes those consumer processes that are directly related to marketing mix decisions—product, place, price, and promotions. Specifically, it can be easily argued that the information derived from understanding the model's behavioral principles can easily accommodate the marketing managers' normative orientation. In other words the marketing manager making marketing mix decisions needs direct information concerning each marketing mix element. Traditionally, the study of consumer behavior has been somewhat divorced from the decision-oriented environment of the marketing manager. Consumer behaviorists usually feel guilty about not doing an adequate job of tying marketing management and consumer behavior together. To cope with this sense of guilt, they usually have nice little "implications" sections at the end of each consumer-behavior topic which does a mediocre job in bridging the gap of the two disciplines. I have to admit that this bridge is yet to be built.

An attempt to build this bridge is made through the use of this model. Specifically, with respect to product decisions, those stages involving product image perception, product need recognition, brand image perception, brand preference, brand choice, brand performance perception, brand satisfaction, brand image revision, and brand loyalty are most important.

Pricing decisions can be enhanced by considering how price is used as a perceptual cue in affecting every psychological process involved in every stage of the decision cycle.

Place decisions can be effectively made with the information base derived from behavioral principles involved with store image perception, store preference, and store choice.

Finally, with respect to promotion decisions, behavioral principles stemming from every stage of the consumer-decision cycle depicted here can be used to make effective creative copy decisions. Once alternative creative copies are generated, copy testing can be conducted effectively by adhering to the principles involved with message perception and message evaluation. To make effective media decisions, the marketing manager has to study his/her target market's media image perceptions, media preferences, and media choices of alternative media vehicles. The knowledge base extracted from the study of consumer behavior using the model here is argued to be applicable directly to the decision environment of the marketing manager.

With respect to public policy makers, understanding the consumer-decision cycle described in the model presented here can enhance the formulation of consumer information, education, and/or protection policies. For example public policy makers can develop programs to provide factual and functional information to consumers to help them perceive products, brands, stores, and media images more accurately and guide them to use functional-related attributes in their preference and choice of brands, stores, and media.*

---

*It has to be noted that the focus of the proposed model is on a given product type (that is, tangible product, service, organization, person, idea). This analysis, by definition, may deal with a given media or store as the central concepts. In other words suppose that the product type that one might be interested in is a gift store. According to the model, the consumer may perceive those attributes related to a gift store (product image perception) which may lead to a recognition that he/she needs to go to a gift store (product need recognition). He/she searches his/her memory for information related to gift store (product familiarity) which may lead to a recognition that he/she needs additional information about the various gift stores (information need recognition). He/she thinks about the various information outlets about gift stores and evaluates them (media image perception and media preference). He/she finally chooses to look in the Yellow Pages (media choice). In this specific instance the information relayed in the Yellow Pages would induce both brand image perception and store image perception. That is, the consumer will evaluate the various locations where gift shops are located (store image perception). This may lead to a location preference (store preference) and a behavioral decision (store choice). Once a location is selected, the various gift shops within the selected location are evaluated and a decision is made (brand image perception, brand preference, and brand choice). The reader should note that store-related dynamics can occur within the context of brand evaluation and not necessarily preceding it. Once the consumer visits the selected gift shop and experiences it, he/she will revise his/her beliefs about the attributes of the gift shop in light of the marketplace experience (brand performance perception, brand satisfaction, and brand image revision). This reevaluation would determine the consumer's future disposition toward this gift shop (brand loyalty).

SUMMARY

Social cognition theory was argued to play an important role in consumer behavior as defined by Level IV along the developmental dimension. In other words social cognition theory plays a central role in explaining, describing, and predicting those psychological structural and process dynamics of individuals who consume an economic or noneconomic good exchanged by a profit or nonprofit organization for the purpose of satisfying consumers at a maximal profit, protecting and educating consumers in the marketplace, satisfying consumers at a minimal cost to them, and/or eliciting a social response. Social cognition theory applied to consumer behavior is positioned to deal only with the individual level (not family, organization, large group, or society), with micro/macro psychological processes (not micro and macro processes), and is applicable across all marketing mix elements (product, price, place, and promotion), across both product levels (brands and generics), and across all product types (tangible products, services, organizations, persons, and ideas).

A consumer-decision cycle was developed also to describe directly those processes that can be explained, described, and predicted by social cognition theory. The model contains seven stages. Stage I describes product image perception and product need recognition. Stage II illustrates those processes related to media image perception, media preference, and media choice. Stage III indicates the dynamics involved with message perception and message evaluation. Store image perception, store preference, and store choice are processes described in Stage IV. This is followed by brand image perception, brand preference, and brand choice in Stage V. Stage VI describes the processes related to brand performance perception and the resulting brand satisfaction. Finally, in Stage VII the consumer undergoes brand image revision leading to brand loyalty.

PART II
The Theory
In
Pure Form

CHAPTER 5
Cognitive Congruity

In this chapter the main thrust of the proposed social cognition theory will be presented in social psychological language. That is, the theory will be discussed in general social psychology jargon and not necessarily restricted to consumer behavior. This chapter is divided into three major segments:

- psychological structures
- psychological needs
- psychological congruity

The psychological structures section presents the major psychological variables involved in the congruity process. Following this, the cognitive needs that function to activate and guide psychological congruity are discussed. Then the type and degree of interactions among structural variables and their resultant responses are described.

PSYCHOLOGICAL STRUCTURES

The structure of an individual psychological system involves the identification of the different types of cognitions distinguished along functional properties and the description of how those cognitions are arranged within the individual's psychological system.

Structural Anatomy of the Cognitive System

Five major types of cognitions are identified: (1) concepts, (2) percepts, (3) values, (4) perceptions, and (5) beliefs (cf. Fishbein and Ajzen 1975; Rokeach 1960, 1972).

A concept is a mental representation of a set of objects or events stored in the cognitive structures or memory banks of an individual (cf. Paivio 1971). This construct has its parallels in a number of theoretical systems. At the level of neuropsychological theory the mental representation process can be regarded as corresponding to Hebb's (1949, p. 60) cell assembly—the simplest instance of a representative process (image or idea). It is similar to Osgood's (1953) representational process. It corresponds to Simon and Feigenbaum's (1964) definition of "image."

A percept, on the other hand, is a concept placed in the focus of attention. Concepts are placed in the focus of attention to be perceptually processed or evaluated. The psychological processes involved with perception and evaluation will be discussed in detail in a following chapter.

Percepts and concepts when placed on the "perceptual platform" (that is, in the focus of attention) are said to have certain attributes. Attributes are concepts that are used to describe the characteristics of the percept and concept in question. For example a consumer product may be a percept when it is perceived or evaluated; however, it remains a concept when it is simply stored in the memory structures. The perception or evaluation process of a given percept is done through a comparison between the attribute value of the percept and the attribute value of the corresponding evoked concept. These attribute values are extracted from the same attribute dimension that is elicited with the evoked concept (see Figure 5.1).

A value denotes the degree of positivity or negativity (highness or lowness) placed around an attribute. Therefore, it can be said that for every percept there is a perceptual value (PV), and for every evoked concept there is an evoked value (EV).

The value of a percept or concept has been traditionally referred to as "meaning" (cf. Osgood 1953).

Perceptions (PB) are psychological links or connections between a percept and a perceptual value. Perceptions vary along a certainty dimension. An individual can perceive a relation (for example, car X is reliable) as processed from an incoming message with high certainty, moderate certainty, or low certainty (cf. Brunswik 1956). Perceptions can be measured

Figure 5.1 Cognitive Structures Involved in a Congruity Process

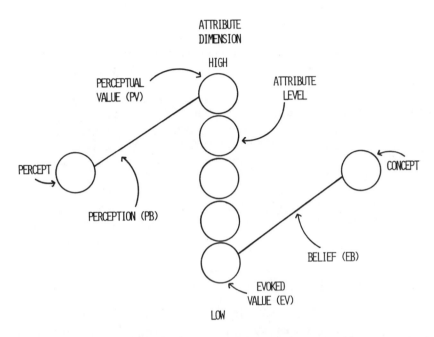

as probability estimates (for example, the likelihood that percept X is related to perceptual attribute Y [Fishbein and Ajzen 1974; Wyer 1974]) or magnitude estimates (that is, the judge is given a set of alternative categories and is asked to assign the object to the category to which it is most likely to belong [Wyer 1973]).

Beliefs (EB), on the other hand, are psychological links or connections between concepts and evoked values (EV). They, like perceptions, vary in strength and can be measured as probability or magnitude estimates. So by definition, beliefs are different from perceptions in that they are psychological relations linking concepts with conceptual attributes, whereas perceptions link percepts with perceptual attributes.

Beliefs can be viewed as representing different types of psychological relations. Beliefs can describe prior knowledge, desires, ideals, norms, expectations, anticipations, referent states, and so on.

Structural Arrangement in the Cognitive System

The structural arrangements of these cognitions can be described in terms of attitude structure, and frame of reference.

An attitude structure refers to those salient perceived and evoked cognitions which are activated in any given moment in time for the purpose of perceiving or evaluating a percept (see Figure 5.1).

Figure 5.1 shows an attitude structure that is not only composed of a percept and its associated attributes as traditionally construed (Atkinson 1957; Edwards 1954; Fishbein 1967; Lewin 1951; Porter and Lawler 1968; Rosenberg 1956; Rotter 1954; Tolman 1955; Vroom 1964), but also contains the evoked concept and its associated attributes (March and Simon 1958). The determinants of an attitude will be addressed in a later chapter.

Rokeach (1972) elaborated on attitude structures. He asserted that each belief within an attitude of organization is conceived to have three components:

(1) a cognitive component representing a person's knowledge held with varying degrees of certitude about what is true or false, good or bad, desirable or undesirable (in terms of the attitude structure construct presented here, this cognitive component involves the perception construct—PB)

(2) an affective component representing the affect aroused centering around the object of belief (with respect to the construct presented here, this affective component is determined by one or more congruities occurring between perceptual and evoked values—PV minus EV—which will be addressed in some detail in the latter part of this chapter)

(3) a behavioral component reflective of a response disposition of varying thresholds which must lead to some action when activated (this behavioral component will be referred to as the resulting affect from the congruity process which also will be dealt with in this chapter)

The traditional measurement of attitude structure has involved tapping salient attributes in the perceptual and evoked sets. This is usually accomplished by a variety of techniques such as, free-elicitation procedure (Kanwar, Olson, and Sims 1981), conjoint analysis (Robinson 1980), Kelly repertory grid (Kelly 1955; Frost and Briane 1967) factor analysis (Sirgy 1982b), information display board (Jacoby, Szybillo, and Busato-Schach 1977), and determinant analysis (Myers 1970), among others.

A frame of reference denotes the specific conceptual structure or cognitive schema activated at a given moment in time. It includes those evoked cognitions which are subjected to the congruity process. A given frame of reference may have three characteristic components: (1) concept characteristics, (2) situation characteristics, and (3) time characteristics (cf. Anderson and Bower 1974).

Concept characteristics of an activated frame of reference refer to those primary concepts and attributes (produced from memory repertoire). The situation characteristics of a given frame of reference refer to those secondary attributes characterizing the perceived situation. Time characteristics, on the other hand, refer to the time orientation of the perceived situation represented also as an attribute.

Also, social cognition theorists advanced the concept of "scripts and vignettes" (Abelson 1976; Schank and Abelson 1977). It should be noted that a frame of reference is the smallest unit in a vignette or script. It includes those psychological relations that are actually activated in a given moment in time, while scripts and vignettes refer to a network of conceptual relations which are "primed" or become more accessible to activation.

A given frame of reference, which traditionally has been referred to as "cognitive category," "schema," "evoked set," "conceptualization," among others, varies along at least four dimensions: (1) centrality, (2) differentiation, (3) category width, and (4) articulation.

Centrality refers to the degree of interrelatedness of the evoked beliefs with other beliefs stored in the memory structures. Centrality of beliefs has been conceptually defined by Sherif, Sherif, and Nebergall (1965) in terms of ego involvement. They assumed that variations in ego involvement with a specific issue are overtly manifested by the latitude of rejection. Eagly (1967) defined it in terms of the number of other concepts dependent on it. She assumed that self-beliefs are more central than nonself-beliefs. Rosenberg (1960) defined it in terms of the importance to which it is perceived to be instrumental to the furtherance or hinderance of important values. Rokeach (1972) defined the centrality dimension solely in terms of connectedness, as it is assumed here. He asserted that the more a given belief is functionally connected or in communication with other beliefs, the more implications and consequences it has for other beliefs, and therefore, the more central the belief. Rokeach went further to classify beliefs according to this centrality dimension. He effectively argued that there are at least five types of beliefs varying along the centrality dimension. These are: (1) primitive beliefs—100 percent consensus, (2) primitive beliefs—zero consensus, (3) authority beliefs, (4) derived beliefs, and (5) inconsequential beliefs.

Primitive shared beliefs (100 percent consensus) are most central and are learned by direct encounter with the object of belief and reinforced by a unanimous social consensus among all of one's reference persons. An example of a primitive shared belief may be "I believe this is a table, chair, house, mother, and so on."

Primitive unshared beliefs (zero consensus) are incontrovertible beliefs involving existence and self-identity that are learned by direct encounter with the object of belief; however, their maintenance does not depend on others' consensus. An example of this type of belief may be "I believe that the world is doomed. I believe, but no one else could."

Authority beliefs are those beliefs that render judgment on the degree of credibility of an authority figure. For example there are general beliefs concerning the credibility of professors in the context of university education, political scientists in the context of political affairs, economists in the context of economic affairs, and so on.

Derived beliefs are those beliefs derived from those authority figures. For example, "The surgeon general declared that cigarette smoking is hazardous to your health, and I believe it."

Inconsequential beliefs, of course, are low involvement types of beliefs and the ones that concern us the most in the study of consumer behavior. The major portion of these beliefs is directed to arbitrary matters of taste and individual preferences.

The reader should note that there is an important distinction between strength of a conceptual relation and centrality of a conceptual relation. Rokeach (1972) puts it this way.

> While there is undoubtedly a positive correlation between centrality and intensity (strength), the relationship is by no means a necessary one. Many inconsequential or trivial beliefs can be intensely held and strongly defended. One may, for example, intensely believe that rare steaks are tastier than well-done steaks, or that more enjoyable vacations await us at the seashore than in the mountains. Such beliefs are nevertheless inconsequential because they have relatively few connections with, and if changed, have relatively few consequences for, other beliefs (p. 13).

Furthermore, centrality of conceptual relations can also refer to the extent to which they are abstract versus concrete or general versus specific (Brown 1965; Paivio 1971; Wyer and Carlston 1979).

Differentiation is defined as the degree of attributes evoked in a given frame of reference. A highly differentiated frame of reference is therefore one which contains a high number of conceptual attributes (concept, situation, and/or time attributes). A low differentiated frame of reference, conversely, would contain a low number of conceptual attributes. This construct parallels that of Rokeach in his discussion of attitude structure. It also has its basis in the individual difference variable of cognitive complexity. Driver and Streufert (1969) distinguished between "cognitively simple" and "cognitively complex" individuals. Cognitively simple individuals are described as having a conceptual system representing an inaccurate and/or oversimplified picture of reality. Using statistical jargon, cognitively simple individuals see the world in terms of "main effects," which is usually inaccurate, whereas cognitively complex people see the world in terms of "interaction effects."

The reader should note that the differentiation construct presented here is a situation-specific individual difference variable and not a general-personality individual difference variable as theorized by Driver and Streufert (1969).

Category width refers to the extent to which the attribute dimension of a specific belief within a given frame of reference is broadly or narrowly categorized. For example suppose an advertising message for an automobile presents the fact that the automobile has an EPA rating of a 20 MPG. Now the question is how this message would be perceptually categorized in the minds of the audience. One consumer may evoke a broadly defined economy dimension containing low economy versus high economy and may therefore categorize the 20 MPG stimulus as low economy, whereas, another consumer having evoked a narrowly defined economy dimension (for example, extremely high economy, very high economy, high economy, moderately low economy, low economy, very low economy, and extremely low economy) may classify the advertised car as a moderately low economy type of car.

Pettigrew (1958) viewed this construct from a general-personality individual difference perspective. He maintained that some persons have stable dispositions to broadly categorize across a variety of situations while others do the opposite. It should be noted that category width as treated here, is a situation-specific construct and not a general-personality construct.

What is the interrelationship between centrality, differentiation, and category width, if there is any? It is very conceivable that highly central evoked cognitions may have a frame of reference that contains highly differentiated cognitions involving attributes of narrow category width. This assertion seems quite plausible since those highly central cognitions are highly salient for that individual. Due to the projected saliency of the perceived situation, the individual is likely to pay close attention to the incoming stimuli, allocate greater cognitive effort, and by doing so the perceptual process is likely to involve a differentiated frame of reference with attributes of narrow category width to facilitate an optimal perceptual decoding process. This process will be addressed in greater detail in a later chapter.

The articulation dimension refers to a verbal versus nonverbal dimension. Some concepts are well articulated or encoded in a semantic or verbal form, whereas others are not well articulated and encoded only in an affective or sensory form (Kosslyn and Pomerantz 1977; Paivio 1971). Within a given frame of reference, some cognitions may be highly articulated while others are lacking in articulation but still exerting significant psychological effects. The structure of cognitions along the articulation dimension is extremely important from a methodological point of view, since less articulated cognitions are usually not tapped by traditional survey and explicit verbal techniques. It also could be possible that self-report measures force respondents to articulate affectively encoded constructs.

Verbal and nonverbal cognitions are interrelated. Aspects of a visual or emotional experience are linked with verbal concepts. The interrelatedness of sensory and semantic memory systems has been an issue of both theoretical and empirical interest to investigators as Abelson (1976), Kosslyn and Pomerantz (1977), Paivio (1971), and Pylyshyn (1973).

PSYCHOLOGICAL NEEDS

The motivational dynamics underlying any psychological process involve one of three primary cognitive needs. These are: the need for cognitive enhancement, the need for cognitive consistency, and the need for cognitive differentiation (Sirgy 1981b).

The need for cognitive enhancement is involved with the motivational dynamics inherent in the value content of the activated concepts. It is defined as a propensity to maintain and enhance one's conceptual system by acting in ways to minimize negative emotions and maximize positive emotions. Individuals maximize their pleasures and enhance their self-esteem by behaving in ways to satisfy their psychogenic and biogenic needs (for example, need for achievement, need for approval, need for power, and need for self-esteem). Individuals attempt to minimize their pains by avoiding noxious stimuli and are specifically motivated to do so by avoidance needs (for example, need to avoid disapproval, need to avoid failure, need to avoid self-abasement).

Specifically, the need for cognitive enhancement can be described along two different psychological levels: genotypic level and phenotypic level. The genotypic state of the need for cognitive enhancement is the dormant state of this need. However, once this need is activated, its phenotypic state takes over. The phenotypic state of this need can be construed along a homeostatic dimension. Perceptual outcomes that serve to inform the individual that a desired state is achieved or maintained would trigger a homeostatic phenotypic state of this need in the form of positive emotion. On the other hand, perceptual outcomes informing the individual that the perceived state is discrepant from the desired state (evoked belief) would trigger a phenotypic deviation state (that is, deviation from homeostasis) in the form of negative emotions.

Therefore, two types of phenotypic states are identified--positive emotion (homeostatic level of the need for cognitive enhancement) and negative emotion (deviation level of the need for cognitive enhancement). These phenotypic states will be elaborated upon later.

Such a cognitive need is essential to the human organism since it serves to enhance the growth and maintenance functions of the individual. This concept parallels Freud's (1933) psychoanalytic notion of tension reduction, Hull's (1943) behavioral theory of consummatory reactions, goal accomplishments of cognitive theorists (for example, Lewin, Dembo, Festinger, and Sears 1944; Tolman 1955; Edwards 1954; Rotter 1954; Vroom 1964; Porter and Lawler 1968), Epstein's (1973) phenomenological principle of self-esteem maintenance and enhancement, and Katz's (1960) utilitarian, ego defensive, and value-expressive functions of attitudes.

The need for cognitive consistency refers to the need of any individual to assimilate the data of reality in terms of a conceptual or psychological theory unique to every individual. Such a psychological theory is essentially needed to allow the individual to make sense of himself/herself and of the external world. However, a psychological theory, like all scientific theories, is formulated by a set of beliefs which are consistent with one another. Inconsistencies contribute to the invalidation of one's psychological theory and therefore threaten the individual with conceptual disorganization, which is anxiety provoking (cf. Epstein 1973; Lecky 1969).

The homeostatic phenotypic manifestation of this need is cognitive consistency or reinforcement. It is defined as a positive affect state, which is triggered when a perceptual outcome is found to be highly consistent with the evoked conceptual relation (that is, belief). The deviation state of this need is cognitive dissonance, which reflects a negative affect state triggered by an inconsistency between a perceptual outcome and an evoked belief. This will be discussed more fully in following chapters.

This phenotypic state has its roots in cognitive dissonance theory, originally proposed by Festinger (1957), and later extended by Brehm and Cohen (1962), Aronson (1969), and Wicklund and Brehm (1976).

The need for cognitive differentiation refers to the propensity of an individual to assimilate the data of reality (Sirgy 1981b). From the perspective provided by the theory presented here, it is defined as the need to form, reinforce, or strengthen salient evoked belief relations. This need functions to motivate the individual to form a representational image of reality as means for coping with the environment.

As with the needs for cognitive enhancement and consistency, the need for cognitive differentiation has a homeostatic phenotypic state. The homeostatic state is referred to as information assimilation. This state is defined as a positive affect state reflective of the formation of new belief relations or the strengthening of existing belief relations. The deviation state is referred to here as information acquisition. It is defined as a negative affect state triggered by an evoked belief of low certitude. This will be treated in greater depth in following chapters.

This construct parallels Epstein's (1973) notion of the tendency to assimilate the data of reality, Kelly's (1955) choice corollary, Piaget's (1954) assimilation tendency, and Katz's (1960) knowledge function of attitudes.

PSYCHOLOGICAL CONGRUITY

This theory posits that psychological processes involved in goal-directed behavior can be explained by the simple process called congruity. Congruity points to the psychological comparison between perceptual set and an evoked frame of reference (cf. March and Simon 1958). A perceptual set refers to one or more perceptions related to a specific percept. The evoked set refers to those corresponding beliefs that are elicited from the person's cognitive structures for perceiving or evaluating the percept.

This view is consistent with the theories of Bruner (1957), Hebb (1949), and Paivio (1971). According to these theories, perception consists of some kind of matching process involving sensory input and neuronal model. The present view posits that like lower-level perceptual process, higher-order motivational phenomena involved in goal-directed thought are determined by basically the same psychological process, namely a match or a comparison process between a perceptual (or sensory) state and an internally evoked cognitive state. In essence it is argued that the psychological process involved in perception is essentially the same as in problem-solving, decision-making, or goal-directed thought.

Therefore, congruity is defined here as the degree of discrepancy occurring between a perceptual value (PV) and an evoked value (EV). Reference to congruity therefore means small or negligible discrepancies between a PV and its corresponding EV. Incongruity refers to a significant discrepancy between a PV and a corresponding EV. The directionality of a congruity (or incongruity) also can be noted. The congruity construct can be classified into (1) positive congruity, (2) positive incongruity, (3) negative congruity, and (4) negative incongruity.

Positive congruity refers to a negligible or zero discrepancy between a positively valued perception (+PV) and a positively valued evoked belief (+EV). A positive incongruity signifies a significant discrepancy between a positively valued perception (+PV) and a negatively valued evoked belief (-EV). A negative congruity describes a condition in which there is negligible or zero discrepancy between a negatively valued perception (-PV) and a negatively valued evoked belief (-EV). Moreover, a negative incongruity is said to involve a significant discrepancy between a negatively valued perception (-PV) and a positively valued evoked belief (+EV).

The homeostatic phenotypic states pertaining to the needs of cognitive enhancement, consistency, and differentiation discussed earlier involve positive emotion, cognitive consistency, and information assimilation, respectively, and are all positive outcome states. In terms of cognitive congruities, the homeostatic phenotypic state of the cognitive enhancement motive can be described in terms of positive congruity or incongruity. It will be shown in a following chapter that individual evaluation of percepts is directed by the need for cognitive enhancement. A congruity process directed by this need resulting in either positive congruity or incongruity is argued to induce a positive emotional state. A positive emotional state associated with the need for cognitive enhancement is the homeostatic phenotypic state of this need. Conversely, the deviation state of this need can be expressed in terms of negative congruity or incongruity conditions. Specifically, when a percept is evaluated and the resultant process is either negative congruity or incongruity, a negative emotional state will be felt. Negative emotional states directly associated with the need for cognitive enhancement are deviation states prompting the individual to act to reduce this deviation state and bring it to homeostatic balance (positive emotion).

The perceptual process will be shown to be mostly directed by the need for cognitive consistency. In perception the individual strives to categorize percepts into cognitive categories enabling him/her to make sense of the world. In doing so the individual is constantly matching perceptual stimuli with evoked cognitions. In other words those percepts that highly match the evoked cognitive categories are categorized as such. This matching process can be expressed by the congruity variable. A good fit or a good match can be viewed in terms of either positive or negative congruity, and a bad fit can be expressed in terms of positive or negative incongruity. Specifically, the homeostatic phenotypic state of the cognitive consistency motive (that is, cognitive consistency) can be viewed as the affect state resulting from positive or negative congruity, whereas the deviation state of the same motive (that is, cognitive dissonance) can be expressed by positive or negative incongruity. The experiential state of cognitive dissonance propels the individual into action for the purpose of reducing this dissonance state to bring it back to homeostasis.

With respect to the need for cognitive differentiation, the phenotypic homeostatic state of this motive (that is, information assimilation) is described as a state in which information processing is conducted in an environment of certainty. In other words those congruities occurring in either perception or evaluation have strong belief components (strong EB). A congruity process occurring under the direction of either the enhancement or consistency motives that is found to contain a weak evoked belief (weak EB) would trigger the differentiation motive, and the deviation state of this motive (that is, information acquisition) will be felt. This would prompt the individual to seek information to reduce this deviation state and bring about a homeostatic balance (that is, information assimilation).

The focal point of this argument is that negative outcome states (or deviations states) are responsible for goal-oriented behavior. That is, to reduce an experienced deviation state, the individual is aroused to seek and evaluate alternative courses of action. These alternative courses of action are assessed for their degree of instrumentality in reducing a given deviation state.

Now the key question is: What is the nature of the congruity involved in approach/avoidance motivation in determining goal-oriented behavior?

It is argued here that the degree of approach/avoidance motivation toward an alternative course of action can be described by the congruity dynamics directed by the enhancement motive. In other words the precise conditions applied to describe positive/negative emotion can be used to describe approach/avoidance motivation. However, that is not to say that these two constructs are theoretically equivalent or interchangeable. To reiterate, positive/negative emotion is an outcome of intrinsic state, whereas approach/avoidance motivation is an instrumental state. However, both can be described in terms of congruities involving evaluation dynamics as directed by the enhancement motive.

SUMMARY

There are three primary needs in humans. These are the need for cognitive enhancement, consistency, and differentiation. Each has an adaption or homeostatic level. Individuals or consumers behave in many ways to maintain these homeostatic levels. By the same token, deviations from ranges of homeostatic stability form the basis of behavior. A perceived situation (object, person, or event) is compared with an evoked conceptual relation and any resulting type of congruity or incongruity as directed by one of the three motives forms the basis of individual motivation and emotion. A congruity or incongruity state characterizing a deviation state motivates goal-oriented behavior for the purpose of restoring homeostasis. Goal-oriented behavior, in turn, determined by congruity dynamics, is directed by the enhancement motive and reflected in evaluation of alternative courses of action.

Based on these three primary motives, the degree and directionality of congruity conditions associated with the homeostatic and deviation levels of each of these cognitive needs can be specified. With respect to the need for cognitive enhancement, the homeostatic state is specified in terms of positive emotion.

Deviation from homeostasis can be construed in terms of negative emotion. Positive congruity or incongruity usually induces positive emotion, whereas negative congruity or incongruity induces negative emotion.

In regards to the need for cognitive consistency, the homeostatic state is specified in terms of cognitive consistency. Deviation from homeostasis is construed as cognitive dissonance. The type of congruity dynamics involved in determining cognitive consistency is expressed in positive or negative congruity. Conversely, positive or negative incongruity induces cognitive dissonance. This motive is mostly operative in perceptual processing.

The homeostatic level pertaining to the need for cognitive differentiation is that of information assimilation. The deviation from homeostasis is in the form of information acquisition. Information assimilation involves a congruity or incongruity state that is inflicted by one or more weak evoked beliefs.

A deviation state, whether it may be that of negative emotion, cognitive dissonance, or information acquisition makes a network of schemas accessible in the individual's cognitive structure. Therefore, those situations that provide opportunities for goal attainment (reducing the deviation state in the direction of effecting homeostasis) are evaluated under the direction of the enhancement motive, and the resultant affect is said to determine approach/avoidance motivation and goal-directed behavior.

CHAPTER 6
Modelling Goal-Oriented Congruity

In the preceding chapter components of individual cognitive structures, genotypic and phenotypic states of the needs for cognitive enhancement, consistency, and differentiation, as well as congruity mechanics underlying each of the cognitive motives, were briefly discussed (see Table 6.1).

As the table indicates, the three cognitive needs have phenotypic states. Each phenotypic state varies from a homeostatic level to a deviation level. Specifically, the need for cognitive enhancement has a homeostatic state reflected in positive emotion and a deviation state indicated by negative emotion. Although reference to these levels of the phenotypic state of the enhancement motive is made in terms of two extreme categories, the reader should note that it is more appropriately viewed as a phenotypic bipolar dimension varying from complete homeostasis to significant deviation levels. The phenotypic dimension of the enhancement motive will be referred to hereafter as the Enhancement Affect, and an attempt to mathematically model this phenomenon is made here.

Similarly, the phenotypic state of the need for cognitive consistency will be referred to hereafter as the Consistency Affect. Remember that this phenotypic state varies from cognitive consistency (homeostasis) to cognitive dissonance (deviation state). The same can be said with respect to the need for cognitive differentiation. The phenotypic dimension pertaining to this motive is referred to here as the Information Affect, which varies from information assimilation (homeostasis) to information acquisition (deviation state). As with the Enhancement Affect, mathematical models will be constructed to describe these pheno-

Table 6.1 Major Characteristics of the Enhancement, Consistency, and Information Affect Models

Model	Genotypic State	Phenotypic State (Homeostasis)	Type of Congruity	Phenotypic State (Deviation Level)	Type of Congruity
Enhancement Affect Model	Need for cognitive enhancement	Approach motivation or positive emotion	Positive congruity or incongruity	Avoidance motivation or negative emotion	Negative congruity or incongruity
Consistency Affect Model	Need for cognitive consistency	Cognitive consistency	Positive or negative congruity	Cognitive inconsistency	Positive or negative incongruity
Information Affect Model	Need for cognitive differentiation	Information assimilation	Congruity with strong belief component	Information acquisition	Congruity with weak belief component

typic bipolar dimensions by using the congruity construct. The reader is cautioned not to treat these models as valid models but as initial propositions toward developing valid models.

THE ENHANCEMENT AFFECT MODEL

As stated previously, the enhancement motive determines both approach/avoidance motivation and positive/negative emotion. Instead of speaking in terms of either motivation or emotion, the standard term of enhancement affect, denoting approach/ avoidance motivation or positive/negative emotion will be adopted.

As previously noted, positive congruity or incongruity was argued to induce high enhancement affect, whereas negative congruity or incongruity was said to induce low enhancement affect (see Figure 6.1).

Figure 6.1 shows the degree as well as the directionality of the experienced enhancement affect as a result of differential congruity conditions. Specifically, under the positive congruity condition (+PV/+EV), the individual perceives a stimulus that is associated with a positive attribute; therefore, he/she evaluates this percept (stimulus object) positively. In other words he/she develops a favorable attitude toward the stimulus object. This favorable evaluation of this stimulus object may be reflected in the form of a positive affective disposition such as positive emotion or approach motivation directed toward this stimulus object. For example let us say that a consumer is using his/her automobile as a reference point to evaluate an advertised automobile. The automobile gives the consumer 40 MPG and he/she believes that 40 MPG is high gas mileage (+EV). The advertised car provides 40 MPG. This would automatically assign a positive value to the perceptual attribute (+PV). In this situation alone, the individual will evaluate the advertised car positively.

Under positive incongruity conditions (+PV/-EV), the individual is comparing a percept (stimulus object) that is associated with a positive attribute with a negative referent. This will result in a positive evaluation of the stimulus object. This is because the perceived object is viewed to be better than the referent object. For example suppose that the referent automobile in the previous example gives the consumer 20 MPG, not 40 MPG. This will result in a positive evaluation of the advertised car. Furthermore, it should be noted that the degree of positive evaluation of the stimulus object in this condition is more positive than in the positive congruity condition. This is because the person is judging the stimulus object to be better than the

Figure 6.1 Congruity as Directed by the Enhancement Motive

	+PV	-PV
+EV	POSITIVE CONGRUITY	NEGATIVE INCONGRUITY
-EV	POSITIVE INCONGRUITY	NEGATIVE CONGRUITY

	+PV	-PV
+EV	MOD + ENHANCEMENT AFFECT	HI - ENHANCEMENT AFFECT
-EV	HI + ENHANCEMENT AFFECT	MOD - ENHANCEMENT AFFECT

referent object in the positive incongruity condition, whereas the stimulus object is judged to be "as good" as the referent object in the positive congruity condition.

Under negative congruity conditions (-PV/-EV), the percept is compared with a negative referent (concept) and is found to be "as bad" as the referent object along a specific attribute dimension. Using the automobile example, the consumer uses the present car, which is giving him/her 20 MPG as a referent object to evaluate the advertised car, which also provides a minimal of 20 MPG. In this situation the consumer will not "think much" of the advertised car. Instead, the consumer would feel that the advertised car is "as bad" as his/her present car. The resultant affect toward the stimulus object therefore will be negative.

Under negative incongruity conditions (-PV/+EV), the percept is compared with a positive referent and is found to be "worse than" the referent object. The resultant affect is predicted to be more negative than in the negative congruity condition. For example the consumer here is comparing the advertised car, which is claimed to provide only 20 MPG with his/her present car, which gives 40 MPG. In this case the consumer would feel that the advertised car is worse than the present car and consequently develops a negative attitude toward the advertised car.

However, it can be easily shown that the enhancement affect or evaluation stemming from any of these congruity conditions is moderated by the strength of the perception(s) and the evoked belief(s). Take for example the positive incongruity condition. Given a weak perception and/or a weak evoked referent relation (belief), the resultant highly positive evaluation will be tempered due to the uncertainty associated with involved cognitive relations. Using the same MPG example above, the consumer is told that the advertised car can provide 40 MPG (+PV) but he/she does not trust advertising claims (uncertain or $\downarrow$PB). The consumer compares the advertised car with the present car, from which he/she thinks (uncertain or $\downarrow$EB) that he gets 20 MPG. In this case the positive enhancement affect felt toward the percept (advertised car) is moderated by the uncertainty associated with both the perception and the evoked belief.

By including the PB and EB constructs in the enhancement affect function, the theoretical predictions can be tabulated and shown, as in Figure 6.2.

As shown in Figure 6.2, under weak perception/weak referent conditions ($\downarrow$PB and $\downarrow$EB), the enhancement affect generated is expected to be minimal (or neutral). Under weak perception/strong referent conditions ($\downarrow$PB and $\uparrow$EB), low to moderate positive (and negative) enhancement affect is expected, depending on the exact type and degree of congruity (see Figure 6.2). In the case of positive congruity (+PV and +EV), low positive enhancement affect is expected. In the case of positive congruity (+PV and -EV), moderate positive enhancement affect is predicted. For negative incongruity (-PV and +EV), moderate negative enhancement is expected. And finally, for negative congruity (-PV and -EV), low negative enhancement affect is expected.

With respect to the strong perception/weak referent conditions ($\uparrow$PB and $\downarrow$EB), it is argued that the need for cognitive differentiation will be activated here because of the $\downarrow$EB, which would induce information acquisition. However, would the operation of the need for cognitive enhancement be activated under these conditions? Yes, it is possible; the same type of affect pattern is expected as that generated from the weak perception/strong referent conditions, but with lesser magnitude.

Finally, under strong perception/strong referent conditions, the pattern of expected enhancement affect of the previous two sets of conditions ($\downarrow$PB and $\uparrow$EB and $\uparrow$PB and $\downarrow$EB) is expected to apply here, however, with greater intensity.

The question now becomes: How can these categorical hypotheses be transformed into a continuous mathematical function?

Figure 6.2 Type and Degree of Enhancement Affect as Theoretically Expected from the Different Congruity Conditions

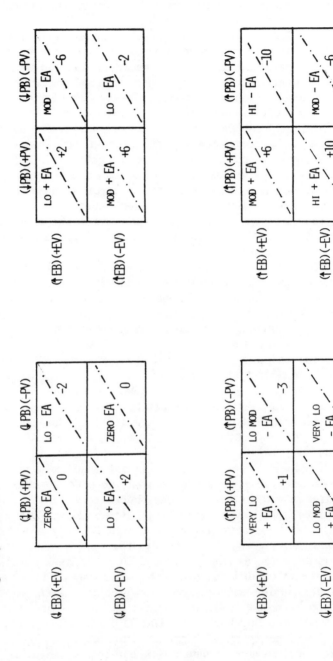

Let's start by suggesting a discrepancy measure between perceptual value (PV) and evoked value (EV) and assuming that both strength of perception and referent are high (PB and EB).

Before we proceed any further, the quantitative character-istics of the scales used here to tap the PV, PB, EV, and EB constructs should be described. The value constructs (PV and EV) will be measured using hypothetical bipolar rating scales (-10 to +10 with zero point deleted). The strength constructs (PB and EB) will be measured using hypothetical probability rating scales (.00 to 1.00). These scales should be construed as ratio scales for our theoretical purpose.

Equation 1

$$EA_{ik} = PV_{ik} - EV_{ik}$$

where i = attribute (i)
      k = individual (k)
   EA_{ik} = enhancement affect pertaining to attribute
        (i) of individual (k)
   PV_{ik} = perceived value of attribute (i) of
        individual (k)
   EV_{ik} = evoked (referent) value of attribute (i)
        of individual (k)

In the case of positive incongruity, a positive score is expected, and in the case of negative incongruity, a negative score is expected. In both positive and negative incongruity conditions, the predicted scores from Equation 1 are consistent with the theoretical predictions as shown in Figure 6.2. How-ever, in the case of both positive and negative congruities, Equation 1 produces zero scores, which are not quite consistent with the theoretical expectations as indicated in Figure 6.2. For the time being let us shelve this problem; later we will come back to it with a solution.

As stated previously, any value (perceived or evoked) is moderated by the strength of the connecting percept or concept. In other words, if a person expects that car X will give him 40 MPG and positively values the 40 MPG level, the value placed on the 40 MPG attribute is moderated by the extent to which his 40 MPG expectations is strong, moderate, or weak. A high posi-tive or negative value is neutralized by a weak relation, and conversely, is reinforced or strengthened by a strong relation. This is accounted for by multiplying the value constructs with the strength constructs. Therefore:

Equation 2

$$EA_{ik} = PB_{ik} \, PV_{ik} - EB_{ik} \, EV_{ik}$$

where PB_{ik} = perceived strength of attribute (i)
of individual (k)
EB_{ik} = belief strength of attribute (i) of
individual (k)

Going back to the theoretical distinction between positive
and negative congruity conditions that is yet unaccounted for
by Equation 2, the enhancement affect function can be modified
in such a way that will (1) positively increase EA_{ik} under positive
congruity conditions while simultaneously negatively increase
it under negative congruity conditions, and (2) insure that the
resulting EA_{ik} scores under $\downarrow EB / \uparrow PB$ pattern scores are of
lesser magnitude compared with those of $\uparrow EB / \downarrow PB$, as theoretically expected. As theoretically predicted and explained,
the enhancement affect is theorized to be greater under positive
congruity than under negative congruity conditions. Also, the
enhancement affect was postulated to be minimized under weak
belief conditions ($\downarrow EB / \uparrow PB$) due to the interference of the activation of the differentiation motive.

To accomplish this task, the square of ($EB_{ik} \, EV_{ik}$) is
introduced in Equation 2, or the square of the evoked components
to be multiplied with the perceptual components $PB_{ik} \, PV_{ik}$ as
shown in Equation 3:

Equation 3

$$EA_{ik} = [(PB_{ik} \, PV_{ik})(EB_{ik} \, EV_{ik})^2] - [EB_{ik} \, EV_{ik}]$$

The resultant EA_{ik} scores using this function are strongly
consistent with the theoretical expectations as shown in Figure
6.2.*

---

*Why this particular function, the reader may ask? It
may be argued that other functions may be tried. For instance
the square of the evoked component can be treated as a parameter
to be estimated.

$$EA_{ik} = [(PB_{ik} \, PV_{ik})(EB_{ik} \, EV_{ik})^{\alpha}] - [EB_{ik} \, EV_{ik}]$$

The model of the enhancement affect as represented in Equation 3 is limited to the activation and operation of one attribute (i). In most cases more than one attribute (i) might be involved with a given frame of reference. However, the question remains whether to use a compensatory decision rule or a noncompensatory one (refer to Chapter 11 for a social cognition treatment of decision rules). According to the literature on decision making, compensatory and linear decision rules seem to be more predictive than their noncompensatory and nonlinear counterparts (see Slovic and Lichtenstein 1975; Einhorn 1971). But based on the works by Anderson (1965, 1967) in cognitive algebra, the averaging rule seems to be as predictive as the summative rule. Based on the above notions, it may be argued that a compromise rule can be generated, that is, a decision or integration rule that possesses both qualities of averaging and summation. In other words the resultant cognitive response may be affected by the number of attributes processed in a monotonic manner rather than in the ordinary linear form.

It is postulated that the first attribute processed may have more impact on the resulting cognitive response relative to the second attribute. And similarly, the second attribute may play a more salient role in the overall resulting cognitive response than attribute three, and so on. What is needed is a "counting

---

Also, multiplying the perceptual component by two or some other estimated parameter may also do the job.

$$EA_{ik} = 2(PB_{ik} \, PV_{ik}) - (EB_{ik} \, EV_{ik})$$

$$EA_{ik} = \alpha (PB_{ik} \, PV_{ik}) - (EB_{ik} \, EV_{ik})$$

Better still adding the perceptual component to the discrepancy between the perceptual and evoked components may also produce a data pattern consistent with the theoretical expectations.

$$EA_{ik} = (PB_{ik} \, PV_{ik}) + [(PB_{ik} \, PV_{ik}) - (EB_{ik} \, EV_{ik})]$$

The point of all of this is not to argue for a specific function but to show possible tentative variations of the EA model that are consistent with theoretical predictions. Of course these functions (and possibly others) have to be tested for their predictive validity.

rule" of some sort that systematically places more weight on those attributes depending on their sequential position.

This can be done as follows:

Equation 4

$$EA_k = \sum_{i=1}^{I} \frac{1}{m} [(PB_{ik} PV_{ik})(EB_{ik} EV_{ik})^2 - (EB_{ik} EV_{ik})]$$

where m = sequential position of attribute (i), 1,2, ..., nI

Therefore, it may be proposed that the intensity of enhancement affect is a function of the sum of the adjusted (adjusted for sequential attribute processing) discrepancy between the perceptual and evoked sets as shown in Equation 4.

However, one must also acknowledge that parallel processing does occur, as stated earlier. Parallel processing can be captured best by the linear compensatory decision rule. Mathematically indexed:

Equation 5

$$EA_k = \sum_{i=1}^{I} [(PB_{ik} PV_{ik})(EB_{ik} EV_{ik})^2] - [EB_{ik} EV_{ik}]$$

THE CONSISTENCY AFFECT MODEL

This model describes the extent to which the comparison or congruity between perception and evoked belief relations will induce cognitive dissonance or cognitive consistency.

As stated in the previous chapter, positive or negative congruity is said to determine high consistency affect (cognitive consistency), whereas positive or negative incongruity is argued to induce low consistency affect (cognitive dissonance). This is shown in Figure 6.3.

In the case of the positive or negative congruity, the perceptual attributes are said to "fit" or closely correspond to the evoked attributes. In other words there is consistency between what is perceived and what is known or expected. This type of consistency is reflected in high consistency affect. On the other hand with positive or negative incongruity, there is a lack of a "goodness-of-fit" between the perceptual attributes

Figure 6.3 Congruity as Directed by the Consistency Motive

	+PV	-PV
+EV	POSITIVE CONGRUITY	NEGATIVE INCONGRUITY
-EV	POSITIVE INCONGRUITY	NEGATIVE CONGRUITY

	+PV	-PV
+EV	CONSISTENCY AFFECT	INCONSISTENCY AFFECT
-EV	INCONSISTENCY AFFECT	CONSISTENCY AFFECT

and the evoked counterparts. This will generate a feeling of dissonance, forcing the individual to reduce this dissonance.

The consistency affect is only prevalent in perceptual-related phenomena as will be treated in the following chapter. To illustrate the congruity dynamics involved with the consistency affect, an example might be in order. Suppose that a consumer through previous experience knows that the Ford Escort gives 30 MPG (EV). The same consumer then becomes exposed to an ad claiming that the Ford Escort gives 40 MPG (PV). In this situation the consumer will experience positive incongruity, which will cause a certain amount of dissonance (low consistency affect).

It should be noted, however, that congruity-inducing consistency affect (like congruity-inducing enhancement affect) is moderated by the strength of both perception and belief components (PB and EB). Theoretical predictions can be derived under each different congruity condition. These are shown in Figure 6.4.

As shown in Figure 6.4, cognitive dissonance (and cognitive consistency) were only expected under strong beliefs conditions (↑EB). Under weak perception/strong belief conditions (↓PB and ↑EB), moderate amounts of cognitive dissonance were expected for both positive and negative incongruity situations, whereas moderate amounts of cognitive dissonance were expected for both positive and negative congruity conditions. The same

Figure 6.4 Type and Degree of Consistency Affect as Theoretically Expected from the Different Congruity Conditions

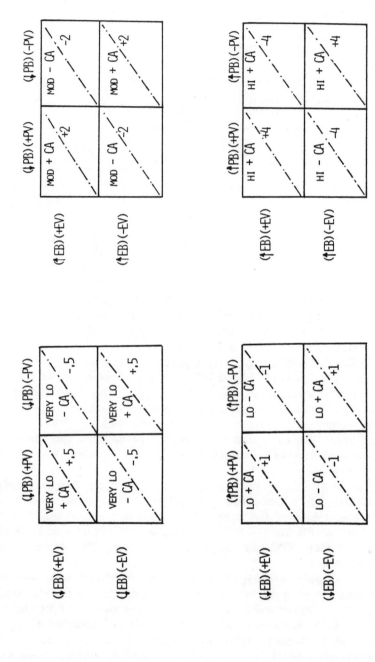

pattern of consistency affect is expected under strong perception/strong belief conditions (↑PB and ↑EB) but with greater intensity.

Under strong perception/weak belief conditions (↑PB and ↓EB), it can be argued that this would be a situation in which the need for cognitive differentiation becomes activated. However, does this mean that the need for cognitive consistency will remain completely dormant? It is proposed that the same cognitive consistency/dissonance affect will be induced but with a lesser magnitude compared to the strong perception/strong belief (↑PB and ↑EB) and weak perception/strong belief conditions (↓PB and ↑EB). This is shown in Figure 6.4

With regard to the weak perception/weak belief condition (↓PB and ↓EB), this will almost amount to message dismissal; however, a negligible similar pattern might occur.

Now, can this consistency affect function be mathematically modelled? To start with, the reader can note that the multiplicative product of the perceptual and evoked values may be a good starting point. That is:

Equation 6

$$CA_{ik} = PV_{ik} EV_{ik}$$

where CA_{ik} = consistency affect pertaining to attribute (i) of individual (k)

This function does provide positive scores for congruity conditions reflecting cognitive consistency and negative scores for incongruity conditions reflecting cognitive dissonance.

But as noted before, the need for cognitive differentiation can be activated under congruity conditions involving weak ↓EBs. If information acquisition affect is generated under weak ↓EB conditions, then, theoretically speaking, the consistency affect pattern in these conditions should be weaker than under strong ↑EB conditions. However, how can the perceptual and belief strength variables be incorporated in such a way to get lower cognitive consistency/cognitive dissonance scores under strong perception/weak belief conditions (↑PB and ↓EB) relative to the weak perception/strong belief conditions (↓PB and ↑EB) to meet our theoretical expectations? By introducing the square of (EB_{ik}) and the (PB_{ik}) as multiplicative variables to $PV_{ik} EV_{ik}$, then the resultant scores are found to be quite

quite consistent with the theoretical expectations (see Figure 6.4).* Therefore:

Equation 7

$$CA_{ik} = (PV_{ik} \, EV_{ik})(EB_{ik})^2 \, PB_{ik}$$

As it was argued for the multiattribute situation for the enhancement affect, the same decision rules can be used in the consistency affect function. Therefore, Equation 8 represents sequential attribute processing and Equation 9 indicates parallel processing.

Equation 8

$$CA_k = \sum_{i=1}^{I} \frac{1}{m} [(PV_{ik} \, EV_{ik})(EB_{ik})^2 \, PB_{ik}]$$

Equation 9

$$CA_k = \sum_{i=1}^{I} [(PV_{ik} \, EV_{ik})(EB_{ik})^2 \, PB_{ik}]$$

It is proposed, therefore, that affective intensity related to cognitive consistency/dissonance is a function of the sum of the adjusted (or unadjusted for sequential attribute processing) product of the perceptual and evoked value intensities, the square of the strength of the evoked beliefs, and the strength of the perceptions.

---

*As it was argued for the enhancement affect model, other variations of the consistency affect function are equally plausible. For example it may be easier to accept the fact that the power of the EB_{ik} component has to be estimated as a parameter rather than being treated as a constant.

$$CA_{ik} = (PV_{ik} \, EV_{ik})(EB_{ik})^\alpha \, PB_{ik}$$

Other models may be attempted and compared for their predictive validity.

THE INFORMATIONAL AFFECT MODEL

As presented in the congruity discussion, the need for cognitive differentiation is activated under weak belief or referent conditions ($\downarrow$EB). Weak beliefs generally result in an information acquisition response.

The information affect felt with a weak belief relation is more intense when the perception is strong ($\uparrow$PB) compared to when it is weak ($\downarrow$PB).

As shown in Figure 6.5, information affect is expected to be felt the strongest under strong perception/weak belief or referent conditions ($\uparrow$PB and $\downarrow$EB), followed by weak perception/weak belief conditions ($\downarrow$PB and $\downarrow$EB), followed equally by both $\uparrow$PB/$\uparrow$EB and $\downarrow$PB/$\uparrow$EB conditions.

These theoretical predictions can be mathematically modelled by first taking an index of the primary instigator of the need for cognitive differentiation, namely $\downarrow$EB. $\downarrow$EB can be mathematically represented as:

Equation 10

$$IA_{ik} = 1 - EB_{ik}$$

Since it is also expected that the value of both PV and EV affects the degree of informational affect experienced, a multiplicate index of both PV and EV combined (the absolute value of this index) can be incorporated into the informational affect function. Therefore:

Equation 11

$$IA_{ik} = (1 - EB_{ik})\ |PV_{ik}\ EV_{ik}|$$

And to insure that the $\uparrow$PB/$\downarrow$EB conditions will generate higher IA scores related to the $\downarrow$PB/$\downarrow$EB conditions, the PB variable can be introduced into Equation 11 to do just that. Therefore:

Equation 12

$$IA_{ik} = (1 - EB_{ik})\ |PV_{ik}\ EV_{ik}|\ (PB_{ik})$$

By applying Equation 12 to the different congruity conditions, the reader may note that the resulting scores are consistent with the theoretical expectations (see Figure 6.5).

Figure 6.5 Type and Degree of Information Affect as Theoretically Expected from the Different Congruity Conditions

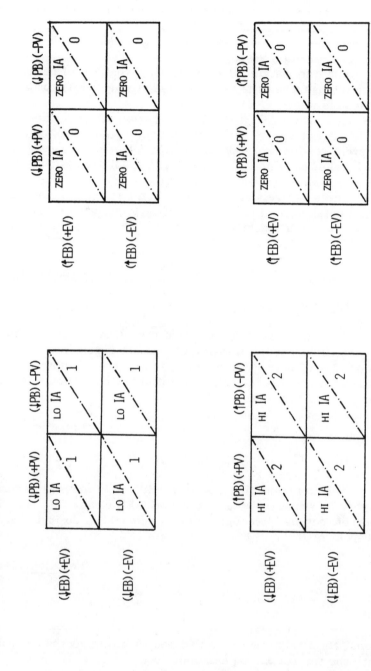

With respect to the multiattribute situation, the information affect function of Equation 13 can best represent sequential attribute processing, and Equation 14 can best represent parallel processing.*

Equation 13

$$IA_k = \sum_{i=1}^{I} \frac{1}{m} [(1 - EB_{ik}) |PV_{ik} EV_{ik}| (PB_{ik})]$$

Equation 14

$$IA_k = \sum_{i=1}^{I} [(1 - EB_{ik}) |PV_{ik} EV_{ik}| (PB_{ik})]$$

Therefore, it is proposed that the affective intensity of information assimilation/acquisition is a function of the sum of the adjusted (or unadjusted for sequential attribute processing) product of (1) the inverse strength of the evoked belief, (2) the absolute product of both perceptual and evoked value intensities, and (3) the strength of the perceptual component.

SUMMARY

The enhancement affect was construed to be mainly dependent on the degree of the positivity or negativity of a congruity state in evaluating a stimulus object as represented by a percept. Specifically, positive incongruity was expected to generate strong positive enhancement affect, positive congruity to induce moderate positive enhancement affect, negative congruity to induce moderate negative enhancement affect, and negative incongruity to be responsible for strong negative enhancement affect. Using a continuous function, enhancement affect was construed to be a function of the sum of the adjusted (or unadjusted for sequential attribute processing) discrepancy between the perceptual and evoked sets.

---

*As with the enhancement and consistency affect models, the models generated for information affect are highly tentative and require validational support.

The consistency affect was viewed to be dependent on the degree of congruity or incongruity occurring in perceptual-related phenomena. Specifically, consistency affect is postulated to be high under positive or negative congruity, and low under positive or negative incongruity. The continuous mathematical form of this model was formulated also. Accordingly, consistency affect was construed to be a function of the sum of the adjusted (or unadjusted for sequential attribute processing) product of the perceptual and evoked values, moderated by the strength of both perceptions and evoked beliefs.

Finally, the information affect was postulated to be determined by congruity conditions in either perception or evaluation-related phenomena involving weak evoked beliefs. Mathematically indexed, information affect was theorized to be a function of the sum of the adjusted (or unadjusted for sequential attribute processing) product of the uncertainty of the evoked beliefs, the absolute product of the perceptual and evoked values, and the strength of the perceptions involved.

CHAPTER 7
Perception

The classic triad of perception-evaluation-behavior has been construed for many years as the essence of attitude conceptualization efforts. An attitude toward an object represented as a percept is said to be determined by the beliefs associating the object itself with a set of attributes (perception) together with the value projected to these attributes (evaluation). The resultant process is a global affect state reflecting a predisposition to approach or avoid that object (behavior) (Fishbein and Ajzen 1975).

As shown in Figure 7.1, consequential cognitive phenomena that are usually described in terms of the perception-evaluation-behavior triad are described here to show how perceptual as well as evaluative phenomena are processed in (1) congruity operations, (2) resultant affect, (3) decision making, and (4) cognitive labeling.

In this chapter an attempt is made to elaborate on the dynamics involved with perception. The discussion is broken down into:

●perceptual congruity and resulting perceptual affect
●perceptual decision making
●cognitive labeling of beliefs

PERCEPTUAL CONGRUITY AND PERCEPTUAL AFFECT

The resulting affect from perceptual operations is nothing more than the consistency affect as described in the preceding

Figure 7.1 Cognitive Processes Involved with Perception
and Evaluation

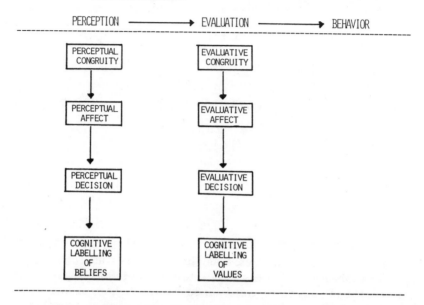

chapters. In other words the affect generated from congruity
dynamics as directed by the need for cognitive consistency and
as modelled by the consistency affect function is the same affect
operative in perception.

To briefly restate what has been described in discussing
consistency affect, perceptual affect can be in the form of
cognitive consistency (homeostasis) or cognitive dissonance
(deviation state). Cognitive consistency is determined by a
congruity state, irrespective of its directionality. In other
words both positive and negative congruities directed by the
cognitive consistency motive will generate consistency affect,
and both positive and negative incongruities directed by the
same motive will produce inconsistency affect.

This perceptual affect is a direct result of what has been
called "categorization" (Bruner 1957), "pattern recognition"
(Neisser 1967), "template matching" (at the attribute level
rather than the whole) (Selfridge and Neisser 1960; Uhr 1963;
Gibson 1963), and "feature analysis" (Selfridge 1959; Sutherland
1959).

It is proposed, therefore, that perceptual congruity involves the testing of "goodness-of-fit" between perceptions and
corresponding belief relations evoked within a given frame of
reference. Based on this proposition it can be argued that

consistency or dissonance affect may be associated with any categorization attempt. Specifically, a perceptual categorization attempt that lacks a "goodness-of-fit" will cause cognitive dissonance, which, in turn, motivates the individual to resort to alternative means to bring about a consistency state. One possible means may involve the activation of other frames of reference or cognitive categories to successfully complete the categorization or identification of the incoming stimulus object. Consequently, the degree of the "goodness-of-fit" can be precisely modelled and predicted by the consistency affect function.

Kahneman and Tversky (1972, 1973; Tversky and Kahneman 1974) referred to this categorization process as the "representativeness heuristic." The essence of this principle is that the individual assesses the degree to which each salient perceptual value pertaining to the stimulus object is representative of, or similar to, the evoked value of the activated frame of reference.

A number of other social psychology theories have direct bearing on the use of the consistency affect model in describing, explaining, and predicting perceptual categorization. These include implicit personality theory, social judgment theory, and cognitive dissonance theory.

Implicit personality theory refers to the tendency for an observer to use one or more perceptual cues associated with a given actor to categorize or stereotype the actor, and, therefore, other personality characteristics of that actor can be inferred (Bruner and Taguiri 1954; Cantor and Mischell 1979). This process is highly similar to the perceptual categorization described here.

With respect to social judgment theory (Sherif, Sherif, and Nebergall 1965), messages that are perceived to be falling within the assimilation effect region (consistent with the recipient's position) will be accepted, whereas messages falling with the contrast region (inconsistent with the recipient's position) will be rejected. Message acceptance and rejection seem to involve higher-order perception in which the message is already perceived. However, it can be easily argued that the same congruity dynamics applied to lower-order perception also apply to higher-order perception. In the case involving assimilation contrast effects, it was stated that the consistency affect model can be applied to predict acceptance or rejection of the message—assimilation means high consistency, whereas contrast means inconsistency or dissonance. When a perception does not fit or is inconsistent with the evoked cognitive category, cognitive dissonance will ensue motivating the individual to activate alternative cognitive schemas for better fitting.

A salient factor in Sherif's et al. social judgment theory is the concept of involvement. It was argued that in the case of high involvement, the assimilation region becomes narrowed, and conversely, in the case of low involvement, the assimilation region widens. How can this be explained by the proposed theory? It is simple. Remember what has been said about the centrality dimension as it is related to category width. It was mentioned that the more central the evoked frame of reference, the greater the likelihood that the involved attributes may have narrow attribute dimensions. This situation can be construed as a direct translation of the involvement concept in assimilation contrast effects. That is, low involvement means the activation of a noncentral frame of reference that has attribute dimensions with broad category widths.

Cognitive dissonance theory (Festinger 1957) tells us that discrepancy between a perception and an evoked belief may cause dissonance, which motivates the individual to act in one way or another to reduce this dissonance. From a lower-order perception point of view, it can be easily argued that people attempt to match or categorize incoming stimuli using consistency criteria. Those stimuli that are found to be inconsistent with an evoked category arouse dissonance, which serves to do more perceptual screening in an attempt to identify the stimulus object. On a higher-order perceptual level, it can be argued that a perceived message may be compared with previous associations (belief relations) regarding the percept, and in the presence of salient inconsistencies, the individual experiences dissonance. Dissonance, as an affective state indicating a deviation state from homeostasis, serves to arouse the individual to engage in further perceptual processing with the specific goal of reducing the experienced discrepancy, or bringing about a consistency or consonant cognitive state.

The magnitude of the dissonance has been mathematically expressed as:

$$D_k = \sum_{d=1}^{D} I_d \left/ \left[\sum_{d=1}^{D} I_d + \sum_{c=1}^{C} I_c \right] \right.$$

where D_k = magnitude of dissonance associated with cognitive element (k)

I_d = importance of dissonant element (d)

I_c = importance of consonant element (c)

D = number of cognitive elements in a dissonant relation with element (k)

$$C = \text{number of cognitive elements in a con-}$$
sonant relation with element (k)

This mathematical formulation can be evaluated based on the proposed theory. First, the precise mechanics elaborating how cognitions are dissonant or consonant with one another are not represented by the formula. Second, the strengths of the involved cognitions are not considered as moderator variables. And third, the formula forces us to consider cognitive interaction in terms of only two broad categories, namely dissonant versus consonant elements, and therefore can be viewed as "very crude."

It should be noted that the consistency affect model can be used with interval (relative) measures rather than with the ratio (absolute) measures described previously (ratio scales are used throughout this book for theoretical purposes only). To operationally represent the consistency affect model the importance of each involved belief has to be accounted for, as is done by Festinger's cognitive dissonance formula. Theoretically the importance measure is not needed since the importance weights are automatically reflected in the absolute magnitude of the value components. Since most operational self-report measures fail to tap the absolute magnitude of both perceptual and evoked values as well as the resulting affect, introducing the importance weights as separate variables can add to the predicted variance. The belief importance construct, of course, can be theoretically and operationally accounted for by belief centrality (BC_{ik}). Therefore, the operational form of the consistency affect model can be construed as:

$$CA_k = \sum_{i=1}^{I} \frac{1}{m} [BC_{ik} (PV_{ik} EV_{ik}) (EB_{ik})^2 (PB_{ik})]$$

or,

$$CA_k = \sum_{i=1}^{I} [BC_{ik} (PV_{ik} EV_{ik}) (EB_{ik})^2 (PB_{ik})]$$

The process of categorization is said to be influenced by the accessibility of certain cognitive schemas or categories to activation relative to others. With respect to the determinants of concept accessibility, at least four factors may be noted:

(1) the activation of a script in a specific situation

(2) goals in the form of affect felt as a result of experiencing one or more deviation states

(3) the strength of those beliefs involved in the activated script

(4) the degree of belief centrality involved within the evoked frame of reference.

When a consumer, for example, goes to the supermarket, the supermarket script is activated. This script contains a network of conceptual relations reflecting general expectations of objects, persons, and events occurring in the supermarket. By definition those conceptual relations involved in that script will be automatically more immediately accessible for activation and processing compared to a script involved with, let's say, studying for an exam (cf., Abelson 1976).

Accessibility of concepts and conceptual relations are also affected by the goals set by previous experiences of deviation states associated with the activation of one or more cognitive needs. For example suppose that a consumer in a previous situation having evaluated different brands of cars reached a decision regarding his/her need to acquire additional information regarding a specific brand. This can be in the form of a goal. The information acquisition affect translated into a goal will thus "prime" or make those conceptual relations related to the designated brand of automobile more accessible given a situation involving automobile advertising, visits to a car dealer, discussing cars with his/her friends, and so on.

Given the activation of a cognitive script and the accessibility of those beliefs stated in terms of goals, it is argued that those conceptual relations that are strong are more likely to be activated than are weak ones. This is a self-reinforcing tendency in which those strong conceptual relations, because of their strength, become more accessible and are further strengthened, whereas those weak beliefs gradually become extinguished.

Finally, the degree of belief centrality is argued to be a major determinant of concept accessibility. This seems to be rather obvious and commonsensical. Those beliefs and other conceptual relations of high importance to the individual will become more susceptible to perceptual activation compared to those which are not salient.

Tversky and Kahneman (1974) referred to the "availability heuristic" in describing the factors associated with concept accessibility to the processes of perception, memory, or construction from imagination. Nisbett and Ross (1981) made reference to the "vividness criterion." It is defined as information that is likely to attract and hold our attention because it may be emotionally interesting, concrete and imagery provoking, and/or proximate in a sensory, temporal, or spatial way.

More recently Cohen (1981) raised the question about the relative memorability of information that is consistent and inconsistent with a social category (cf. Rothbart, Evans, and Fulero 1979; Hastie and Kumar 1979). The relative memorability of concepts, of course, is directly relevant to the notion of concept accessibility introduced here. The findings were that both consistent and inconsistent information are memorable. These findings can be directly explained by the second and third factors related to concept accessibility. Inconsistent information will lead to cognitive dissonance, and the goals set associated with cognitive dissonance would serve to make the information that led to this dissonance more accessible for cognitive activation, or to make them more memorable. On the other hand, the memorability of consistent information is tied to the strength of the conceptual relation factor. It was argued that those cognitive categories having strong belief relations are more accessible for activation (memorability) than weak cognitive categories having weak belief relations. It seems quite plausible that the way social cognition researchers have operationally treated this construct had a lot to do with the strength of belief relation (Cohen 1981). That is, consistent information as manipulated by the experimenter has been in the form of a particular cognitive category, which is not only consistent with the incoming information but also has a strong link between the evoked concept and that attribute used to identify the perceptual attribute.

The discussion pertaining to perceptual congruity has been so far directed by the consistency affect model. Perceptual categorization was argued to be a process involving a match between a perception and a belief relation of an evoked cognitive category. Consequently, congruity involving the need for cognitive consistency has been the central point in this address. However, distinction had to be made between strong beliefs and weak beliefs involved with perceptual congruity. This distinction is important since the consistency affect model only applies under strong belief conditions. Under weak belief conditions, the information affect model becomes more applicable.

Therefore, it is argued that in case of weak beliefs the resultant process will involve information acquisition motivating the individual to seek external and/or internal information sources to strengthen the weak evoked beliefs.

But how and under what conditions does the individual allocate greater or lesser amounts of cognitive effort to perceptual processing? Or why do individuals under certain conditions attend to greater detail of the environment? More technically put, what are the determinants of perceptual intensity or attention and how do they relate to perceptual affect? Using social cognition terminology, greater attention to the stimulus object means the evocation of highly differentiated rather than non-differentiated frames of reference (cognitive categories or schemas). These, in turn, may have been evoked as a direct result of the evocation of a central or "ego-involving" conceptual relation in a congruity state, and/or an affective state related to either a homeostatic or deviation state of a particular motive. In other words attention as a psychological phenomenon can be predicted by taking into account the type and degree of congruity occurring at any specific time.

In the information processing literature, cognitive psychologists have described these phenomena in terms of "automatic versus deliberate pattern recognition" (Anderson 1980). Information processing theory posits that individuals can identify patterns by processes that recognize feature configurations. If the pattern is familiar, the stimulus will be recognized automatically (automatic processing) without the intercession of attention; if the pattern is unfamiliar, attention is directed to the stimulus to synthesize the features into a pattern (deliberate processing). Using the proposed theory, the unfamiliar pattern will involve an incongruity state between the perceptual set and the evoked frame of reference. This incongruity state causes cognitive dissonance, which, accordingly, determines the level of "attention." Familiar patterns, on the other hand, would be responsible for a lower level of attention.

It is also interesting to note that information processing theorists (for example, Anderson 1980) make the distinction between "top-down versus bottom-up processing." Top-down processing is perceptual processing directed by the individual's internal psychological dispositions (that is, needs, interests, attitudes), whereas bottom-up processing is the type of processing directed by the environment. From the social cognition perspective proposed here, this distinction is not made, because the notion of concept accessibility to perceptual activation is argued to implicitly describe this process. With a specific frame of reference, the individual can direct himself to process most of the incoming stimuli (for example, reading a book) or to actively seek only those stimuli that are to be compared with highly accessible conceptions (for example, listening to a verbal speech in a noisy room). The former state is said to be bottom-up processing and the latter state said to be top-bottom processing. Whichever type of processing is involved, it can be addressed in terms of degree of concept accessibility to sensory stimuli. In the bottom-up case a large set of cognitive categories becomes accessible to sensory stimuli, whereas the top-bottom type of processing, a select number of schemas become highly accessible to the incoming sensations.

But how do we explain surprising, novel, potentially threatening, or unexpected stimuli and their effect on our perceptual system? Information processing theorists explain these phenomena in terms of automatic and bottom-up types of processing (cf. Kahneman 1973). From the perspective proposed here, it is argued that a surprise affect is construed in terms of an emotional response resulting from the perception of an outcome compared with a highly incongruent belief as directed by the consistency motive.

Two remaining issues plague the literature of attention. These are: (1) parallel versus sequential processing, and (2) conscious versus unconscious processing (Broadbent 1958; Dixon 1971; J. Duncan 1980; Neisser 1976; Posner 1982). Parallel versus sequential processing refers to the notion of whether the mind can process more than one piece of information at a time (sequential processing) or whether it is capable of processing a number of information pieces simultaneously (parallel processing). Conscious versus unconscious processing refers to the extent to which unconscious processing can occur during conscious processing and whether this unconscious processing affects the operation of conscious processing.

Based on a recent assessment of the psychological literature of attention, Posner (1982), a renowned scholar in this area, presented cumulative evidence suggesting that parallel and sequential processing and conscious and unconscious processing do occur. Knowing this, how does the proposed theory treat these phenomena?

This author argues that there is no incompatibility between the congruity process discussed in this theory and the phenomena involving parallel versus sequential processing and conscious versus unconscious processing. If forced to take a stand on these issues, this author's position would be that more than one congruity process can occur simultaneously. Furthermore, the simultaneous occurrence of these congruity processes are "facilitated" if they are from different sensory channels rather than if they were from the same sensory channel. However, this is not to say that simultaneous congruities can only occur at a sensory lower-order level. Simultaneous congruities can occur at a higher-order level quite removed from sensory stimulation. Attention or cognitive effort, described by the proposed theory as an affective state resulting from previous congruities and directed to guide future congruities, can then be differentially allocated. A congruity process can occur with a low degree of allocation of cognitive effort or attention, and therefore can be characterized as "unconscious." Conversely, a congruity process having a greater attention allocation is said to be "conscious."

PERCEPTUAL DECISION

Perceptual decisions are nothing more than the formation of new beliefs or a change (or reinforcement) of existing beliefs. There are at least three types of perceptual decisions: (1) decisions linking the percept with the evoked concept referred to here as perceptual categorization, (2) decisions linking the percept with a conceptual attribute referred to as perceptual inference, and (3) decisions linking the percept with a modified attribute, which, in turn, is addressed in terms of belief change.

Perceptual Categorization

Decisions arising from perceptual categorization are decisions linking a percept with an evoked concept. These perceptual decisions are a direct result of perceptual categorization in which a stimulus object becomes identified by associating it with the evoked cognitive category (evoked concept). See Figure 7.2 for an illustration of this principle.

This process can be represented mathematically as:

$$CA_{ik} = (PV_{ik} \, EV_{ik})(EB_{ik})^2 \, (PB_{ik})$$

This would produce a score reflective of the consistency affect, which, in turn, may be taken as an indicator of the strength of the perceptual decision formed linking the percept with the evoked concept. In order to transform this CA_k score to a score standardized to zero-1.00 scale (the theoretical ratio scale used to represent strength of both belief and perception), a scaling transformation is needed. This is accomplished by dividing the CA_k score with the maximum possible CA_k score given perfect congruity (goodness-of-fit). This may be denoted as follows:

$$DB_k = CA_k / CA_k^{max}$$

Figure 7.2 Perceptual Categorization

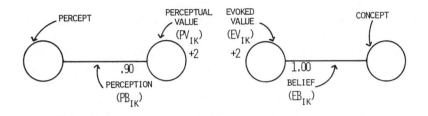

$$CA_K = (PV_{IK} \, EV_{IK})(EB_{IK})^2 (PB_{IK})$$

$$= (+2)(+2) \quad (1.00)^2(.90)$$

$$= +3.60$$

$$DB_K = CA_K / CA_K{}^{MAX}$$

$$= 3.60 / 4.00$$

$$= .90$$

Operationally, the belief centrality construct (BC_{ik}) has to be included in deriving CA_{ik} as shown previously.

Therefore, it is proposed that the strength of the perceptual decision (DB) linking the percept with the evoked concept is a direct function of the resulting consistency affect.

As shown in Figure 7.2, the degree of consistency affect experienced in this situation is close to maximal, that is, 3.60 out of 4.00 possible. The maximal consistency affect that can be experienced in any given situation can be derived by setting each perceptual value (PV) equal to each corresponding evoked value (EV), and setting the strength of both perception and corresponding beliefs equal to 1.00 (maximal strength). By dividing the experienced consistency affect with the maximal consistency affect that can be obtained in that particular situation, a value ranging from 0 to 1 can be obtained, indicating the strength of the stimulus object with the evoked cognitive category.

Perceptual Inference

Decisions arising from perceptual inference are decisions linking a percept with a conceptual attribute. Perceptual inference is a psychological process from which the stimulus object, through perceptual decoding or categorization, becomes directly associated with one or more attributes of the evoked concept. These conceptual attributes referred to here are not attribute dimensions that are used to categorize the percept but other related attributes directly linked with the evoked concept.

As with perceptual decisions linking a percept with an evoked concept, the perceptual dynamics involved with perceptual decisions linking a percept with a conceptual attribute can be described in terms of perceptual categorization and modelled through the consistency affect function (with minor alterations).

As argued earlier, the degree of a given perceptual categorization can be modelled through the consistency affect as follows:

$$CA_{ik} = (PV_{ik} \ EV_{ik})(EB_{ik})^2 \ (PB_{ik})$$

The resultant consistency affect is then standardized along the zero-1.00 belief strength scale as follows:

$$CA_k^! = CA_k \ / \ CA_k^{max}$$

However, for the percept to make connection with a conceptual attribute belonging to the evoked cognitive category, the belief strength linking the evoked concept with the conceptual attribute in question will moderate the resultant decision. This is intuitively highly plausible given the fact that under perfect "fit," the percept is categorized as the evoked concept. Given that the percept and the concept are now the same (contentwise), and given that the concept is associated with the conceptual attribute at a given strength, it is only logical to conclude that the resultant decision will be highly affected by the strength of this belief. In other words:

$$DB_k = (CA_k^!) \ (EB_{xk})$$

In operationalizing this model, the belief centrality construct (BC_{ik}) has to be included in deriving CA_k, as shown previously.

For example a consumer is exposed to a number of perceptual cues involving a stimulus object of an automobile. The evoked frame of reference used to identify or categorize this

automobile may be that of "Ford automobiles." Within the evoked
frame of reference of "Ford automobiles" may be a number of
attributes associating "Ford automobiles" with "unreliability"
and "low economy." A perceptual inference, in this case, may
be formed directly linking the stimulus object as a "Ford automobile" with "unreliability" and/or "low economy" (see Figure
7.3).

Hence, it is proposed that the strength of the perceptual
inference is a direct function of the degree of goodness-of-fit

Figure 7.3 Perceptual Inference

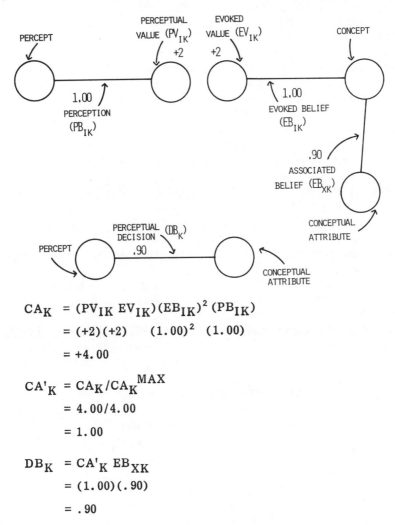

$$CA_K = (PV_{IK} \, EV_{IK})(EB_{IK})^2 \, (PB_{IK})$$
$$= (+2)(+2) \quad (1.00)^2 \quad (1.00)$$
$$= +4.00$$

$$CA'_K = CA_K / CA_K^{MAX}$$
$$= 4.00/4.00$$
$$= 1.00$$

$$DB_K = CA'_K \, EB_{XK}$$
$$= (1.00)(.90)$$
$$= .90$$

between the perceptual and the evoked sets as reflected by cognitive consistency or dissonance, and the strength of the belief associating the cognitive category (evoked concept) with the conceptual attribute in question.

Perceptual inference has been discussed extensively in the social psychology literature in terms of attribution, rules for perceptual organization, nonverbal communication, trait inferences, and so forth.

The attribution process is a perceptual process in which a consumer uses cognitive rules (or strong beliefs) to arrive at an inference or to form a new conceptual relation. These rules are referred to as the discounting, augmentation, and covariation principles.

These principles are derived from the works of Heider (1958), Jones and Davis (1965), Bem (1967, 1972), and encompassed within Kelley's attribution theory (1967, 1973). Kelley described the attribution process within an analysis-of-variance framework. He introduced the covariation principle based on multiple observations over time and configuation principles involving discounting and augmentation based on single observations.

The covariation principle refers to the extent to which an individual will infer the characteristic of an entity based on the distinctiveness, consistency, and consensus of perceptual cues. Distinctiveness refers to the attribution of the effect to the entity if it occurs uniquely when the entity is present and does not occur in its absence. Consistency is a twofold criterion. One is consistency over time—each time the entity is present, the individual's reaction must be the same. The other is consistency over modality—the reaction must be consistent even though the mode of interaction with the entity varies. Consensus describes the effect of an entity as perceived the same way by all observers.

The covariance principle was argued by Kelley to parallel the F-statistic used in statistical inference with analysis-of-variance designs. Thus:

$$\text{Naive } F = \frac{\text{distinctiveness criterion}}{\text{consistency and consensus criteria}}$$

An example of this principle is borrowed from Mizerski, Golden, and Kernan (1979, p. 128).

> A consumer's product experience illustrates this concept. If Kathy observes that her car runs

smoothly (the effect) on Brand A gasoline, but
knocks and misses (also effects) with all other
brands, she may think that smooth operation is
uniquely associated with Brand A. If Kathy further
finds that Brand A is associated with smooth operation every time she uses this brand, she should be
more confident that her initial observations were
valid. Similarly, she will also be more confident
if she finds that this effect is present in both city
and country driving. Finally, Kathy will have more
confidence in her perceptions to the extent that
other drivers recognize the same association between
the brand and smooth engine performance.

In this example Kathy observed that smooth engine operation was distinctive with Brand A gasoline as was consistently
smooth driving the four times she used Brand A in both city
and country driving. Her inference that the "cause" for smooth
engine operation must be something about Brand A is strengthened by the consensus information provided by other drivers.

The discounting principle (or "multiple sufficient schema")
describes the situation in which the perceiver believes that
any number of plausible causes could individually prompt an
observed effect, with any specific cause discounted when the
perceiver believes other causes are also present. This can be
illustrated with the automobile purchase example used by
Mizerski et al. (1979, p. 130),

The consumer (Brian) was attempting to infer the
true motivation (causal attribution) for the salesman's unfavorable comments (the effect to be attri-
buted) about the more expensive BX-70 automobile
(the stimulus object). Notice Brian's perception
of the plausible causes for a salesman providing
favorable (Case 1), as compared to unfavorable
(Case II), information about BX-70:
These perceptions are derived from Brian's
past experience with salesmen, information from
other individuals, and other sources (for example,
Consumer Reports and home economics literature),
using the covariance process. Brian has learned
to believe that there are many plausible causes
(nonstimulus attributions) other than the product's
actual performance that could prompt the salesman
to provide favorable product information. Therefore, Brian discounts the possibility of a stimulus

Table 7.1 An Attribution Example

	Case I	Case II
Observed effect:	−Says favorable things about the BX-70	−Says unfavorable things about the BX-70
Plausible causes:	−Believes what he says −Would lose his job if he didn't −Makes a higher commission on BX-70 −Would say anything to sell a BX-70	−Believes what he says

cause—that is, that the salesman was giving his honest opinion—and is unable to make a very strong or confident attribution for the salesman's comments. Unfavorable information presents a substantially different plausible causal array. In Case II, Brian finds it difficult to think of any nonstimulus causes. Because this situation involves no discounting of the plausible stimulus cause, Brian would tend to infer that the BX-70's poor performance prompted the unfavorable information.

The augmentation principle (or "compensatory schemata"), unlike the discounting principle where a simple presence or absence of plausible causes determines the strongest perception, operates where the nonstimulus cause(s) may be inhibitory for the observed effect. That is, the presence of the nonstimulus cause(s), such as constraints, costs, sacrifices, or risks involved in taking an action, serves to heighten the inferred perception that a stimulus cause is present.

Now, how are these rules or cognitive principles interpretable in terms of the proposed theory? These "rules" can be viewed as strong belief relations that are evoked for the purpose of using perceptual cues (or relations) to arrive at an inference concerning the cause of an observed effect. The cause can be represented as the perceptual decision (DB), the effect as the perception (PB).

For example, using the augmentation principle a consumer might observe an advertising message claiming both positive and negative characteristics in a product. Here, the consumer, based on his/her past experience, knows that it involves a high cost or sacrifice on the part of the manufacturer since the manufacturer may end up losing money by exposing the negative features of the product. Therefore the conceptual relation (or belief) generated in this case might be "advertisers who inform consumers about both positive and negative attributes of their products are honest." The perception in this situation might be "advertiser X is informing us about both the positive and negative features of a product." This comparison between a belief and a perception will induce a congruity process activating the need for cognitive consistency, and the resultant decision, "advertiser X is honest" will then be a direct function of the variables involved in the consistency affect model.

How about an example of the discounting principle. Let us use a somewhat similar example involving an advertiser informing its target audience only about the product's positive features and not its negative features. Here, the consumer might activate a cognitive category describing the typical advertiser who only informs its audience about the positive features of its product. This cognitive category involves the attributes of profit motive, having a truly superior product, or countering competition's claim. What is argued here is that the consumer has three various beliefs explaining why the advertiser informs its audience only about the positive features of its product. This is to be contrasted with the augmentation principle in which one belief relation is usually activated. The resultant inference explaining why that advertiser informs its audience only about the product's positive feature will become influenced by the strength of each belief relation involved and by the corresponding value intensities.

This process is described in two stages. The first stage involves the match between the perception and the cognitive category, through which inferences are made linking the percept to each conceptual attribute pertaining to the evoked cognitive category. Once these inferences are made, the extent to which an overall response would occur is dependent on the degree of the resultant congruity (second stage).

With respect to the covariation principle, the cognitive process can be described in two stages. The first stage involves a congruity between the perception and the evoked cognitive category that has the attribute of distinctiveness, consistency, and/or consensus in its conceptual network of relations. This allows an inference to be made linking the percept with any one of those attributes (distinctiveness, consistency, and/or consensus). The second stage involves the resulting inference acting as a perception and being compared to the cognitive category involving the particular perceptual attribute. This evoked cognitive category, in turn, is most likely associated with those attributes that reflect the disposition of the stimulus object, person, or event. In both of these cases, the consistency affect model can be used to predict the strength of the resultant perceptual decisions.

Nonverbal communication studies in the social sciences have been rapidly accelerating for the last two decades (Knapp 1972). Nonverbal communication has been studied to determine those implicit rules that people use to infer psychological disposition of nonverbal interpersonal interaction. These nonverbal communication principles introduced here are primarily due to Mehrabian's (1968, 1971, 1972) research. Mehrabian asserted that the total impact of an interaction can be partialled as .07 verbal + .38 vocal + .55 facial. Though the relative variances are questionable, this assertion underscores the notion that perception using nonverbal cues is an important psychological study.

Mehrabian's research consisted of an extensive series of investigations designed toward partialling the components of nonverbal behavior along the two basic dimensions of: (1) evaluation or liking, and (2) potency or social control.

The evaluation principle refers to the notion that an observer would infer an actor's evaluation of the observer or another as being positive using one or more of the following cues: head nods, uh-huh, rhythmic following, close proximity, touching, eye contact, forward lean, higher speech rate, lengthier communication, frequent verbal reinforcers, gesticulation, smiling, less frequent self-references, and/or open arrangement of arms. On the other hand, inference of a negative evaluation can be derived using the cues of reclining position, backward lean, avoiding or shifting eye contact, avoidance of close proximity, closed arrangement of arms, torso orientation away from the addressee, and/or finger tapping.

The potency principle, on the other hand, describes those perceptual cues used to make inferences about the status of the actor. A high status inference is generally arrived at using the following cues: direct eye contact while speaking, moderate eye contact when listening, relaxed posture, arm position asymmetry, sideways lean, hand relaxation, neck relaxation, head nodding, gesticulation, increased facial activity, low speech-error rate, halting speech with eye contact, active speech rate, strong speech volume, chest expanded, backward lean, and/or direct body orientation.

A low status inference involves the following cues: looking away before speaking, steady eye contact when listening, hesitations, halting speech with shifting eye contact, high speech-error rate, inactive communication, depressed posture, forward lean, bowed head, dropping shoulders, sunken chest, and/or shifting body orientation.

These principles represent the congruity process in which nonverbal cues are associated with personality dispositions as conceptual relations or beliefs. These beliefs are activated when a nonverbal cue is perceived, decoded, or placed in a cognitive category, and the resulting inference of the actor's disposition becomes the multiplicative function of the degree of the goodness-of-fit and the strength of the noverbal-personality belief relation.

As stated above, the inference derived from the nonverbal cues can be modelled using the consistency affect formula. For example let's say that we are using an advertising communicator who is supposed to give the impression of high status, since high status people are usually perceived as more credible. In other words we want the communicator to use a set of nonverbal cues to induce an inference or perception in the target audience that the communicator (and therefore the communication) is credible.

Rules of perceptual organization involve those firmly rooted (primitive) beliefs that allow the individual to make distinctions between figure and ground. Stimuli tend to organize themselves in accordance with the gestalt principles of perception. These principles include the principle of proximity, similarity, good continuation, closure, and symmetry (Anderson 1980).

Sensory elements which are proximally close to one another tend to organize into units as dictated by the principle of proximity. The principle of similarity refers to the notion that sensory objects that look alike tend to be grouped together. The principle of good continuation rules that sensory elements that have good continuation in form will be perceived as objects. The principle of closure illustrates the fact that when elements group themselves in form, we tend to perceive them in terms of objects while filling in any gaps. The symmetry principle points to the notion that sensory elements grouped together having symmetrical form will be perceived as objects compared to non-symmetrical forms.

As with the attribution and nonverbal communication principles, these psychological principles are construed in terms
of congruity using the social cognition perspective proposed
here. Strong beliefs such as proximal objects, similar objects,
and objects with good continuation may all represent figure
rather than ground. These belief relations are matched with
stimulus objects, and the resulting congruity will determine
the extent to which these stimuli will be identified or categorized
as form or ground. That is, cognitive consistency would result
in a "form" perception, whereas cognitive dissonance would
determine a "ground" perception.

Trait inference refers to the inference of a network of
personality traits from information that may be relevant to a
single or few traits. This has been referred to as "stereotypic
perception," and is the essence of implicit personality theory
(Asch 1946; Schneider 1973; Bruner and Taguiri 1954). Ebbesen
and Allen (1979) used two different models to describe this in-
ferential process: (1) the exemplar scanning model, and (2)
the feature comparison model.

The exemplar scanning model posits that the inference of
traits is dictated by the evocation of an "exemplar" category.
To use the same example provided by Ebbesen and Allen (1979),
if a person is asked to verify whether "a witty person is also
generous," he/she might retrieve one or more of the known
persons who possess the trait "witty" and examine this sample
to determine whether "generous" is a trait that these exemplars
possess. Therefore, the strength of the resulting inference is
dependent on the extent to which the exemplars possess both
traits (cf. Kahneman and Tversky 1972; Walker 1975).

With respect to the feature comparison model, the trait
inference is argued to be a function of the overall similarity
between lists of features that the two traits activate in memory.
When the similarity between the two feature sets is above a given
threshold, the resultant inference is strong. When this similarity
falls below that threshold, the resultant inference is weak (or
no inference is made). When the similarity falls right around
the threshold, a second stage of processing is hypothesized.

Ebbesen and Allen (1979) conducted a number of experiments to test the predictive validity of these two models. The
findings indicated that the two models are equally "plausible."

Let us try to explain the trait inference process through
the direct application of the consistency affect model. The
exemplar scanning model describes a situation in which, using
social cognition language, a cognitive category of the "typical"
or "exemplar" persons is evoked. One trait (for example,

"witty") associated with a perceptual cue is used to activate its cognitive category counterpart (that is, exemplar "witty" person). The resultant inference associating the percept ("witty") with "generous" depends on the goodness-of-fit and the strength between the concept ("exemplar witty person") and the conceptual attribute ("generous").

As far as the feature comparison model is concerned, we also can use the consistency affect model to describe its internal dynamics. Using social cognition theory, it can be argued that one trait can be depicted as a percept and the other as a concept. The percept, of course, is associated with one or more perceptual cues or attributes. These perceptual attributes are directly matched against their corresponding attributes related to the evoked concept. The resulting congruity may be that of cognitive consistency or dissonance. With cognitive consistency, the resultant inference would associate the percept with the conceptual attribute. The precise mechanics of this process is elaborated upon in some detail in the following section.

Belief Change

Decisions reflecting belief change can be viewed as decisions linking a percept with a modified attribute. The decisions emanating from a perceptual categorization involving a "good fit" that result in the formation of a new belief arise directly from perceptual processes involving cognitive dissonance. For example suppose that an advertising message advocating "Ford Escort gives 40 MPG" is compared with a frame of reference involved with prior experience with the Ford Escort. Furthermore, suppose that a salient belief in this frame of reference is "Ford Escort gives only 25 MPG based on my own past experience with this automobile." The perception will be found to be inconsistent with the evoked conception. The resultant state is cognitive dissonance.

Among the possible alternative strategies in reducing this dissonance are: (1) cognitive change involving the perceptual value component (PV), (2) cognitive change involving the evoked value (EV) component, or (3) cognitive change involving both the perceptual and evoked components.

The magnitude of change can be modelled and predicted by taking the average of the perceptual and evoked components together. Specifically, the value of the newly formed decision (DV) can be predicted as follows:

$$DV = (|PV| \; / \; |PV| + |EV|)PV + (|EV| \; / \; |EV| + |PV|) \, EV$$

This is directly borrowed from Osgood and Tannenbaum's (1955) congruity principle as will be discussed in a following section. However, to improve on this belief-change model, the moderating effects of PB and EB can be incorporated in the equation. This is done by multiplying each PV variable with its corresponding PB, and similarly each EV is multiplied with its corresponding EB. The resulting function can be represented as follows:

$$DV = (|PV| \ PB \ / \ |PV| \ PB + |EV| \ EB) \ PV \ PB +$$
$$(|EV| \ EB \ / \ |EV| \ EB + |PV| \ PB) \ EV \ EB$$

And the strength of the newly formed belief (DB) can be modelled by taking the weighted average of both PB and EB. The weights involve the PB and EB constructs. Therefore:

$$DB = (PB^2 + EB^2)/(PB + EB)$$

Therefore, it is proposed that the perceptual decision formed would have a value that is a function of the average of the weighted values of the perceptual and evoked value components. The weight of the perceptual value is its perceptual strength, whereas the weight of the evoked value is its belief strength. Furthermore, the strength of the perceptual decision linking the percept with a modified attribute is a function of the weighted average of the strength of both perception and evoked belief components.

Now let us take a few minutes to relate these propositions to three social psychology theories directly addressing this phenomenon. These are: (1) Osgood and Tannenbaum's (1955) congruity principle, (2) Rokeach's (1972) principle of belief congruence, and (3) Jaccard's (1981a) belief-change theory.

Osgood and Tannenbaum's (1955) congruity principle is designed to predict the outcome of a cognitive interaction between two psychological relations based on the direction and degree of polarization of the two relations. The formula used to predict the outcome of this cognitive interaction is as follows:

$$Dcs = |Dc|/(|Dc| + |Ds|) \ Dc + |Ds|/(|Ds| + |Dc|) \ Ds$$

where $|D|$ is deviation or polarization from neutrality on
        the scales regardless of sign,
    D is deviation from neutrality with respect to sign
    cs is a characterized subject
    s is a subject
and c is a characterization

Figure 7.4 Belief Change

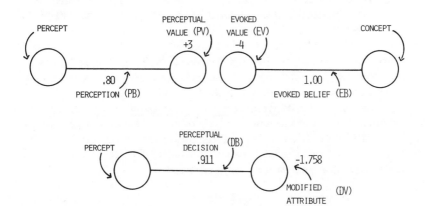

$DV = (|PV| \text{ PB } / |PV| \text{ PB} + |EV| \text{ EB) PV PB} +$

$\quad (|EV| \text{ EB } / |EV| \text{ EB} + |PV| \text{ PB) EV EB}$

$\quad = |+3| \ (.80) \ / \ |+3| \ (.80) + |-4| \ (1.00)) \ ((+3)(.80)) +$

$\quad (|-4| \ (1.00) \ / \ |-4| \ (1.00) + |+3| \ (.80)) \ ((-4)(1.00))$

$\quad = -1.758$

$DB = (PB^2 + EB^2) \ / \ (PB + EB)$

$\quad = ((.80)^2 + (1.00)^2) \ / \ (.80 + 1.00)$

$\quad = .911$

     Using an example provided by Rokeach (1972), if one strongly admires college professors (+3) and moderately deplores extramarital sexual relations (-2) and then learns that the former approves of the latter, the outcome of this cognitive interaction can be viewed as a belief change linking the percept "college professors" with a modified attribute value reflecting a decrease in valence toward the percept.

     By translating this principle into the language of the proposed theory, the reader may note some of the shortcomings of this principle. For instance the congruity principle does not tell us anything about how the individual came to value the subject or the characterization. We also do not know anything about the strength of these beliefs.

     By making some assumptions about these unknown variables, the psychological mechanics described above can be explained using the proposed social cognition theory. The process can be viewed as involving at least three stages. The first stage involves the evocation of a conceptual relation that answers the perceptual question. The second stage evaluates the percept in direct relation to the link between the subject and characterization. The mechanics of this stage will be covered in some depth in the section involving "evaluation." The third stage shows how two conflicting psychological relations are compared and how the resulting decision is derived.

Rokeach's (1972) <u>principle of belief congruence</u> is essentially quite similar to Osgood and Tannenbaum's (1955) congruity principle with a minor deviation. This deviation involves the construct of belief centrality as operationalized in terms of perceived importance. Mathematically represented:

$$Dcs = (W)Dc + (1 - W)Ds$$

where (W) and (1 - W) refer to the perceived importance of Dc and Ds relative to one another in the context of cs.

For example using the same example involving college professor (s) and extramarital sexual relations (c), the cognitive interaction and outcome are not solely dictated by the intensity and direction of the value of both Dc and Ds but also by their relative importance weights.

The position taken by this author is that belief centrality or perceived importance is usually reflected in the magnitude of the value associated with a given attribute. Therefore, the inclusion of importance weights is theoretically redundant; however, they should be included in operationalizing the functions. This may be done as follows:

$$DV = (|PV| \, PB \, BC \, / \, |PV| \, PB \, BC + |EV| \, EB \, BC) +$$
$$(|EV| \, EB \, BC \, / \, |EV| \, EB \, BC + |PV| \, PB \, BC)$$

and

$$DB = BC \, (PB^2 + EB^2)/(PB + EB)$$

However, the central problem with Rokeach's mathematical formulation of the principle of belief congruence is one of scaling. The linear combination of the cognitive elements would only produce the correct theoretical predictions given that one cognitive element is positive and the other negative (using a bipolar scale). However, given that the two cognitive elements are both positive or negative, the function would yield equivocal results. Based on this argument, it can be said that Osgood and Tannenbaum's function is more effective with bipolar scales than Rokeach's function.

Jaccard's (1981a) belief-change theory argues that the immediate psychological determinants of belief change are the discrepancy of the source's position from the individual's own position, the confidence the individual has in his/her own position, and the confidence the individual has in the source.

Jaccard's theory of belief change is highly akin to the principle involving the linkage of the percept with a modified attribute. According to Jaccard's theory, the nature of the newly formed belief, which can be represented as DV, is dependent on the discrepancy of the source's position and the individual's position. The source's position can be represented in terms of the PV component and the individual's position becomes the EV component. The perceived discrepancy between the two components is mathematically represented in the average of the two components. This, of course, is moderated by the confidence of the individual's position and the perceived credibility of the source's position. These two moderator constructs are represented by the strength of the perception, PB (confidence in source's position), and the strength of the evoked relation, EB (confidence in the individual's own position).

As noted, Jaccard's theory describes the direction of belief change (DV) but does not touch upon the strength of the resulting belief (DB).

COGNITIVE LABELING OF BELIEFS

The strength of a given belief, whether it is a perceptual decision, playing the role of a perception, or evoked from the cognitive structure can be verbally labeled to signify the degree of strength. For example a belief having a strength of, let's say .90, may be labeled as "very strong," whereas a .20 may be labeled "weak."

How do beliefs get labeled? This is done by perceptual categorization and inference as was described repeatedly in the preceding sections. In other words the belief that is to be labeled is placed on the perceptual platform playing the role of a percept. The perceptual attribute would represent, in this case, the strength of the belief (perception). A cognitive category representing the percept is evoked to identify the percept using the same attribute dimension. The perceptual

Figure 7.5 Cognitive Labeling of Beliefs

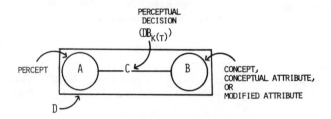

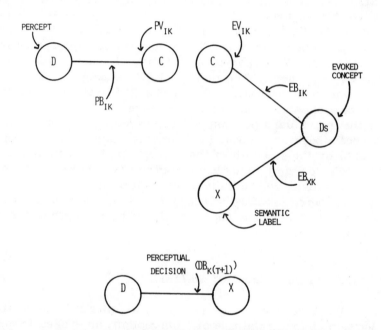

process used to describe perceptual inference can be used here to describe cognitive labeling of beliefs. This process is exemplified in Figure 7.5.

SUMMARY

Perceptual congruity was described in terms of congruity directed by the consistency motive and the resulting affect in terms of consistency affect. Both positive and negative congruities were argued to generate high consistency affect, while positive and negative incongruities were said to induce low consistency affect (dissonance).

Perceptual categorization was viewed as a perceptual decision linking a percept with an evoked concept. A mathematical argument was introduced to describe this process and its resulting outcome. This was done within the framework of the consistency affect model.

Perceptual inference was viewed as a perceptual decision linking a percept with a conceptual attribute. A mathematical formulation was also provided to describe this process and its outcome. This again was accomplished within the overall framework of the consistency affect model.

Belief change, in turn, was construed in terms of a perceptual decision linking a percept with a modified attribute. A mathematical representation of this process was attempted also.

The discussion of these perceptual processes and outcomes was related directly to existing social cognition theories.

CHAPTER 8
Evaluation

In contrast to perception, which is argued to be mostly directed by the consistency motive, the evaluation process will be argued as a function of the enhancement motive. Evaluative affect is construed to be the direct result of evaluative congruity, and therefore both phenomena will be treated conjunctively. Also, the process involving evaluative decision making and cognitive labeling of values will be treated in this chapter.

EVALUATIVE CONGRUITY AND EVALUATIVE AFFECT

The enhancement affect felt as a direct result of evaluative congruity is an affective disposition toward the object in question. It is equivalent to the concept of attitude propagated in the social psychology literature. However, a further distinction has to be drawn between attitude toward an object (A-object) and attitude toward an act (A-act). The enhancement affect resulting from evaluative congruity is more akin to the A-object construct than the A-act construct. The verbal manifestation of this attitude (enhancement affect) has usually been referred to as opinions and will be treated in some depth in the evaluative decision section.

Evaluative congruity involves the direct use of the enhancement affect model. Specifically, the evaluation of a stimulus object or percept is done by assessing the value differences between perceptual and evoked values. Once the perceptual attributes attain their value through perceptual encoding or through the assessment of the value difference, it is just a matter of applying the traditional multiattribute attitude formula, involving the sum of the product of the value of each perceptual attribute with the strength of the corresponding perception

$$\sum_{i=1}^{I} PB_{ik}\, PV_{ik}$$

This is the traditional expectancy-value model highly publicized in the social and consumer psychology literature (Fishbein and Ajzen 1975; Lutz 1981).

It is being argued here that the enhancement affect model described in the previous chapter, and represented as:

$$EA_k - \sum_{i=1}^{I} \frac{1}{m} \left[(PV_{ik}\, PB_{ik})(EV_{ik}\, EB_{ik})^2 - (EV_{ik}\, EB_{ik}) \right]$$

or

$$EA_k = \sum_{i=1}^{I} \left[(PV_{ik}\, PB_{ik})(EV_{ik}\, EB_{ik})^2 - (EV_{ik}\, EB_{ik}) \right]$$

is not an alien formula of attitudes. It is based on the traditional expectancy-value model and has the advantage of accounting for the precise mechanics pertaining to the evoked frame of reference (see Figure 8.1).

So, in other words, it can be easily argued that the two models can be used interchangeably. The sole requirement for using the expectancy-value model as shown above is control of the evoked frame of reference. To reiterate, the multiattribute attitude model can be used more effectively given that respondents make their evaluations in direct comparison with a specified standard—that standard may be another comparative stimulus object or their own expected, desired, or deserved criterion of evaluation restricted to that object category.

Another point involves the relative versus absolute or interval versus ratio scaling of the attitude component. The traditional expectancy-value model produces scores that are meaningless in an absolute form but meaningful when one attitude score is compared to another. In contrast the enhancement affect function provided here can be construed as a ratio measure. That is, a score derived from the direct application of this formula is meaningful by itself, and in relation to other scores.

Figure 8.1 Evaluative Congruity and Affect

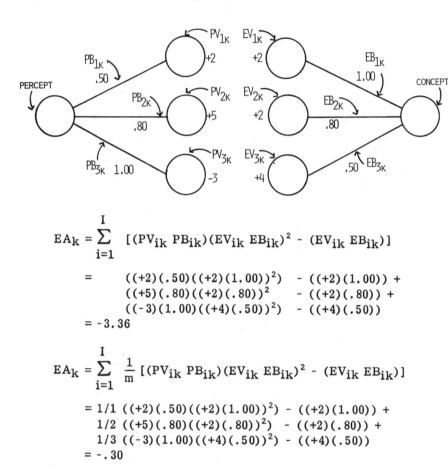

$$EA_k = \sum_{i=1}^{I} [(PV_{ik} PB_{ik})(EV_{ik} EB_{ik})^2 - (EV_{ik} EB_{ik})]$$

$$\begin{aligned}
= \quad &((+2)(.50)((+2)(1.00))^2) \quad - ((+2)(1.00)) + \\
&((+5)(.80)((+2)(.80))^2 \quad\;\; - ((+2)(.80)) + \\
&((-3)(1.00)((+4)(.50))^2) \quad - ((+4)(.50))
\end{aligned}$$

$$= -3.36$$

$$EA_k = \sum_{i=1}^{I} \frac{1}{m} [(PV_{ik} PB_{ik})(EV_{ik} EB_{ik})^2 - (EV_{ik} EB_{ik})]$$

$$\begin{aligned}
= \;\; &1/1 \;((+2)(.50)((+2)(1.00))^2) - ((+2)(1.00)) + \\
&1/2 \;((+5)(.80)((+2)(.80))^2) \;\; - ((+2)(.80)) + \\
&1/3 \;((-3)(1.00)((+4)(.50))^2) - ((+4)(.50))
\end{aligned}$$

$$= -.30$$

Therefore, it is proposed that the degree of evaluation of an object percept is a function of the sum of the discrepancy between the perceptual set and the corresponding evoked set adjusting (or unadjusting) for sequential attribute processing. The perceptual set for a specific attribute dimension involves the product of perceptual value of that attribute with its perceptual strength weighted by the square of the evoked component of the same attribute dimension. The evoked component involves the product of the evoked value of the same attribute dimension and its evoked strength.

In operational form, since the ratio scales cannot be used in their absolute form, the belief-centrality variable (BC_{ik})

should be included in the theoretical version of the enhancement affect function. The operational form of the enhancement affect model employed to describe evaluative affect can be designated as follows:

$$EA_k = \sum_{i=1}^{I} \frac{1}{m} [BC_{ik} (PV_{ik} PB_{ik})(EV_{ik} EB_{ik})^2 - (EV_{ik} EB_{ik})]$$

or

$$EA_k = \sum_{i=1}^{I} [BC_{ik} (PV_{ik} PB_{ik})(EV_{ik} EB_{ik})^2 - (EV_{ik} EB_{ik})]$$

This model can be used operationally if the investigator is in a position to measure the reference point. On the other hand the investigator can control the reference point by specifically instructing the individual to evaluate the stimulus object in comparison with a designated other. Under controlled conditions the investigator may opt not to measure the cognitive elements associated with the reference point. In this case the traditional expectancy-value model may suffice. The measurement aspects of the traditional expectancy-value model can be improved slightly by introducing the belief-centrality construct into the traditional formula when comparisons are made between stimulus objects derived from different object classes (for example, different products rather than different brands of the same product).

$$A_k = \sum_{i=1}^{I} [BC_{ik} PV_{ik} PB_{ik}]$$

Also, the sequential decision rule can be employed under conditions when the order of attribute processing is controlled and/or measured.

$$A_k = \sum_{i=1}^{I} \frac{1}{m} [BC_{ik} PV_{ik} PB_{ik}]$$

Next, the concept of attitude toward objects as treated in the social psychology literature will be reviewed. Then, an attempt will be made to discuss alternative attitude formulation in light of the above discussion on evaluative congruity.

The concept of <u>attitude</u> has been conceptualized by social psychologists as an organized predisposition to respond in a favorable or unfavorable manner toward a specified class of social objects (Shaver 1981).

Based on this conceptual definition of attitude, attitude theoreticians and researchers conceive three separate components of an attitude: a cognitive component, an affective component, and a behavioral component (Krech, Crutchfield, and Ballachey 1962; Fishbein and Ajzen 1975; Allport 1935). The <u>cognitive</u> component refers to the sum total of knowledge, beliefs, or perceptions associating the stimulus object with a set of attributes. The <u>affective</u> component involves the sum total of the values, emotions, and affective dispositions toward each of the attributes in question. The <u>behavioral</u> component has been thought of as the "predisposition to respond"—which reflects both the beliefs about the attitude object and the evaluative judgments made of the object.

The major alternative to the three-component view of attitude treats attitude as a single dimension of affect for or against an object. Fishbein (1967) argued that the evaluative or affective component is usually treated as the attitude. Katz and Stotland (1959) and Rosenberg (1956) asserted that an attitude includes both cognitive and affective components and should not necessarily include the behavioral component. This is the two-component view of attitude (Bagozzi and Burnkrant 1979).

The social cognition position proposed here, of course, is that of the <u>two-component</u> view of attitude.

This concept of attitude has been treated from a number of theoretical perspectives. These are: (1) theory of syllogistic thinking, (2) learning theory, (3) expectancy-value theory, (4) consistency theory, and (5) attribution theory. Each of these theoretical treatments will be addressed and an attempt will be made to establish a connection between the traditional theoretical treatments of attitude and the principle of evaluative congruity presented here.

With respect to the <u>syllogistic</u> model, Jones and Gerard (1967) and Bem (1970) attempted to explain attitude organization in terms of syllogistic thought mechanisms. A syllogism is a form of logical reasoning in which two premises are related to each other to produce a conclusion. The essence of this attitude theory is that the minor premise can be a <u>belief premise</u> and the major premise is the <u>evaluative premise</u>, and the conclusion can be construed in terms of the resultant attitude.

For example:

Cars provide a form of transportation (minor premise: belief)
Transportation is good (major premise: evaluation)
Cars are good (conclusion: attitude)

This syllogistic view of attitude is not incompatible with the proposed theory. A minor premise can be construed as a perception linking the percept (cars) with the perceptual attribute (transportation). This perceptual attribute (transportation) is matched against its corresponding evoked attribute (transportation), which is associated with a concept (good). A perceptual inference would therefore result linking the percept (transportation) with the conceptual attribute (good). The evoked conceptual relation in this case is the major premise. The conclusion that is represented as the attitude is therefore a decision stemming from this perceptual process and described in terms of the cognitive labeling of beliefs.

This process can be precisely modelled using the consistency affect function and the propositions involving perceptual congruity.

With respect to the <u>learning theory</u> of attitudes, attitude is defined as a learned, implicit anticipatory response. Classical conditioning has been used to explain how specific associations are formed between perceived objects and their attributes. Instrumental conditioning was applied to explain the evaluative responses associated with the object attributes (Fishbein and Ajzen 1975).

Fishbein (1967) argued that an attitude toward any object is a function of the beliefs about the object and the implicit evaluative responses associated with those beliefs, expressed in this form:

$$A_k = \sum_{i=1}^{I} b_{ik} e_{ik}$$

where A_k = attitude toward some object (o)
of individual (k)
b_{ik} = belief (i) about (o) of individual (k)
e_{ik} = the evaluation of attribute (i) of
individual (k)
I = number of beliefs

This model can be directly translated in terms of the proposed social cognition theory as:

$$EA_k = \sum_{i=1}^{I} PB_{ik} \; PV_{ik}$$

And as stated previously, this model is criticized as inadequate because it does not take into account the elements involved with the evoked set. It also assumes parallel processing in a linear summative form, which cannot be theoretically justified by itself.

The essence of <u>expectancy-value theory</u> of attitude is that people have certain expectations about the attributes associated with an object. These attributes can have either positive or negative valence, that is, benefits or costs. Among the numerous versions of expectancy-value models of attitudes, two will be referred to. These are Edward's (1954) subjective expected utility model (SEU) and Rosenberg's (1960) instrumentality-value model.

Edward's <u>subjective expected utility</u> model is expressed as follows:

$$A_k = \sum_{i=1}^{I} SP_{ik} \; U_{ik}$$

where SP_{ik} = subjective probability that alternative (o) will lead to outcome (i) for individual (k)

U_{ik} = subjective value of utility of outcome (i) of individual (k)

Rosenberg's <u>instrumentality-value</u> model can also be expressed as:

$$A_k = \sum_{j=1}^{J} I_{jk} \; V_{jk}$$

where I_{jk} = instrumentality or probability that (o) will lead to the attainment of goal (j) for individual (k)

V_{jk} = value importance or degree of satisfaction or dissatisfaction associated with goal (j) for individual (k)

Of course both models are highly similar to one another and also similar to Fishbein's (1963) model. The SP , I , and b can all be expressed in terms of the perceptual strength (PB) associating the stimulus object O with the attribute i's. The U , V , and e are all akin to the value associated with the perceptual attributes that are associated with the stimulus object O (PV). Moreover, the same argument used to criticize the Fishbein model can also be applied in the context of the expectancy-value models.

Consistency theory of attitude is a macro theory that contains Heider's (1958) balance theory, Osgood and Tannenbaum's (1955) cognitive congruity theory. Each will be covered briefly.

Heider's balance theory is an interpersonal theory of consistency that is concerned with how "unit formation" between a person (O) and an object (X) will lead to liking or disliking by a person (P) (see Figure 8.2).

The essence of the theory is that an attitude of a person (P) toward a person (O) can be formed if the attitude of (P) toward (X) and the attitude of (O) toward (X) are known. The formation of this attitude is dictated by the rules of balance and consistency.

Similarly, an attitude of a person (P) toward an object (X) can be formed given the knowledge of the attitude of (P) toward (O) and the attitude of (O) toward (X).

For example let us construe a situation involving a consumer (P), his friend (O), and a sports car (X). Consumer (P) can form an attitude toward the sports car (X) if he knows his friend's (O) attitude toward sports cars (X) and his attitude toward his friend (O). If his friend's (O) attitude toward sports cars (X) is positive and he has a positive attitude toward his friend (O), then balance theory argues that consumer (P)'s attitude toward the sports car (X) will most likely be positive to maintain balance or cognitive consistency.

The concept of balance here is highly equivalent to the theory of syllogism of attitudes and a similar social cognition translation can be offered here.

Osgood and Tannenbaum's (1955) congruity theory goes one step beyond balance theory in that it postulates the degree of attitude change given an imbalanced or incongruous state. Osgood and Tannenbaum's congruity theory and Rokeach's (1972) principle of belief congruence have been used previously to describe belief change or the formation of decisions linking the percept with a modified attribute. Therefore, the reader is referred to the previous section in which these theories were treated in some detail. These theories are not designed to explain the organization of an attitude, but its principles of change, and therefore are more appropriately covered under perceptual decision making.

Figure 8.2 Balanced versus Imbalanced States

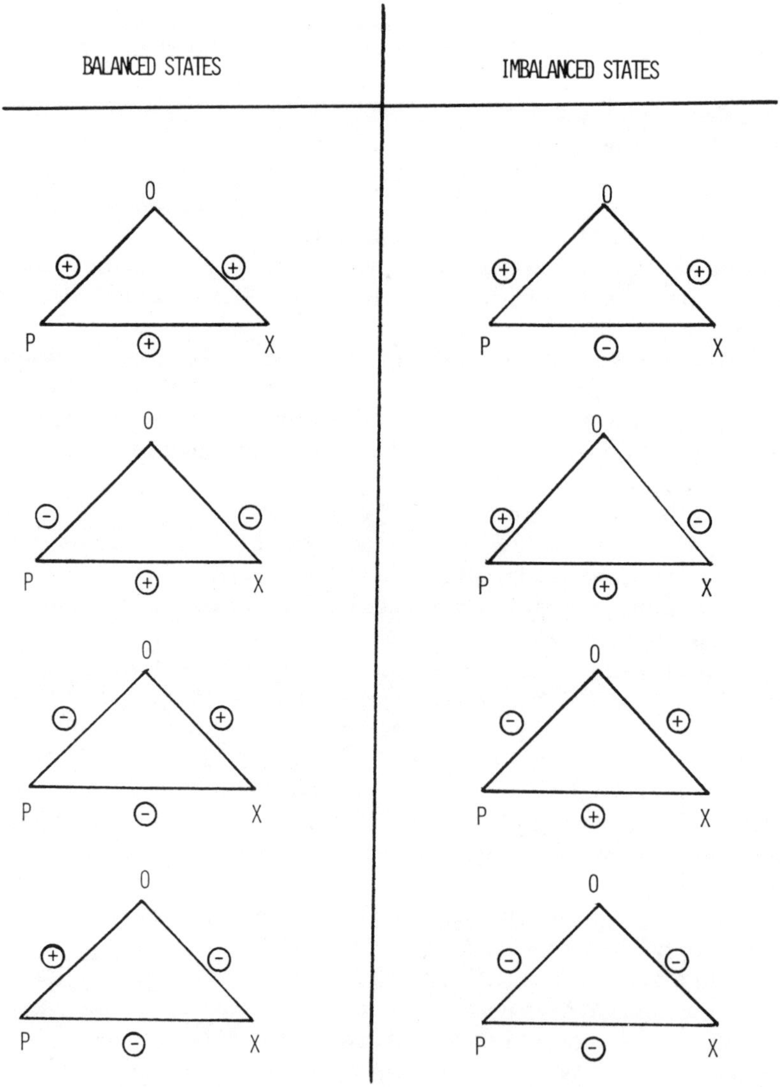

Cognitive dissonance theory (Festinger 1957), on the other hand, denotes the tendency to form attitudes toward objects and persons in the direction that would insure cognitive consonance and minimize cognitive dissonance. As with balance theory and congruity theory, the same social cognition explanation offered with respect to the syllogism theory of attitude also applies to cognitive dissonance theory of attitude.

Like consistency theory, attribution theory is a macro theory that contains a number of micro theories. Among these are Heider's (1958) naive psychology theory, Kelley's (1973) attribution theory, Jones and Davis' (1965) correspondent theory, Weiner et al. (1972) achievement motivation attribution theory, and Bem's (1972) self-perception theory. Only Bem's self-perception theory has a direct bearing on the concept of attitude as discussed in the present context and therefore will be addressed. The reader is referred to the perception section in which a formal analysis of attribution theory was presented in the light of the proposed social cognition theory.

Bem argued that an attitude toward an object can be formed not necessarily and directly by considering the benefits and costs associated with that object but by observing our own behavior. Through self-observation of behaviors that are relevant to the object being evaluated, a person can attribute an attitude toward that object. For example a person can form an attitude toward a sports car based on his or her observation of himself or herself having owned one. The scenario might be as follows: "I own a sports car; people who own sports cars must like sports cars; therefore, I like sports cars."

Note that a syllogism was used to explain the mechanics of self-perception theory, and as previously shown, syllogistic thinking related to attitudes has been translated in light of the proposed theory.

EVALUATIVE DECISIONS AND COGNITIVE
LABELING OF VALUES

Traditionally, in the social psychology literature, reference is made to opinions as verbal manifestations of an attitude (Hovland, Janis, and Kelley 1953).

For example let's say that an individual experiences a -10 enhancement affect score toward an evaluated object, let's say a Ford Escort. This degree of negative affect displaced toward the Ford Escort can be represented as an evaluative decision linking the percept "Ford Escort" with a semantic attribute having a value level that corresponds to the degree of the evaluative affect induced. This attribute value can take a verbal form such as "bad" or "very bad," or some similar verbal counterpart. This has been referred to as cognitive labeling of values. It is defined as a perceptual categorization of enhancement affect experienced toward a percept being evaluated into a cognitive category providing a semantic label to this evaluation. The enhancement affect experienced is semantically labeled along an evaluative semantic dimension varying from "very positive" to "very negative," or some other verbal counterpart. Remember how perceptual decisions (DB)s were labeled? It was argued that a perceptual categorization process is used to semantically label the resulting beliefs. The same can be said with regard to evaluative decisions labeling evaluative affect (EA).

What about evaluative decisions? An evaluative decision is defined as the outcome of the derivation of the value intensity of a perceptual decision (or DV). Evaluative decision making was discussed indirectly under the topic of belief change and modelled accordingly. The reader is referred to the previous chapter to review the dynamics of evaluative decision making.

SUMMARY

Evaluation has been construed as a process through which a percept representing a stimulus object attains a value reflecting enhancement affect toward that object. This process involves evaluative congruity, affect, decision making, and labeling. Evaluative congruity and the resultant affect have been addressed directly using the enhancement affect model. In other words the affect resulting from evaluative congruity was modelled in terms of the enhancement affect. Traditional attitude formulations were also related to evaluative congruity and affect.

Evaluative decision making was also addressed within the model described for belief change. Cognitive labeling of values, as with labeling of beliefs, was described in terms of perceptual categorization.

CHAPTER 9
Behavior

As shown in the preceding chapters, decisions are made at both perceptual and evaluative levels. But the question is, do these decisions translate into overt behaviors? This has been a controversial issue in the social/consumer psychology literature for quite some time now.

The controversy regarding the relationship between attitudes and behavior has been "hammered to death." For many years social scientists have attempted to explain why the relationship between attitudes and behavior is weak (Wicker 1971; Ehrlich 1969; McGuire 1969). One explanation involves the identification of nonmotivational variables such as ability which moderates this relationship. For example if an individual has a favorable attitude or disposition toward an object, but he/she doesn't have the resources to carry it out, then it is most likely that this attitude would not translate into behavior (Fishbein and Jaccard 1973). Another explanation involves the applicability of the attitude-behavior relationship to predict broad-based behavioral patterns. General attitude measures are said not to be relevant to the prediction of specific behaviors (Weigel and Newman 1976; Fishbein and Ajzen 1974).

Yet another explanation lies in the specificity argument. Ajzen and Fishbein (1977) argued that behavior can be predicted from attitudes that are highly specific to the situation at hand and not from general attitudes.

More recently, Bagozzi and Burnkrant (1979) argued that the findings revealing a weak attitude-behavior relationship may be due to methodological artifacts rather than to theoretical considerations. They were able to demonstrate that the two-component model of attitude (beliefs/evaluations) is more predictive of scaled and multiple-indicator measures of behavior than of unscaled and single-act behavior criteria.

How can this issue be resolved in light of the proposed theory? The position advocated here is rather simple. The proposed social cognition theory says that motivated behavior functions to reduce a deviation state involving one or more activated cognitive needs (that is, need for cognitive enhancement, consistency, and differentiation). The activation of a need is a transformation of that need from its genotypic state to its phenotypic state. The phenotypic state of a need is represented in terms of a deviation state from homeostasis. For example an achievement situation can present itself as an opportunity. This situation is perceived and compared with the desired level of achievement given that situation. The desired level of achievement may be represented as evoked beliefs involving desired expectancies. The result of this evaluative congruity manifests itself through enhancement affect. This enhancement affect can be construed as an achievement-related affect or an emotional reaction, which is translated into an evaluative decision. That evaluative decision represents the achievement goal "I want to achieve in this situation." This achievement-related affect accompanied by its verbal manifestation of goal setting is the deviation state. This deviation state prompts the individual to seek one or more alternative ways to attain the achievement goal and reduce this deviation state. Guided by this goal, the individual evaluates one or more alternative ways to attain this goal, and in doing so he/she evaluates one alternative course of action against another, against an exemplar, or against certain criterion standards. This is conducted through evaluative congruity, evaluative affect, and evaluative decision. Of course the evaluative decision would automatically reflect the variation of the evaluative affect he/she had toward each of the examined alternatives, and the evaluative decision can be construed as an intention to act or a synonym for the behavior itself.

The essence of this argument is that motivated behavior can be predicted through evaluative congruity, affect, and decision, given a specific goal, or for the purpose of reducing a deviation state.

By the way, in the last example a deviation state stemming from the need for cognitive enhancement (that is, achievement) was used; however, this is not to say that other deviation states stemming from the two other needs—the need for cognitive consistency and the need for cognitive differentiation—are excluded.

The same argument applies to these other two needs. In other words a deviation state involving cognitive dissonance or information acquisition can and does occur. These, in turn, would induce the individual to set goals to reduce the deviation states and prompt him/her to evaluate alternative courses of action. The activation of a cognitive dissonance deviation state is modelled using the consistency affect function, and the information acquisition deviation state is modelled using the information affect function, as previously described. However, the evaluation of one or more courses of action related to the reduction of any of these deviation states is modelled using the enhancement affect function.

Now let us examine in some depth how motivated behavior has been theorized and modelled in the social psychology literature and make an attempt to establish a rational connection between these models and the proposed social cognition theory. The three selected models to be examined here are Fishbein's extended attitude model, Wyer's probabilistic attitude model, and Jaccard's behavioral alternative attitude model.

Fishbein and Ajzen (1975) have modified their beliefs/ evaluation model to include social norms involved in the situation and the individual's motivation to comply. This has come to be known as the Fishbein extended model, and it is positioned as such to further enhance attitude prediction of behavior. Expressed mathematically:

$$B_k \approx BI_k = \sum_{i=1}^{I} b_{ik} e_{ik} + \sum_{j=1}^{J} b_{jk} m_{jk}$$

where B_k = overt behavior of individual (k)
BI_k = behavioral intention on individual (k)
b_{ik} = belief about consequence of engaging in behavior (i) of individual (k)
e_{ik} = evaluative aspect of belief about consequence (i) of individual (k)
b_{jk} = normative belief (j) about what others expect of individual (k)
m_{jk} = motivation to comply with normative belief (j) of individual (k)

This model is not only an extension of Fishbein's (1967) beliefs/evaluation model but a reformulation of the original model. This is because the dependent variable is no more designed to measure attitude toward the stimulus object per se but the individual's disposition to act toward a particular behavioral alternative.

This model can be construed, like its predecessor, to be composed of the sum of the product of the perceptual attribute values and the strength of the connecting perceptions

$$\sum_{i=1}^{I} PB_{ik} PV_{ik}$$

at the behavioral level. The social norm ($b_{jk} m_{jk}$) component does not have to be treated independently of the attitude ($b_{ik} e_{ik}$) component, since its attributes can be decomposed into attribute costs and benefits associated with compliance with significant others' expectations.

The major shortcoming of this model, from the perspective of the proposed theory, is that the reference point for these evaluations is not known. Also, based on the functional perspective advocating that motivated behavior is designed to reduce deviation states pertaining to one or more cognitive needs, it seems clear that the individual in his/her evaluation of the various alternatives has to consider those behavioral consequences associated with alternatives that would instigate future negative deviation states. For example to what extent would the selection of an alternative course of action be inconsistent with his/her self-perception (cognitive dissonance deviation state). Or to what extent would it place him/her in an unfamiliar surrounding (information acquisition deviation state). Normally, those behavioral consequences associated with the enhancement affect are considered but to the exclusion of both consistency and information affects.

With respect to Wyer's (1974, 1975) probabilistic theory of attitudes, the main postulate seems to be that the attitude-behavior relationship can be predicted better by measuring the relevance instead of the valence of each attribute. This is based on Wyer's probabilistic theory of cognitive consistency adapted to the study of behavioral intentions (Wyer and Goldberg 1970; Wyer 1974, 1975; Jaccard and King 1977). The essence of this relevance component lies in the discrepancy between the estimate of the probability that the individual will act, given a belief is true and the estimate of the probability that he/she will act, given the same belief is false. The greater the discrepancy, the greater the relevance of that attribute in predicting behavioral intention or behavior itself.

The relevance notion is based on the dynamic treatment of attitude change. Working with the traditional Fishbein two-component attitude model, its dynamic version can be represented as (Danes and Hunter 1980):

$$A_{act} \text{ or } BI_k = \sum_{i=1}^{I} b_{ik} e_{ik}$$

The aforementioned relevance component replaces the (e) component in the dynamic version of the two-component model. Therefore,

$$BI_k = \sum_{i=1}^{I} \Delta b_{ik} r_{ik}$$

where r_{ik} = degree of relevance of attribute (i) of individual (k) to change behavior intention (BI)

At least three models have been formulated to mathematically model the (r) component (Danes and Hunter 1980). These are: (1) the consistency relevance, (2) the contingency relevance, and (3) the discrepancy relevance.

The <u>consistency relevance</u> is represented as follows:

$$r_{ik} = p(BI_k|b_{ik}) - p(BI_k|b'_{ik})$$

where $p(BI_k|b_{ik})$ = the probability that individual (k) will intend to behave in a certain way given attribute (i) is true

$p(BI_k|b'_{ik})$ = the probability that individual (k) will intend to behave in a certain way given attribute (i) is false

The <u>contingency relevance</u> is represented as follows:

$$r_{ik} = p(b_{ik}) \, p(BI_k|b_{ik}) - p(BI_k)$$

where $p(b_{ik})$ = the probability of the initial belief involving the presence of attribute (i) of individual (k)

$p(BI_k)$ = the probability of initial behavioral intention

Finally, the <u>discrepancy relevance</u> is formulated as:

$$r_{ik} = p(BI_k|b_{ik}) - p(BI_k)$$

In a test of these three models, Danes and Hunter (1980) found the discrepancy relevance to be more predictive of behavioral intention than both the consistency and contingency relevance functions.

What does this mean in light of the proposed social cognition theory? Nothing much, really. This probabilistic theory of attitude has its value in predicting those salient attributes that do play a significant role in the evaluation process. But the problem with Wyer's model is that it lacks explanatory power. We can know by applying this model that a particular attribute would have an effect or no effect on behavioral intention. But how does this come about?

In terms of the proposed social cognition theory, this model can be used in conjunction with the enhancement affect model to operationally select those salient attributes that might be activated within a given situation.

Finally, with respect to Jaccard's (1981b) behavioral alternative theory of attitudes, the essence of this theory seems to lie in the notion that attitudes should be measured in direct relation to alternative behaviors. He argued that behavior cannot be solely predicted from an attitude toward one alternative; the full distribution of attitudes across the behavioral alternatives have to be known. Based on this argument, he developed a "behavioral alternative" model that was demonstrated to predict behavior slightly better than the single-component attitude model.

To illustrate the behavioral alternative model, let us go through the same example supplied by Jaccard (1981b) in his article (see Table 9.1).

The emphasis of this model, unlike the traditional two-component model, is on within-subject variation rather than between-subject variation.

Table 9.1 Hypothetical Example of Three Individuals' Attitudes toward Voting Alternatives

Individual	$A_{Democrat}$	$A_{Republican}$	$A_D - A_R$
1	13	19	-6
2	10	12	-2
3	7	5	2

The traditional two-component attitude model would predict that individual 1 would be more likely to vote for the democratic candidate than individual 2 and individual 3, respectively. In contrast the behavioral alternative model predicts the opposite pattern. Knowing something about the distribution of attitudes across the behavioral alternatives, the behavioral alternative model would predict that individual 3 is more likely to vote for the democratic candidate followed by individual 2 and individual 1, respectively.

This model is in perfect harmony with the proposed evaluative congruity principle. This is because the emphasis as projected by this model is on comparison between one alternative and another, and this is exactly what the congruity process is all about—a comparison between a percept and a concept. Of course the concept is represented by the behavioral alternative model as a behavioral alternative. Although the concept of comparison between behavioral alternatives is an extremely important one, Jaccard does not incorporate in his model a comparison between a behavior alternative and an ideal alternative, or a deserved alternative, or a predicted alternative, among other possible types of reference points. In other words Jaccard's model can be viewed to be restricted to those referent relations involving other stimulus objects.

SUMMARY

Goal-oriented behavior was construed as behavior designed to reduce deviation states or bring about homeostatic states associated with the needs for enhancement, consistency, and/or differentiation. These deviation or homeostatic states are represented as goals or beliefs about behaviors. These goals prompt the individual to evaluate alternative courses of action. This is done through evaluative congruity and evaluative affect associated with alternative courses of action. The resultant evaluative decisions represent the cognitive counterparts of actual behaviors.

These propositions were related to the traditional treatments of the attitude-behavior relationship in the social psychology literature.

PART III
The Theory Applied To Consumer Behavior

CHAPTER 10
Consumer Perception

In this chapter perceptual congruity and outcomes are
applied to explain consumer-related perceptual phenomena.
These include product image perception, media image perception,
message perception, brand image perception, brand performance
perception, and brand image revision.

The first thing that should be noted is that product-related
phenomena should be distinguished from brand-related phenomena.
Usually, when reference is made to product-related attributes,
for example, product benefits and costs are addressed. For
instance an automobile may have transportation, social, and
esteem benefits. However, brand-related attributes, although
capable of being addressed in terms of product attributes, are
usually treated in such a way as to differentiate one brand from
its competition. For example Ford Escort can be characterized
along such dimensions as MPG, United States versus foreign,
price, roominess, style, and so forth. These are the kind of
attributes that serve to distinguish one brand from another.

PRODUCT IMAGE PERCEPTION

With respect to product image perception, the consumer
perceives the attributes or features associated directly with
current product performance. The performance benefits of a
given product are viewed to be varied. The evaluation of these
benefits against a referent standard may create feelings of
satisfaction/dissatisfaction with that product. Dissatisfaction
with current product induces the consumer to recognize that
he/she needs a new product.

Product image perception is not a mere listing of the attribute levels associated with current product performance. As discussed previously, the process of perception involves mainly the process of categorization and inference. It is interesting to note that product benefit perception is influenced by how a product benefit is categorized and the extent that such categorization may lead to inference of related benefits not originally seen by the consumer. For example suppose that a consumer X's car is having a transmission problem. This may be a perceptual cue used to categorize the situation. He/she may use this cue to categorize this situation in an evoked cognitive category involving "the car is breaking down." This evoked frame of reference may contain a number of belief attributes related to the characteristics of "the car is breaking down" concept, for example, "tuneup problems," "engine problems," "radiator problems," and so on. It is very possible that the percept "the car" becomes associated with any of these additional attributes through the sheer process of perceptual inference.

The aforementioned product perception involves product image perceptions that are involved in problem recognition. However, product need recognition is not exclusively problem recognition. It also incorporates the concept of opportunity recognition. This is brought up here to make the point that the type of perception responsible for problem recognition is not the same as that for opportunity recognition. In opportunity recognition the consumer is not confronted with an existing product but exposed to a product in the marketplace. This is said to lead to opportunity recognition because the consumer essentially examines this new product for its benefits and assesses its opportunity to satisfy one or more particular needs or wants.

Accordingly, the perception is directed to a new product. This is done as follows: A perceptual cue associated with that product is used to evoke a cognitive category involving that product. The evoked cognitive category represents a set of attributes or benefits associated with the evoked concept (that is, new product). These attributes may be functional or symbolic in nature. For example "I see a sports car" may be viewed as a perceptual cue. I decode this cue using my conception of a sports car. From prior knowledge I know that a sports car is associated with youthfulness, sex appeal, and having a good time. These are symbolic or personality attributes related to the evoked concept of the sports car.

The degree to which I would categorize what I see as a sports car is dependent on the matching cue(s) that I use to evoke the sports car concept. In other words this perceptual categorization is dependent on the goodness-of-fit between the perceptual cue(s) and the matching attribute(s) within the evoked cognitive category.

Also, the extent to which I would make an inference about an attribute involving the sports car (for example, youthfulness) is dependent on the goodness-of-fit and the strength of the belief relation associating the concept (sports car) with that attribute (youthfulness). The models describing perceptual decision linking a percept with an evoked concept (perceptual categorization) and linking a percept with a conceptual attribute (perceptual inference) can be used here to derive the resulting perceptual decisions involving product image perception.

MEDIA IMAGE PERCEPTION

Marketing communication researchers realize that the communication environment contributed by a media source can have a substantial effect on the nature of the resulting communication. For example print media, because of their association with news stories, could be perceived as more objective, and this, in turn, may affect the selection of the media or the acceptance of messages transmitted through these media.

Aaker and Myers (1982) consider the following media image attributes as important on both message acceptance and media selection. These are: (1) unbiasedness, (2) expertness, (3) prestige, and (4) mood created.

The degree of unbiasedness perceived may affect media preference and selection. For example a consumer looking for product-related information may select a medium such as Consumer Reports rather than a salesperson because of the unbiasedness attribute.

Expertness also seems to be an important factor in the selection of media. A consumer would resort to a car mechanic for information regarding the purchase of an automobile rather than a salesperson because of this factor.

Prestige and status can also be considered as a determinant attribute in media preference and selection. Consumers may purchase the New Yorker magazine not only for its content but because of the prestige factor associated with it.

Mood created is an important image factor in media preference and selection. The consumer's perception of the degree to which a specific medium is capable of creating a desired mood such as relaxation, excitement, and learning is used in evaluating and deciding upon the various media vehicles.

Axelrod (1963) conducted a study in which he attempted to identify those mood factors affecting media preference. He tested nine dimensions of moods: concentration, aggression, pleasantness, activation, deactivation, egotism, social affection, depression, and anxiety. Multiple indicators were used for each of these media image factors. For example the involved attributes for activation were vigorous, energetic, and active. Measures of these media mood attributes were taken before and after the respondents watched a movie. It was found that the mood was significantly altered along eight of the nine dimensions by the movie. Also, these attributes were found to significantly predict respondents' attitudes toward the movie.

Wolfe and his associates conducted a major image study involving 3,000 respondents (cited in Aaker and Myers 1982). The study attempted to determine the image of eleven large-circulation magazines in terms of ten dimensions: dynamic, informational, entertainment, cultural, intelligence, influence, format, scope, moral, and good will.

The marketing manager can greatly benefit from media image research. Knowing his/her target market and the kinds of media images that the target market is mostly influenced by in its exposure habits is extremely important because the marketing manager can select those media for his/her marketing communication campaign partly based on these image factors.

It should be noted that the managerial perspective espoused here is that of the marketing manager who is using media as a support service. These implications may or may not apply to the media institution at large.

MESSAGE PERCEPTION

Message perception includes a number of research areas such as message awareness, message comprehension, and message belief. Each of these research topics will be treated in some depth.

Message Awareness

Message awareness refers to perceptual categorization, which means the identification of the message's product in an appropriate cognitive category. It is extremely important to know something about those cognitive categories that are used by the target consumer to identify the message's product (that is, the stimulus product). This is because some cognitive categories may enhance the advertised product while others may do just the opposite. For example in an advertising message involving Ford Escort, one consumer may categorize Ford Escort as a Ford car, making no distinctions among the various Ford brands. Based on his/her previous experience with Ford cars, he/she may have developed a negative value toward Ford cars. Therefore, the mere perceptual categorization of this product may be quite harmful to Ford's market position with respect to this particular market segment.

However, if we take another consumer who may use the cognitive category of "American-made cars" to classify the product "Ford Escort," and given that he/she has positive experiences with "American-made cars," the overall result may be a positive attitude toward the advertised product.

As previously discussed, the goodness-of-fit can be directly assessed through the application of the consistency affect model. The resulting consistency affect can therefore be used as an indicator of the strength of the perceptual decision connecting the stimulus object with the evoked concept.

Furthermore, it is argued here that message awareness involves a perceptual categorization process that classifies the stimulus object in an appropriate cognitive category. And, of course, the extent to which a cognitive category may be more accessible than another is dependent on (1) the activation of a script, (2) goals set by past perceptual and/or evaluative congruity decisions, (3) the strength of the conceptual relations involved in the activated script, and (4) the degree of belief-centrality involved with the evoked beliefs.

To illustrate the operation of these factors on message awareness, let's go back to the Ford Escort example. It is likely that the cognitive category of Ford cars can be activated if one or more perceptual cues were used to activate the entire script involved with the consumer experience with Ford cars.

Also, those cognitive categories that are not strongly associated with a set of conceptual attributes are less susceptible to activation compared to those that are. Using the Ford Escort example, it can be argued that this frame of reference was activated instead of others because the strength of the involved belief relations was strong. Given that they were weak, they may have been less accessible for activation.

Finally, with respect to belief-centrality, the question becomes how important or unimportant is this cognitive category in the realm of things. In the example of Ford cars, to what extent is this concept important to this consumer in a relative

or absolute manner? One good indicator of the importance of
a given concept is the value intensity associated with that concept. In the case for the "Ford cars" concept, it is -3, which
is moderate. Using the bipolar scale ranging from -10 to +10,
we know that concepts taking values of around + or - 10 are
highly important for that consumer. The associated attributes
would constitute central beliefs. Conversely, concepts taking
on low values (for example, + or -1) involve peripheral beliefs.

Message Comprehension

This is another term for information assimilation. As
previously described, information assimilation as a psychological
process is the outcome of perceptual categorization.
In the consumer-behavior literature two independent research programs seem to have direct bearing on message comprehension. These are low-involvement learning, and information
load.

Low-Involvement Learning

Most purchase decisions are low in consumer involvement
(Maloney and Silverman 1979; Wilkie 1979). A low-involvement
purchase is that type of behavior that is considered not important
to the purchaser. It is not important to his/her belief system
and he/she does not identify himself/herself with it.
Kassarjian and Kassarjian (1979) put it this way:

Subjects just do not care much about products; they
are unimportant to them. Although issues such as
racial equality, wars, and the draft may stir them up,
products do not. Hence, the emerging conclusion
must be that true attributes about these items most
likely do not exist for many subjects. Bicycles, colas,
and toothpaste generally do not have attitudes associated with them. To claim that attitudes about these
products do exist is to claim that subjects "give a
damn" about them. (Most) subjects do not (p. 8).

Low-involvement research in consumer behavior has been
influenced by two theories: (1) social judgment theory (Sherif,
Sherif, and Nebergall 1965) and (2) theory of passive learning
Sherif operationalized the concept of involvement by identifying a latitude of acceptance (the positions the individual

accepts), a latitude of rejection (positions the individual rejects), and a latitude of noncommitment (positions toward which the individual is neutral). A highly involved individual having a definite opinion about the product would accept only a few positions (narrow attitude of acceptance and wide attitude of rejection). An uninvolved consumer, on the other hand, would be more accepting of a wide range of positions (wide latitude of acceptance) or would have no opinion about the product (wide latitude of noncommitment). In other words the highly involved consumer would be more inclined to experience a contrast effect than an assimilation effect, whereas the converse is true for low-involved consumers.

Rothschild and Houston (1977) used social judgment theory in the formulation of their hypothesis. They predicted that high involvement is associated with the use of more attributes in brand evaluation while low involvement is related to the use of fewer attributes. Their findings confirmed their hypothesis using political rather than consumer choice.

Lastovika and Gardner (1978) found a similar set of relationships. They determined the number of car makes that consumers accepted (low involvement), rejected (high involvement), and were neutral (medium involvement). A simpler set of decision rules was used in evaluating brands under low-involvement than under high-involvement conditions.

As previously discussed, the assimilation-contrast theory has already been translated into the language of the proposed theory.

Krugman's passive learning theory, on the other hand, argues in a low-involvement environment (such as TV watching), that the viewer is in a relaxed state and does not pay attention to the message. That means that the consumer does not allocate cognitive effort to the processing of the stimulus object. Therefore, learning occurs through reception but not in such a way that the learned message is linked to the consumer's needs, beliefs, and past experiences. As a result, a consumer can show a high level of recognition for a particular message, but the chances that the message affected his/her attitude toward the advertised product are nil.

Grass and Wallace (1974) conducted a study based on Krugman's theory of passive learning and found that for low-involvement consumers a low-involvement media vehicle (such as TV) is more effective in conveying the message than high-involvement media vehicles (for example, magazines, newspapers).

In light of the proposed theory, it can be shown that in case of low-involvement learning, perceptual categorization of incoming messages is highly fragmented. In other words perceptual decisions resulting from one categorization process may not be linked to the original cognitive category used to categorize the percept in the first place. Under high-involvement conditions, the individual goes beyond the simple process of perceptual categorization. He/she attempts to integrate this information by comparing it to his/her prior beliefs. The newly formed beliefs (arising from message comprehension) may be (in)consistent with the prior beliefs. This involves a belief-change process and hence can be modelled using the belief-change model as described previously (refer to perceptual decision linking a percept with a modified attribute).

Information Load

Because of the direct application potential in both the private and public sectors, consumer-behavior research in information load has been somewhat extensive. From a business point of view, advertisers want to know how much information can be assimilated by consumers. From a public policy point of view, policy makers want to know the extent to which consumers would and can use available objective product information to make "sound" or "rational" marketplace decisions.

Based on the works of Jacoby and his associates (Jacoby, Speller, and Kohn 1974; and Scammon 1977), it was pointed out that giving consumers too much information (information overload) serves only to increase consumers' confidence and satisfaction with their decisions, but does not increase the rationality of the decision.

In terms of the proposed theory, there may be thresholds involving cumulative perceptual categorizations, which beyond particular levels of information processing, become dysfunctional. Simon and Newell (1972) argued that around seven chunks (may be translated into seven attributes) may be the average threshold for most people. Beyond this number message comprehension disintegrates because the individual is forced to use newly created cognitive categories that may or may not be integrated with the prior ones.

Message Belief

This concept refers to high-involvement learning. It is the process that consists of perceptual categorization followed by an attempt to integrate the incoming information with prior knowledge structures.

As described in high-involvement learning, the outcome of this integration can be modelled through the consistency affect model.

As mentioned, message belief involves the integration of incoming information with prior knowledge. The resultant decision involves a compromise between the incoming information and prior knowledge. This process can be modelled through the belief-change model of the proposed theory. However, this compromise is very dependent on the strength of both perception and evoked belief.

Let's focus on the strength of the perception. Let us suppose that we have a situation where the incoming information is perceived as 100 percent credible (1.00 PB). This, of course, may come from examining credible media sources, such as Consumer Reports, or other technical consumer journals. However, in case of advertising, the PB is usually low because of the biased nature of advertising (or at least) how consumers perceive it to be. However, many advertising researchers have looked into the cognitive factors that may increase or decrease the strength of message perception (Settle and Golden 1974; Woodside and Davenport 1976; Busch and Wilson 1976).

The strength of message perception is found to be affected by: source credibility; two-sided message; and communicator/consumer similarity.

Source Credibility

This concept, involving expertness and trustworthiness, affects the strength of message perception (Busch and Wilson 1976; Dholakia and Sternthal 1977). How can this process be visualized from a social cognition perspective?

It all seems to be a question of perceptual categorization, inference, and labeling. The message, as it is associated with the source, is categorized in the cognitive category of the credibility component (that is, trustworthy or expert). The result of this process is a perceptual decision linking the message with credibility as a conceptual attribute.

The strength of this decision, of course, is a direct function of the degree of goodness-of-fit. The resulting decision can be construed as the verbal counterpart of the strength of the message perception and can be measured as such.

Two-Sided Message

With respect to the two-sided message, it has been noted that if the source would covary the product claim (that is, state some product benefits as well as some product costs or weaknesses, instead of the usual all-positive attributes claim), then consumers would more likely attribute or ascribe greater credibility to the source and therefore to the message (Settle and Golden 1974). Attribution theory (the covariation principle) has been used to explain this phenomenon. In terms of the proposed theory, it was argued previously that attribution is merely a process involving perceptual inference.

Communicator/Audience Similarity

Similarly, source credibility has been found to increase under conditions of source/consumer similarity. Research has shown that when consumers see salespersons as similar to themselves, they become more likely to accept the salesperson's message (Woodside and Davenport 1976). Again, this situation can be similarly described using the perceptual inference notions already described.

STORE IMAGE PERCEPTION

With respect to retail investigations, much research has been conducted on store image. This research activity has included a large variety of store attributes or dimensions.

Based on the findings of a study by Hansen and Deutcher (1977-78), those salient store attributes used in the selection of department store and grocery store are shown in Table 10.1.

Table 10.1 Store Attributes for Department and Grocery Stores

Department Store	Grocery Store
Dependable products	Dependable products
Fair on adjustments	Store is clean
High value for money	Easy to find items you want
High-quality products	Fast check out
Easy to find items you want	High-quality products
Fast check out	High value for the money
Helpful personnel	Fully stocked
Easy to return purchases	Helpful store personnel
Easy to exchange purchases	Easy to move through store
Store is clean	Adequate number of store personnel

Store image has been variously defined by various retailing researchers; however, Pierre Martineau's (1958) classic definition still remains the most visible. He defined store image as "the way the store is defined in the shopper's mind, partly by its functional qualities and partly by an aura of psychological attributes" (p. 47). These functional qualities are functional attributes related to merchandise selection, price ranges, credit policies, store layout, and so on. Psychological qualities may be personality or symbolic attributes related to the stereotypic image of the generalized shopper of a particular store or type of store. These attributes can be represented as friendly, formal, high-status, feminine, youthful, and so on.

The distinction between functional and personality attributes has been made with respect to products and brands, and is generalizable to stores. With respect to functional and personality store attributes at least nine universal store image attributes have been identified. These are:

(1) merchandise (quality, selection or assortment, styling or fashion, guarantees, and pricing)

(2) service (service-general, salesclerk service, self-service, ease of merchandise return, delivery service, and credit policies of the store)

(3) clientele (self-images of clientele such as status, gender, age, and so on)

(4) physical facilities (for example, elevators, lighting, air conditioning, washrooms, store layout, aisle placement and width, carpeting)

(5) convenience (convenience-general, locational convenience, and parking)

(6) promotion (sales promotion, advertising, displays, trading stamps)

(7) store atmosphere (customer's feeling of warmth and acceptance)

(8) institutional factors (store's reputation and reliability)

(9) posttransaction satisfaction (merchandise in use, returns, adjustments)

(Lindquist 1974-75; Samli and Sirgy 1981).

Store image has been traditionally measured using a semantic differential methodology (James, Durand, and Dreves 1976). It has been pointed out that the use of the semantic differential alone is not sufficient to tap the full range of those salient attributes. The semantic differential scale would be a good measure only if those salient attributes are included. Perceptual mapping techniques involving multidimensional scaling have been used in the past to detect those salient attributes for the target market (for example, Singson 1975).

The use of the two-component multiattribute attitude model has also been used to find those salient attributes most predictive of store preferences (James, Durand, and Dreves 1976). This is done by employing a pool of store image attributes having belief/evaluation measures. The higher the product of the belief and evaluation measures, the greater the salience. Those attributes that are found highly salient are then regressed to predict store preference, store patronage, store satisfaction, or store loyalty.

This type of conceptualization and operationalization of store image, of course, is highly consistent with the approach of the proposed social cognition theory. Store image research can further benefit by adopting the perspective introduced here.

For example the marketing manager might be interested in knowing those types of retail outlets that are associated with his/her product-brand in his/her consumers' minds. This requires a complete analysis that would distinguish those perceptual cues in this perceptual categorization process and the complete identification of the various evoked cognitive categories.

It should be noted that the managerial implications discussed here apply to the marketing manager who is using retailing as a support service, although some of these principles directly apply to store management. That is not to say that a store manager would not be able to use these principles. On the contrary the store manager, as a marketing manager, would treat his/her store as a brand having its own marketing mix elements (product, place, price, and promotion).

BRAND IMAGE PERCEPTION

This is a perceptual process involving categorization and inference of brand-related attributes. As with product image perception, this phenomenon can be modelled using the proposed categorization and inference models.

In the following section a number of topics traditionally discussed under product perception will be treated in light of the proposed theory. These are: (1) product image, (2) risk perception, and (3) price perception.

Product Image

Product image refers to those attributes associated with a given product or service. Newman (1957) argued that:

> Among other things, a product is a symbol by virtue
> of its form, size, color, and functions. Its signifi-
> cance as a symbol varies according to how much it is
> associated with individual needs and social inter-
> action. A product, then, is the sum of the meanings
> it communicated, often unconsciously, to others
> when they look at it or use it (p. 100).

Products are assumed to have a personality or image, just like people. This image is not determined by the physical characteristics of a product alone, but by a host of other factors such as packaging, advertising, price, and channels of distribution. Images of products are also formed by other associations such as stereotyped image of the generalized or typical consumer who uses a particular store or service (cf. Levy 1959; Grubb and Grathwohl 1967; Britt 1960).

Product images have been classified as being "functional" or "symbolic" (Sirgy 1982b; Samli and Sirgy 1981). Symbolic product images refer to the stereotypic personality images consumers have of a specific product. Examples of stereotypic personality images people may have of a particular store include traditional versus modern, classy versus folksy, sexy versus plain, friendly versus formal, high-status versus low-status, and so on. These symbolic images are differentiated from their functional counterparts in that the latter involve attributes that are related to the tangible benefits of the product and not the stereotypic personality characteristics associated with it (cf. Munson and Spivey 1980).

Product images are usually detected by what consumer behaviorists call "perceptual mapping." Perceptual mapping is designed to construct a product space, discover the shape of the distribution of similarity or dissimilarity of different products or brands, and therefore identify likely opportunities for strategy development involving product development and positioning. Of course perceptual mapping is undertaken under those circumstances when the product images are not or cannot be easily identified. Other procedures such as the free-elicitation method are used to elicit product images. Once product images are identified, self-report measures, such as Likert rating scales, bipolar rating scales, staple scales, semantic differential scales, among others, are used to measure the strength of the associations between a specific product and those elicited images.

Speaking of those symbolic images associated with the stereotype of the generalized shopper or user, the literature of consumers' self-concept is most relevant (see Sirgy 1982b, for a comprehensive review). An example of symbolic images used in self-concept studies predicting product (or store) preference or loyalty is Birdwell's (1968) product image scale (see Table 10.2).

In light of the proposed social cognition theory, product images are formed through the process of categorization. It should be noted that the perceived images or attributes of a product can be quite different depending on which cognitive category the consumer evokes to identify that product. Also, the perceived product attributes will vary depending on whether the evoked category is abstract or concrete. As stated previously, processing of product stimuli using abstract cognitive

Table 10.2 Personality Image Attributes Employed
by Some Consumer Research Studies

Sophisticated	Unsophisticated
Exciting	Dull
Husky	Weak
Happy	Sad
Eccentric	Conventional
Bold	Shy
Young	Old
Nimble	Clumsy
Simple	Complex
Sporty	Businesslike
Obvious	Subtle
Stale	Fresh
Robust	Fragile
Swift	Slow
Elegant	Plain
Lively	Calm
Indulgent	Thrifty
Reliable	Unreliable
Safe	Dangerous
Impulsive	Deliberate
Masculine	Feminine
Spacious	Cramped

categories, by definition, is expected to involve low-level cognitive effort for the consumer. For abstract cognitive categories to be evoked, the incoming perceptual cue has to be highly familiar to the customer. Familiarity is dictated by a congruity involving a strong evoked belief, whereas low familiarity is determined by a congruity between a strong perception and a weak belief. For unfamiliar products the consumer might evoke concrete cognitive categories in which the functional attributes of the product would be more highlighted than personality or symbolic attributes.

Based on this perspective, it seems important to address the following issues in product image research: First, what are the various cognitive categories typically used to describe a specific product for a specific target market? Second, what is the average level of abstractness of the evoked cognitive category of the target market? Third, what are those cues associated with the evocation of the average or typical cognitive category for that target market? Fourth, what are those cues associated with the evocation of a concrete versus abstract cognitive category in that target market? Fifth, what is the strength of the inference made by the target market associating the perceived product with one or more conceptual attributes involved with the evoked cognitive category?

To answer the preceding questions, it seems essential that image research involving protocols and/or free-elicitation methodologies should be used rather than the preconceived biased methodologies of standardized attribute lists. The latter types of methodologies are argued to bias the activation of specific cognitive categories in the respondents; therefore they fail to measure the cognitive categories that are elicited by product-related cues in a specific consumption situation.

Through protocol and/or free-elicitation procedures, the product image investigator can determine the range of the cognitive categories that can be elicited in a given consumption situation. Those cognitive categories can then be classified into general versus concrete categories. Further investigation can determine the nature of the cues that elicit those general versus concrete categories (cf. Belk 1981). Also, research may indicate whether specific dispositional factors are associated with the activation of those general versus concrete cognitive categories (cf. Belk 1981).

Once this is done, the product image investigator can derive the strength of a specific type of inference linking the product to a specific attribute by applying the consistency affect model to assess the degree-of-fit and by taking the multi-

plicative product of the resultant consistency affect score
(transformed) with the strength of the conceptual relation
involving that attribute (refer to the perceptual inference
model describing perceptual decisions linking a percept with
a conceptual attribute).

For example what is the probability that a specific consumer
will see a specific product as being a high-status product, a
high-quality product, a modern type of product, and a continental
type product, given a perceptual cue of high price only? The
degree of certainty or confidence placed on each inference linking
the product with each of those attributes is a function of the
degree-of-fit between the high-price attribute and the correspondent attribute involving price of the evoked cognitive category and the strength of the belief relations involving that
cognitive category (concept) and the attributes of high status,
high quality, modern, and continental. Suppose that the evoked
category may be that of high-priced products. In this case the
resulting degree-of-fit or consistency affect will be high. The
resulting inference between the perceived product and, for
example, high-status image is the multiplicative product of the
consistency affect (transformed to 0.00 to 1.00 scale) and the
strength of the belief linking the concept of high-priced products
with the high-status image.

Risk Perception

Bauer (1960) defined risk perception as follows:

Consumer behavior involves risk in the sense that
any action of a consumer will produce consequences
which he cannot anticipate with anything approxi-
mating certainty, and some of which at least are
likely to be unpleasant (p. 390).

In simple terms the perception of risk in a purchase situation is a function of the possible negative consequences and the
uncertainty involved. The degree of risk that the consumer
perceives and his own tolerance for risk taking serves to influence his purchasing strategies.

According to Schiffman and Kanuk (1978), perceived risk
can be divided into functional risk, physical risk, financial
risk, social risk, and psychological risk. Functional risk is
the risk that the product will not perform as expected. Physical
risk is the risk to self and to others that the product may pose.

Financial risk is the risk that the product will not be worth its cost either in time or in money. Social risk is the risk that a poor product choice may result in embarrassment before others. And psychological risk is the risk that a poor product choice will bruise the consumer's ego (Bauer 1960; Cox 1967; Jacoby and Kaplan 1972; Roselius 1971).

On another dimension perceived risk can be classified as inherent risk or handled risk (Bettman 1973). Consumers perceive inherent risk when thinking about a product class, such as vacuum cleaners, without taking into account particular brands of vacuum cleaners—just how risky are vacuum cleaners generally? Handled risk is the degree of risk involved once the consumer has information about at least one brand. For example a consumer may feel that vacuum cleaners are generally risky products and therefore have high inherent risk. But after talking with a neighbor, the consumer learns that the inherent risk does not apply to a particular brand and therefore perceives low-handled risk.

These formulations of perceived risk are easily interpreted by the proposed social cognition theory. Product risk, from a social cognition perspective, refers to a specific negative attribute associated with a particular product. Using Schiffman's classification, reference can be made to functional, financial, physical, social, and psychological attributes that are perceived as having low valence. Using Bettman's formulation, these negative attributes can be viewed as associated with both product and brand levels.

The notion that perceived risk is a function of both magnitude of negative consequence and perceived uncertainty somewhat parallels expectancy-value logic. The magnitude of negative consequence is the evaluation weight or value component of the object being evaluated and the perceived uncertainty is the inverse of the instrumentality weight or the inverse of the strength of the perception (PB_{ik}) linking the stimulus object with that negatively valued attribute (PV_{ik}). Therefore, if perceived risk is construed to be a function of the uncertainty rather than certainty of those risk attributes (social, psychological, physical, and so forth), it can be mathematically represented as:

$$PR_k = \sum_{r=1}^{R} (1 - PB_{rk})(PV_{rk})$$

where PR_k = magnitude or perceived risk associated with a specific product or brand (p) of individual (k)

$(1-PB_{rk})$ = degree of the uncertainty of risk (r) associated with product or brand (p) of individual (k)

(PV_{rk}) = magnitude of negative consequence of risk (r) associated with product or brand (p) of individual (k)

Although the logic of the expectancy-value theory is consistent with the social cognition formulation presented here, it is argued that the social cognition enhancement affect model is a more powerful model since it incorporates the measurement of the evoked conceptual relations, which, if left unaccounted for, can introduce methodological confounds. The methodological confound is that of lack of direct control (or measurement) of the comparison set—risk compared to what. The value as well as strength of the risk perception are, by definition, dependent on the nature and type of the evoked conceptual relations. Therefore, using the enhancement affect model, the construct of perceived risk can be represented as:

$$PR_k = \sum_{r=1}^{R} [(1 - PB_{rk})(PV_{rk})(EB_{rk}\ EV_{rk})^2 - (EB_{rk}\ EV_{rk})]$$

where EB_{rk} = strength of referent risk (r) involving product (p) of individual (k)

EV_{rk} = magnitude of referent risk (r) involving product (p) of individual (k)

Price Perception

Price is one important attribute that is perceived as a perceptual attribute of a stimulus product or percept. In the price perception literature (see Monroe and Petroshius 1981), the traditional concepts that consumer behaviorists are preoccupied with include: (1) price awareness, (2) price-quality relationship, and (3) price thresholds.

Price Awareness

This concept refers to the ability of the buyer to remember prices. According to Monroe and Petroshius (1981), very little evidence exists in relation to the determinants of price awareness. The scant available evidence points to the following findings: price awareness may be negatively related to income, with the exception of the poor; price awareness may be negatively related to product involvement; price awareness may be positively related to price consciousness.

How can these findings be explained using the proposed social cognition theory? Price awareness can be construed in terms of the strength of the belief relation involving prior price of that product. Price consciousness may refer to the degree of accessibility of the belief relation involving product price in consumption-related settings. From a social cognition perspective, it is very reasonable to assume that accessibility of the price belief relation (stored in memory) may be more salient for high-involving products than low-involving products and for those low-income consumers than for high-income consumers. Product involvement is construed as a motivational state reflective of the activation of the cognitive need for enhancement (affective state indicating the extent to which approaching a particular product might satisfy a particular goal state). As mentioned previously, this cognitive response "primes" (or makes accessible) those conceptual relations that pertain to the consummation of that goal state. And, of course, belief about prior product price, in this case, may very well be a salient conceptual relation.

With regard to the income finding, it may also be very reasonable to surmise that for low-income consumers, because of budget restraints, their belief concerning prior product price may be very accessible. This belief accessibility may be due to the implicit anticipated avoidance motivation response resulting from evaluating the negative consequences associated with overspending.

Price-Quality Relationship

This concept has been defined in the literature as the use of product price as an indicator of product quality (Monroe and Petroshius 1981). According to the comprehensive review of this research as provided by Monroe (1973) and Olson (1977), the perception of product quality was found to be positively related to price. That is, when price is the only differential information available, a positive price-quality relationship is seemingly enhanced when the comparative price differences are accentuated.

How can this finding be explained? Remember what has been said about perceptual decoding in terms of perceptual categorization. This notion can also be applied to explain the price-quality relationship. The unfamiliar product (unidentified percept) perceptually processed with a single attribute of high price (perceptual attribute) is matched with an evoked cognitive category involving "products of high price" and its associated attributes. It seems consensual to most consumers that an important salient attribute of the evoked conceptual attributes involving "products of high price" would include "product quality" (conceptual attribute). Therefore, the unfamiliar product becomes identified or categorized as a product that is associated with high price and high quality, among other less salient attributes.

The categorization of percepts as previously argued is dictated by the rules of the consistency affect model and more specifically the rules of perceptual inference. That is, high congruence between the feature(s) of the stimulus object with those of the evoked conceptual category will induce a response categorizing the percept in that evoked cognitive category. The cognitive category with respect to price is high- (or low-priced) products. Using the consistency affect model, the price-quality relationship can be modelled as follows:

$$CA_{pk} = (PV_{pk} \, EV_{pk})(EB_{pk})^2 \, (PB_{pk})$$

where p = price attribute (p)
$\quad\quad\;\; k$ = individual (k)
and transforming the CA scale (-4 to +4) to an
EB and PB scale (.00 to 1.00)

therefore

$$CA'_{pk} = (CA_{pk})/4$$
$$PQ = CA'_{pk} \, EB_{qk}$$

where PQ $\;\;$ = strength of price-quality relationship
$\quad\quad\quad\quad\quad$ for individual (k)
$\quad\;\; EB_{qk}$ = strength of belief that evoked products
$\quad\quad\quad\quad\quad$ of that price-level have high quality
$\quad\quad\quad\quad\quad$ (q) for individual (k)

For example a consumer is exposed to a price of \$9,000 for a car X (PB_{pk} = 1.00). He/she evokes a cognitive category of cars of a generic type. The price attribute involving the evoked concept involves \$9,000, and it is negatively valued (EB_{pk} = 1.00 and EV_{pk} = -1). In this case the match is perfect (PV_{pk} = -1) and cognitive consistency is high. This leads to the categorization of car X generic product. Of course the strength of this decision is reflected in CA_{pk} (in this case it is +4 which is very high). The extent to which "highly priced products" as a concept is associated with product quality (EB_{qk}) will then determine the strength of the price-quality relationship (PQ). If, in this case, the same consumer believes that "highly priced products" are, by definition, of high quality ($EB_{qk} = 1.00$), therefore the price-quality relationship can be said to be quite high since both percept identification (CA_{pk}) and belief involving the concept "highly priced products" (EB_{qk}) are very high.

Price Threshold

This concept is a twofold consumer behavior phenomenon (Monroe and Petroshius 1981). It involves the absolute price threshold and differential price threshold.

Absolute price threshold refers to the price range that a consumer has regarding a product or product category. A product that is priced above the upper absolute price threshold is unacceptable and, similarly, may be equally unacceptable if priced below the lower absolute price threshold. The differential price threshold, on the other hand, refers to perceived differences between a price level of a given product and its prior price level or a price level of a competing product.

The assimilation-contrast theory (Sherif et al. 1965) has been used in price perception to explain absolute price threshold effects (Monroe and Petroshius 1981). This theory holds that surrounding a given price anchor there is a range or latitude of acceptance region, or the upper and lower limits of the absolute price thresholds. Perceptual stimuli falling within that range will be assimilated and those stimuli falling outside that range will be contrasted and categorized differently (latitude of rejection). For example a consumer may have an absolute price threshold for car X ranging between $5,000 and $7,000. If he/she is exposed to the fact that car X costs $3,000, he/she may be forced to reevaluate his/her beliefs about car X (contrast effect).

The adaptation-level theory (Helson 1964) has also been used to explain the absolute price threshold phenomenon (Monroe and Petroshius 1981). The theory as applied to price perception posits that consumers have specific adaptation levels involving price cues for various products. Each price adaptation level for a particular product serves as a standard from which subsequent or alternative price stimuli are judged. In other words if a consumer's price adaptation level for a specific brand of automobile is $5,000, he/she will perceive a price tag of $6,000 as high and \$4,000 as low. This situation can be contrasted with another consumer whose price adaptation level may be \$7,000. The latter consumer will judge a price tag of \$6,000 as low and that of \$4,000 as very low.

Weber's law applied to perception has been used to explain differential price threshold effects (just noticeable difference or j.n.d.). Weber's law is mathematically represented as:

$$\Delta S / S$$

where ΔS = stimulus change and
$\quad\ \ S$ = the initial stimulus

For example if product X's price is being raised from \$10 to \$13 whereas another product Y's price is changed from \$200 to \$220, which price change will be more perceptually noticeable?

$$\Delta Sx / Sx = (13 - 10)/10 \quad = .20$$

$$\Delta Sy / Sy = (220 - 200)/200 = .10$$

From this example the price change of product X will be more perceptually noticeable than product Y's price change.

In terms of the proposed theory, the stimulus magnitude of the stimulus object as reflected in Weber's formulation can be translated into PV_{ik}. With respect to the assimilation-contrast theory and the adaptation-level theory, the price anchor can be construed in terms of consumers' price referent relations (EV_{ik}). Assimilation effects are therefore analogous to congruity involving the consistency motive, whereas contrast effects are akin to incongruity effects of the same motive.

How are concepts of absolute and differential price thresholds interpretable? With respect to the absolute price threshold, it can be easily argued that the acceptable pricing range as bounded by the absolute price threshold (upper and lower limits) refers to those price expectations that a consumer evokes in a particular marketplace situation. Those price expectations point to the optimal level or range of prices that have been previously evaluated as acceptable to the consumer for a given product under a given set of circumstances.

The differential price threshold (just noticeable difference or j.n.d.), on the other hand, points to the extent to which a consumer will notice a significant difference between the price of the contemplated product and alternative products or between the contemplated and its prior prices. This phenomenon can be treated using the consistency affect model.

BRAND PERFORMANCE PERCEPTION AND
BRAND IMAGE REVISION

The concept of brand performance perception refers to the process involving the categorization and inference of brand-related cues associated with postpurchase performance. With respect to brand image revision, the perceptual process involved here is belief change. The new experiences derived from post-purchase are compared with prior beliefs about the same attributes. The resulting congruities are said to induce belief changes. The degree of belief change can be modelled using the belief-change model described under "perceptual decision linking a percept with a modified attribute."

SUMMARY

Consumer perceptual phenomena were described in terms of perceptual categorization, inference, and labeling as theorized and modelled in the previous chapter. Specifically, product, brand, store, media, and message perceptions were all covered.

With respect to product and brand perception, product and brand image perceptions, product familiarity, brand performance perception, and brand image revision were all discussed. Product and brand image perception were described in terms of perceptual categorization and inference. Product familiarity was referred to as a perceptual process in which the resulting perceptual decision involves a weak relation (DB) which acts consecutively as an evoked belief in further congruity processing. Brand performance perception was also described in terms of perceptual categorization and inference occurring after purchase and usage. Brand image revision was referred to as a perceptual process involving belief change and described accordingly.

Under product and brand perception, the traditional treatment of product image, risk perception, and price perception in the consumer behavior literature was discussed in light of the proposed theory.

With respect to store and media perception, the concepts of store and media image were both treated from the perspective of traditional consumer behavior theory and the perspective introduced here. The models describing perceptual categorization and inference were employed to explain store and media image phenomena.

Under message perception, the concepts of message awareness, message comprehension, and message belief were all treated.

Message awareness was construed in terms of perceptual categorization. Message comprehension was viewed in terms of information assimilation and cumulative perceptual categorization. Distinctions were made between low- and high-involvement learning as directly related to message comprehension. Finally, message belief was described in terms of belief change and modelled accordingly.

CHAPTER 11
Consumer Evaluation

In this chapter the psychological processes of product need recognition, media preference, store preference, brand preference, brand satisfaction, and brand loyalty will all be treated.

PRODUCT NEED RECOGNITION

There are at least two different types of product need recognitions: one involves problem recognition and the other involves opportunity recognition. Problem and opportunity recognitions refer to product need recognitions in which the consumer recognizes that he/she needs to purchase a new product (not specifically restricted to a designated brand). Both problem and opportunity recognition can be treated in terms of the enhancement affect model.

Problem Recognition

With respect to problem recognition, Engel, Blackwell, and Kollat (1978) defined it as "a perceived difference between the ideal state of affairs and the actual situation sufficient to arouse and activate the decision process" (p. 215). The desired state, according to Engel et al., is shaped by a consumer's (1) previous decisions, (2) reference group norms, (3) novelty, (4) marketing efforts, and (5) motive activation.

With respect to the influence of other decisions, Engel et al. argued that a desired consumer state or consumption goal may be set as a result of a direct outgrowth of other consumption decisions. For example a new residence will affect the setting of the need for carpeting and various pieces of furniture as a consumption-related goal.

Reference groups are argued to contribute to the formation of desired states or consumption expectations. For example college students conform to their own dress standards.

Novelty as a desire for change affects problem recognition through the alteration of an existing desired state to a new one.

Marketing efforts, primarily through marketing promotion, are also responsible for the development of unique desired states in consumers' minds.

Motive activation underscores the concept that different needs, such as the physiological need, the safety need, the social need, the esteem need, and/or the self-actualization need can elicit problem recognition. Every consumer possesses these needs with different intensities, which, in the context of a given product-related situation, would be activated and therefore influence directly the experiential level of the desired state.

Dissatisfaction with the actual state was argued to be influenced by changed circumstances and marketing efforts (Engel et al. 1978). Changed circumstances of a consumer refers to the depletion of a presently used product, dissatisfaction with the present or used product, and/or changes in family circumstances such as birth of a child which results in modified requirements for food, clothing, and furniture. Marketing efforts are also said to cause dissatisfaction by underscoring the inadequacy of the present or used product.

Assael (1981) talks about problem recognition in terms of "need arousal." He defined it as a psychological set toward the prospective purchase—that is, his or her needs relative to the product category and his or her attitudes toward various brands. This definition is similar to Engel et al.'s definition of problem recognition. Williams (1982) refers to this concept as "problem perception," but treats it from Engel et al.'s perspective. Schiffman and Kanuk (1978) address the concept of "need recognition," which is also defined similarly to Engel et al.'s concept.

According to the proposed social cognition theory, the "ideal state of affairs" is presented in terms of those expectancies or referents involved in the evoked set which are compared to those perceptions involving the "actual situation." It must be further noted that problem recognition is characterized by a negative congruity or incongruity as determined by the enhancement motive. In this situation the theory equates problem recognition with a negative affective reaction resulting from a significant negative congruity or incongruity effect.

Based on the mathematical formulation of the enhancement affect model, high problem recognition should be represented by high negative EA scores and low problem recognition by low negative or close to zero EA scores.

For example let us conceive of a situation in which a consumer (1) perceives his old car as breaking down and recognizes his need for a new car. Suppose he perceives his car as becoming unreliable (PB = 1.00) and holds a negative value with respect to unreliability (PV = -2). Also, suppose that he strongly desires to have a car that is completely reliable (EB = 1.00) and values reliability (EV = +2). In this situation we would expect that this consumer would have a high problem recognition score. Consumer (1)'s situation is now to be compared with consumer (2)'s situation who perceives his car as highly reliable (PB = 1.00) and holds a positive value on its reliability (PV = +2). Consumer (2) expects also to have a functionally reliable car (EB = 1.00) and highly values automobile reliability (EV = +2). In consumer (2)'s situation we would expect a low or negligible problem recognition score. Now let us apply the enhancement model by plugging in these values and comparing consumer (1)'s problem recognition with that of consumer (2).

$$EA_k = (PV_{ik} \, PB_{ik})(EV_{ik} \, EB_{ik})^2 - (EV_{ik} \, EB_{ik})$$

$$EA_1 = ((-2)(1.00)((+2)(1.00)^2)) - ((+2)(1.00)) = -10$$

$$EA_2 = ((+2)(1.00)((+2)(1.00)^2)) - ((+2)(1.00)) = +6$$

Theoretically, consumer (1), who was expected to have a high problem recognition score ended up with a high negative score indicative of a dissatisfaction state with the current product, while consumer (2), who was expected to have no problem recognition obtained a slightly positive score indicative of a slight satisfaction state with the current product.

A study conducted by Sirgy and Kassem (1982) was specifically designed to test the validity of the problem recognition as conceptualized and formulated by the enhancement affect model. It was hypothesized that problem recognition is strongest under negative incongruity conditions, followed by negative congruity conditions, positive congruity, and positive incongruity conditions, respectively; and that the relationship predicted between problem recognition and evaluative congruity would be stronger under conditions of high certainty (strong perceptions and strong evoked beliefs) than under conditions of low certainty (weak perceptions and weak evoked beliefs).

Three-hundred-and-twenty subjects were randomly assigned to experimental conditions. A 2×2×2×2 factorial design was used in which a positive/negative perception (PV), positive/negative referent evoked belief (EV), strength of perception (PB), and strength of evoked belief (EB) were manipulated. Five self-report indicators of problem recognition were used and high internal consistency among the indicators was demonstrated. Hypothetical consumer situations involving automobile repair experiences were constructed reflective of 16 different congruity conditions.

The pattern of results was highly consistent with the theoretical predictions as derived from the enhancement affect function.

Opportunity Recognition

The need to purchase or acquire a new product does not arise only from comparing desired product attributes with current product attributes, but also from comparing those attributes of a new product (percept) with a set of individual needs (as expressed in evoked beliefs). In other words problem recognition can be manifested as a recognition of an opportunity to acquire a new product to satisfy certain needs. Accordingly, a more suitable label for this process may be "opportunity recognition" rather than problem recognition.

With opportunity recognition, the enhancement affect model is used similarly; however, the point of emphasis does not lie in the negative congruity or incongruity condition as expressed in problem recognition but in positive congruity or incongruity. Also, it should be noted that with problem recognition the percept constitutes the current product, whereas with opportunity recognition the new product is represented by the percept.

MEDIA PREFERENCE

The term media here is broadly defined to include various types of information sources. To further elucidate this point, reference is made to Engel et al.'s typology of sources of consumer information. Information sources were classified along two dimensions: interpersonal versus impersonal and advocate versus independent. Based on this typology four alternative information sources seem available: personal selling (advocate/ interpersonal), word-of-mouth communication (independent/ interpersonal), advertising, sales promotion, and point-of-sale promotion (advocate/impersonal), and publicity and technical reports (independent/impersonal). Each of these general media classes, in turn, can be broken down further along an intra- media dimension. For example advertising can be classified into television, radio, magazines, newspaper, billboards, posters, and so on.

Having touched upon information sources for media alterna- tives, the next question is how does a consumer react to these various media alternatives. This then deals with media prefer- ence. Media preference models in the advertising psychology literature have been mostly borrowed from the brand preference literature. Consequently, the reader is referred to the brand preference section of this chapter.

MESSAGE EVALUATION

There are two different processes involved with message evaluation of marketing communications. One process involves evaluation of message attributes unrelated to the overall objective of the message. This phenomenon is usually referred to as "message interest." The other process involves evaluation of message attributes directly related to the overall objective of the communication. This is called "message persuasion."

Message Interest

The focus of message interest is on the arousal of involve- ment in the message through means usually unrelated to the product. The use of sex and humor appeal usually exemplify this situation. Sex and/or humor are thought to have arousal value that serves to raise the involvement level in message information processing.

This is not to be confused with those product attributes related to sex, humor, fear, and/or other emotional appeals. The use of an emotional appeal therefore may be directly related to the product and designed to enhance product liking or message acceptance, or may be unrelated to the product and designed to arouse interest in the message. The focus of the immediate dis- cussion is on the latter. The use of an emotional appeal as it directly impacts message acceptance will be discussed in the following section.

The extent to which a consumer would be emotionally aroused by a message, using, for example, sex appeal, is mostly dependent on the nature and content of the evoked frame of reference, as well as on the nature and content of the message's sex-related cues (cf. Baker and Churchill 1977). Accounting for these variables, the magnitude of the experienced sexual affect (one type of enhancement affect) can be precisely modelled and predicted.

Let us go through an example. Suppose an ad uses an attractive, sexually provocative female model to advertise a sports car (for example, PV = +7 and PB = 1.00). The extent to which this sexual cue may have an impact depends highly on what becomes compared with this cue. If the consumer compares this perception with his ideal sexy female (for example, EV = +10 and EB = 1.00), then he may experience some positive affect but not as much as if he had compared it with the average female (for example, EV = +4 and EB = .80). If the same consumer has a wife who is sexually nonprovocative (for example, EV = -3 and EB = 1.00) and uses his wife as a reference point, he would experience greater positive enhancement affect toward the ad's sexy model compared to the preceding situations.

Of course there may be other processes going on with sexually related cues such as sexual fantasies that may involve a series of congruity processes, each inducing a certain amount of positive enhancement affect.

In short, what is being argued here is that message interest can be modelled and predicted through the direct application of the enhancement affect function.

With respect to humor research, advertisers appear to agree that humor enhances audience attention (Sternthal and Craig 1973). Leavitt (1970) conducted a study in which he provided some evidence linking humor to the energy level or audience attention to television commercials. In every case humor investigators concede that humorous messages attract attention through the increase of message interest but do not necessarily affect message persuasion (Sternthal and Craig 1973; C. P. Duncan 1980).

Consumer behaviorists and advertising psychologists have used adaptation-level theory and learning theory to explain the effect of humor stimuli on message interest.

Adaptation-level theory (Helson 1964) deals with the capacity of a stimulus to attract attention. An adaptation level exists for different stimuli. Attention is attracted when the individual perceives the focal stimulus to be different from its adaptation level. Although this theory is designed to explain attention or arousal level in general, it has been used repeatedly in the humor research literature to explain humor response. This theory seems to adequately explain the magnitude of the attention or arousal level experienced by an individual, but it fails to address the direction and type of experienced affect. How does this theory differentiate between happiness, sadness, elation, disgust, satisfaction, anger, and so on?

Learning theory, on the other hand, says that through instrumental and classical conditioning of previous stimuli with humor, these stimuli when perceived automatically activate the degree of humor associated with them.

Note that adaptation-level theory explains the magnitude of the experienced emotion and learning theory adequately explains the nature and direction of the experienced emotion. The proposed social cognition theory, in contrast, through the direct use of the enhancement affect model, can explain both the magnitude and the direction of the experienced affect. So far the issue of different types of emotional states, such as anger, sadness, grief, humor, and happiness has not been addressed. Only the directionality of the induced affect was addressed. It is the contention of this author that affect can be differentiated only along a positive-negative quantitative dimension and not along a qualitative dimension. The qualitative aspect that we are all familiar with comes from emotional labeling. It is argued that we have verbal counterparts of positive and negative valences. This labeling process differs depending on the situation and the personality disposition of the individual. This position is consistent with Schachter and Singer's (1962) theory of emotional labeling. According to their view, the individual first becomes aware of diffuse sensations of positive or negative arousal, and if there is no immediate explanation for this arousal, he/she will label this emotional state. When a similar situation occurs, the available emotional label becomes accessible and is used in congruity processing. This theory has been accepted and expanded in the literature of social cognition (see Pennebaker 1980 for a comprehensive treatment of the subject matter). Also, from the perspective of the proposed social cognition theory, the issue of cognitive labeling of values was already discussed in an earlier chapter. These theoretical propositions apply directly to the issue of emotional differentiation discussed here. As noted, enhancement affect is translated into an evaluative decision with a certain attribute value (DV). This attribute value is then subjected to perceptual inference, and, consequently, a semantic label is attached to it.

Message Persuasion

In consumer behavior research message persuasion has
been treated from at least four theoretical perspectives. These
are: (1) the assimilation-contrast theory, (2) the expectancy-
value theory, (3) the cognitive-response theory, and (4)
decision-rule theory.

Sherif and Hovland's (1961) <u>assimilation-contrast theory</u>
suggests that message acceptance is influenced by the discrepancy
between the consumer's beliefs about what the product features
truly are and the marketing claim about the product features.
According to the assimilation-contrast theory, there is a region
in which a range of attributes can be accepted and then assimilated in the consumer's cognitive structures, namely the assimilation region (latitude of acceptance). Conversely, if the product
or message attributes fall outside the region of assimilation, the
product or message will be rejected. This region is labeled the
contrast region (latitude of rejection). Involvement is also expected to influence message acceptance/rejection by widening
or narrowing the latitude of noncommitment.

The assimilation-contrast position has been reinterpreted
in light of the proposed social cognition theory. Product perceptions conveying information about product features (perceptual
attributes) are compared with prior or existing beliefs about
those product features. The resulting perceptual congruity
determines the extent of message acceptance. That is, in the
case of perceptual incongruity, the resultant response involving
cognitive dissonance will induce the consumer to disparage the
message (message dismissal), or make a compromise with the
difference between the perception and belief by forming a new
belief that is positioned somewhere in-between the perception
and the evoked belief (belief change).

In the case of belief congruity the resultant response would
be that of perceptual categorization. Precise message acceptance
predictions can be derived by applying the consistency affect
model. Message acceptance (MA) can therefore be construed
as a direct function of consistency affect.

This consistency affect function comes closer to the
assimilation-contrast function when the range associated with
the assimilation region is comparable to the intervals associated
with the PV and EV measures. And, of course, the consistency
affect function is argued to be more advantageous to the
assimilation-contrast function because it includes the strength
of the incoming message variable (PB) and the strength of the
evoked belief (PB).

The use of the expectancy-value theory in promotional planning has been seminal (Boyd, Ray, and Strong 1972; Wright 1973). The general expectancy-value model assumes that a consumer has a set of needs he/she is seeking to satisfy, and products are seen as being instrumental in satisfying those needs. This model has three essential ingredients: (1) the consumer's perception of the product attributes, (2) the relationship between those attributes and his/her value system, and (3) the hierarchical arrangement of that value system (Wright 1973). There are at least two variations of this model: one is the belief-evaluation model and the other is the belief-importance model. The difference between these two models lies in the evaluation-importance distinction. The evaluation component involves asking the individual to articulate his/her feeling of liking or disliking of each product attribute, whereas the importance component involves reporting the relative importance of a set of product-related needs in his/her value system.

Advertising then functions to restructure the belief component in the target audience. This can come about by creating a new belief, changing an old belief, reinforcing an old belief, and/or extinguishing (unlearning) an old belief.

In light of the proposed theory, it can be argued that both evaluation and importance components relate to the concept of "value." The only problem, as was argued previously, is that the traditional forms of expectancy-value models exclude the treatment of the evoked frame of reference and the interrelationship between the evoked beliefs and their perceived counterparts.

A number of cognitive response modes to message persuasion are suggested based on Greenwald's (1968) cognitive response theory. These are: counterargument, source derogation, and support argument.

Counterargument is activated when a discrepancy is noted between the incoming information and the existing belief system (Wright 1973). The counterargument as a resulting response then serves to neutralize the message evidence. Source derogation focuses on the source of information. It serves as a substitute for counterargument under those conditions when the source is easily viewed as biased (Wright 1973). Support argument is a cognitive response resulting from congruent associations between the incoming information and existing belief structure (Wright 1973).

Wright (1973) in a study investigating the effects of counterargument (CA), source derogation (SD), and support argument (SA) on advertising message acceptance, construed and also found message acceptance to be mathematically a function of:

$$MA_k = Wsa \sum_{i=1}^{I} SA_{ik} - Wca \sum_{j=1}^{J} CA_{jk} - Wsd \sum_{l=1}^{L} SD_{lk}$$

where MA = message acceptance/rejection of individual
(k)
and Wsa, Wca, and Wsd = the weights assigned to
these cue types by the
consumer

Let us see if we can understand counterargument, source derogation, and support argument using social cognition theory. With respect to counterargument Wright (1973) used the following example to illustrate the cognitive dynamics involved with this phenomenon.

> For example, in response to the advertisement's claim that a new food product made from soybean derivatives offers improved cleanliness in packaging operations, the receiver may immediately think of a disadvantage ("side effects from the derivatives") or an alternate solution to the problem cited ("tighter government controls are the best answer") [p. 54].

The nature of the counterargument in this example is a threefold process: (1) perceptual categorization of soybean derivatives in the cognitive structures; (2) comparison of soybean derivatives (percept) to the attributes of the ideal solution (reference point); and (3) comparison of government control attributes as another alternative to soybean derivatives (percept). In other words in the language of the proposed theory, counterargumentation involves one or more evaluative congruities, which use reference points that cause negative congruities and/ or incongruities, and therefore induce a negative evaluative affect toward the product.

How about source derogation? Source derogation can be interpreted in the language of social cognition as a perceptual inference process by which the consumer arrives at a perceptual decision linking the source with noncredibility. This, in turn, undermines the credibility of the message. This is also done through a perceptual inference process.

With respect to support argument, it is construed as the opposite of counterargument. In support argument the consumer uses one or more reference points, which insure positive congruity or incongruity, and therefore induce a positive evaluation toward the advertised product.

The use of decision-rule theory in promotion has been
treated in the consumer/advertising psychology literature
(Wright 1973, 1975). A decision rule refers to the manner in
which a set of perceptions are combined and integrated into an
overall decision. The traditional multiattribute attitude models
use the linear compensatory decision rule in which the sum of
the involved perceptions determines the resultant decision.
This has also been referred to as the "optimizing" rule in the
consumer/advertising literature. Alternative decision rules to
the linear compensatory rule include the conjunctive, disjunctive,
and lexicographic rules. The conjunctive rule involves having
the consumer establish criterion cutoffs on each attribute and
requires that the brand surpass all of these to make a favorable
decision. The disjunctive rule involves having the consumer
require that the brand possess at least one distinctly superior
attribute in order to receive a high evaluation. The lexicographic
rule portrays the consumer making brand comparisons with one
attribute at a time rather than using different attributes con-
currently. The sequence of processing goes from the most
important attribute to the least important. He/she would reach
a decision as soon as significant differences between the brands
are perceived.

In promotion planning advertisers and marketing communication specialists usually attempt to direct the consumer toward
the particular rule that favors the advertiser's position. In
light of the proposed theory and specifically with respect to
the enhancement affect model, two different decision rules denoting parallel and sequential attribute processing are used.
These have been discussed earlier in terms of the traditional
compensatory and noncompensatory rules.

STORE PREFERENCE

The discussion of store preference is lumped with brand
preference. This is done because consumer behaviorists generally
use brand preference models to describe and predict store preference behavior. Therefore, for the sake of simplicity, the term
"brands" is used here to mean both product brands and stores.

BRAND PREFERENCE

This process involves the evaluation of one brand against
another or against a criterion standard.

Four general classes of alternative evaluation models are identified here. These are: (1) unitary models, (2) compensatory models, (3) noncompensatory models, and (4) self-image/brand-image congruity models.

Unitary Models

One unitary model is selected and described here, namely, the affect-referral model (Wright 1975). This model does not focus on attributes or beliefs about alternatives; instead, it posits that evaluation of an alternative is determined by past experiences stored in memory. Wright (1975, 1978) argued that a consumer may not evaluate a brand based on its attributes but, rather, strictly on his/her affective reaction toward that product based on his/her past experience.

This process can be explained as follows: The evoked frame of reference may be that of past experience with that product. This may involve a cognitive category of that product associated with a number of positively and/or negatively valued attributes (based on the consumer's experience with the product). The perceived product with some perceptual cue would activate this cognitive schema.

Since the evoked cognitive category is well established (having strong EBs), those conceptual attributes will be projected onto the perceptual platform, and, in essence, determine the perceptual attributes that relate directly to the percept (stimulus brand). Due to the forced projection of conceptual attributes onto the perceptual platform, then, by definition, there should be perfect congruity. The extent to which this congruity per attribute is positive or negative is automatically transferred onto the stimulus brand in terms of enhancement affect (or evaluative affect) using a compensatory decision rule.

Compensatory Models

Four compensatory models are briefly described and presented.

(1) Beliefs/Evaluation Model: This model states that a purchase decision concerning a specific brand depends on the sum of the product of the probability that the brand has some attribute (b_{ik}) and on the evaluative aspects of that attribute (e_{ik}) (Fishbein 1967).

$$A_k = \sum_{i=1}^{I} b_{ik}\, e_{ik}$$

This model received wide application in marketing (Assael 1981).

(2) Beliefs/Importance Model: This model states that the overall evaluation of a brand is a function of the sum of the product of beliefs about the attributes possessed by a brand (b) weighted by the importance of each attribute (w_{ik}) [Bass and Talarzyk 1972].

$$A_k = \sum_{i=1}^{I} b_{ik}\, w_{ik}$$

(3) Ideal Point Model: This model asserts that a consumer's overall evaluation of a specific brand can be determined by the sum of the weighted (by beta coefficient W) discrepancies between the belief that the brand is associated with a specific attribute (A_{jk}) and the ideal position involving that attribute (I_{jk}) [Lehman 1971].

$$A_k = \sum_{j=1}^{J} W_j (A_{jk} - I_{jk})$$

(4) Beliefs/Only Model: Sheth and Talarzyk (1972) argued for the inclusion of the beliefs component only. In other words overall brand evaluation was found to be a function of the sum of the belief ratings involving the brand attributes.

$$A_k = \sum_{i=1}^{I} b_{ik}$$

In the language of the proposed social cognition theory, the various compensatory models can be explained in terms of congruity effects involving the enhancement affect function.

To begin with, let us concentrate on the beliefs/evaluation model. The belief dimension in this model is directly akin to the perceptual component—PB_{ik}. The evaluative dimension is also directly analogous to the PV_{ik}.

The problem with the beliefs/evaluation model is that the standard of comparison, the frame of reference, or the cognitive "anchor," is not specified. A consumer's evaluative judgment of a specific product attribute can be drastically different depending on the evoked frame of reference. One way out of this is to control the frame of reference in the assessment of the model's components, that is, instruct the respondent to evaluate each product attribute in direct comparison to an alternative product, an ideal product, and so on. This method would provide control of the evoked schema, and the resultant overall evaluation may be highly comparable to that of the enhancement affect function.

Furthermore the model's compensatory rule assumes that each cognitive element (b_{ik} e_{ik} or PB_{ik} PV_{ik}) that is processed will be added on to the effect of the previous one with the same magnitude. In other words the overall evaluation is construed to be a linear function of the number of attributes involved, which corresponds to the parallel forms of the EA model.

With respect to the beliefs/importance model, it may be easily argued that the importance dimension as traditionally measured by the beliefs/importance model is tapping the same evaluation construct as the beliefs/evaluation model. It would only be different if importance of an attribute is measured relative to the other attributes involved. But quite interestingly, to provide an importance rating for each attribute, it may be argued that the respondent will have to use the enhancement congruity function for every attribute involved to make a decision concerning the rating of the importance of that attribute relative to another attribute. To argue for this type of congruity may be only feasible under those conditions in which the evoked cognitive category might not be an integrated whole. An integrated cognitive category or schema have attribute values relative to one another and therefore importance ratings might only duplicate what is already in these.

With respect to the beliefs/only model, it may be easily argued that Sheth and Talarzyk's (1972) finding that the evaluation and/or importance variable did not contribute significantly to the predicted variance because of a method confound, namely the attribute preselection procedure. Once a list of attributes is gathered that insures saliency, by definition, it is very likely that these gathered attributes may be all somewhat equally important or equally evaluated by most of the respondents. This procedure would automatically make the evaluation or importance factor a statistically nonsignificant factor but cannot argue for its theoretical exclusion.

With regard to the ideal point model, the current perceived state of an attribute of a product (A_{jk}) is conceptually equivalent to the social cognition variable of PV_{ik}, whereas the ideal attribute of that product (I_{jk}) may be easily construed as a referent attribute value (EV_{ik}). Lehman's model comes close to the enhancement model in its theoretical formulation but falls short in its exclusion of the strength of the perception and evoked conceptual relations.

Before we leave this topic of compensatory models it should be noted that the direct application of the belief/evaluation, belief/importance, belief/only, and ideal-point models provides us with a measure of affect (or EA) toward an object, not a measure of choice. Choice comes as a result of a perceptual inference in which the object scoring the strongest positive affect is categorized into a decision-rule cognitive category. An example of a decision-rule cognitive category may involve the concept "object inducing the strongest positive affect" linked with a conceptual attribute of "accept decision." This perceptual inference process following evaluative congruity and affect is not only essential to the overall understanding of decision-making psychology, but also essential to the understanding of the psychological use of noncompensatory decision rules in particular. Now we turn our attention to noncompensatory decision models.

Noncompensatory Models

A number of decision rules have been applied in consumer behavior research (Wright 1975). These rules, mostly borrowed from the psychology of decision making, are varied (see Montgomery and Svenson 1976; and Slovic and Lichtenstein 1975, for a comprehensive review).

(1) Dominance Rule: This model prescribes that if alternative A is better than alternative B on at least one attribute, and if A is not worse than B on any other attribute, A will be chosen (Lee 1971).

	A*	B	C
1	3*	1	2
2	4*	2	3
3	4*	3	2

(Asterisks are used to denote selections, and cross-overs denote eliminations).

(2) Conjunctive Rule: This model implies that the attractiveness of every aspect for the chosen alternative must exceed a criterion specific for each attribute and that at least one of the aspects of the other alternative falls below one of the critical

values of the attractiveness (Coombs and Kao 1955; Dawes 1964; Einhorn 1971).

	A*	B	C	Criterion
1	4*	2	3	3
2	5*	3	2	4
3	4*	2	3	3

(3) Disjunctive Rule: This model states that the attractiveness of at least one aspect for the chosen alternative must exceed a criterion specific for that attribute and that all aspects of the other alternative fall below a criterion specific for each attribute (Coombs and Kao 1955; Dawes 1964; Einhorn 1971).

	A*	B	C	Criterion
1	5*	2	1	3
2	2	1	2	3
3	2	3	3	4

(4) Lexicographic Rule: This model implies that the choice will be the alternative that is more attractive on the most important attribute. If the aspects of the attribute are equally attractive, the decision will be based on the attribute next in importance (Fishburn 1974).

	A*	B	C	
1	2	2	2	1st most important
2	2	2	2	2nd most important
3	4*	1*	2*	3rd most important

(5) Elimination-By-Aspect Rule: This model implies that the most important attribute is selected and the alternatives that do not exceed the conjunctive criterion on this attribute are eliminated. This procedure is then repeated with new attributes, selected according to their order of importance until all the alternatives are eliminated but one (Tversky 1972).

	A	B	C	Criterion	
1	4	4	1	3	1st most important
2	5	1		3	2nd most important
3				3	3rd most important

(6) Elimination-By-Least-Attractive-Aspect Rule: This model implies that the decision maker chooses that alternative that is not associated with the least attractive aspect (maximum principle in game theory in Luce and Raiffa 1957).

	A	B	C
1	3	5	2
2	2	3	4
3	2	1	2

(7) Choice-By-Most-Attractive-Aspect Rule: This rule means that the decision maker should choose that alternative that is associated with the most attractive aspect (maximum principle in game theory in Luce and Raiffa 1957).

	A*	B	C
1	6*	4	2
2	2	4	3
3	3	4	4

(8) Maximizing-Number-of-Attributes-With-Greater-Attractiveness Rule: This model implies that the alternative with the greater number of favorable attributes is chosen. That is, if one alternative is more attractive than another alternative on a greater number of attributes, then that alternative is chosen (May 1954).

	A*	B	C
1	4*	2	1
2	1	3	4*
3	3*	2	2

With regard to those noncompensatory decision models, the attractiveness weight for each attribute belonging to each alternative can be viewed to be composed of the PV_{ik} PB_{ik} elements. The reader should also note that attractiveness weights are derived in direct comparison to another alternative or a criterion standard. Comparison with other alternatives or some standard criterion in social cognition terms will automatically render a type of congruity involving referent relations.

The lexicographic rule seems somewhat comparable to the enhancement affect model involving sequential attribute processing. Brand A (perceived) is compared with Brand B (evoked) along the most important attribute. The most important attribute is first selected because of its high accessibility. And an over-all evaluation can be reached right then and there toward Brand A. The brand having the strongest evaluative affect score (and reflected cognitively through labeling of value) will be percep-tually categorized in a decision-rule category in which an "accept-ance" perceptual inference may result. In the presence of a tie between two or more brands, this situation (reflected through cognitive labeling of values) will be perceptually categorized into a decision-rule category reflecting this situation. This decision-rule concept can be viewed as strongly linked with a conceptual attribute involving "consider the next most important attribute."

Thus, a perceptual inference may result linking the per-ceived situation with the attribute "consider the next most important attribute." This perceptual decision may act as a goal motivating the individual to engage in further processing until he/she reaches a decision to accept an alternative.

The elimination-by-aspect rule is also somewhat comparable to the dynamics involved with the enhancement affect model of the sequential type. A perceived attribute is compared with a criterion standard (desired criteria) along the most important attribute and an overall evaluation is attempted. If the evalua-tion of that attribute is less than satisfactory (negative enhance-ment affect), then the consumer rejects the brand and under-takes another brand. This latter process, of course, is dictated by perceptual categorization and inference.

The elimination-by-least-attractive aspect rule can be described from a social cognition perspective as a perceptual categorization process in which that alternative with the least attractive aspect is categorized into the evoked cognitive cate-gory labeled as "alternative with least attractive aspect." A conceptual attribute associated with that category may be "reject that alternative." Therefore, that perceived alternative will be associated with the evoked conceptual relation involving the attribute of "rejection." Consequently, the decision incurred, in this case, is that of rejection.

The choice-by-most-attractive-aspect rule can be similarly explained. The process involves the categorization of that alter-native with the most attractive aspect (perceptual cue) which is linked to the attribute "accept."

With respect to the maximizing-number-of-attributes-with-greater-attractiveness rule, at least three major perceptual operations may be involved. The first set may involve a number of perceptual categorizations that would identify the alternative that has the greatest attractiveness aspect for every attribute dimension. The second set may involve a number of perceptual categorizations that perform counting operations. Finally, the individual identifies the alternative with the maximum number of attributes and makes a perceptual inference linking that alternative with an "accept" conceptual attribute.

The dominance rule can be described as follows: Those features of a specific alternative that indicate whether that alternative is greater or lesser than the other alternative for a particular attribute are identified. These features are matched with the cognitive category involving the dominance rule. High consistency (consistency affect model) will induce the consumer to accept that alternative.

The conjunctive rule is somewhat different from the dominance rule in that comparisons are made with a criterion standard rather than with another brand. As with the dominance rule, a categorization of an alternative is made in the cognitive category testing whether that alternative is better than criterion on every attribute. If there is "goodness-of-fit" (high consistency affect), then a perceptual inference would result, linking the alternative (percept) with an attribute stating that it met the first condition. Then the competing alternative is categorized in such a way as to test whether it falls below the criterion on at least one attribute. Given a perfect "fit," a perceptual inference is made stating that the second condition is met. These perceptual inferences now become perceptual attributes to that alternative (percept), and are entered into another categorization in which a cognitive category representing the rule "if first and second conditions of alternative are met then accept" is evoked and a perceptual inference is incurred.

The disjunctive rule can also be similarly viewed, although with slight variations in the specific content of the evoked cognitive categories.

Before we leave this topic, we need to touch upon a related topic involved in the decision-making literature: decision-rule selection. Bettman (1979) argued that depending on the mode of processing, consumer decisions will be different. This is known in the decision-making literature as contingent decision making. Payne (1982), in a literature review article on contingent decision behavior, reviewed evidence that would suggest that decision-rule selection is moderated by task complexity, response mode, information display, and similarity of alternatives.

Task complexity was argued to affect contingent decision behavior through three factors: number of alternatives, number of attribute dimensions, and time pressure. Specifically, the greater the number of alternatives considered, the greater the use of noncompensatory decision rules. The greater the number of attribute dimensions, the greater the selective perception and use of these dimensions. And, the greater the time pressure in the decision environment, the greater the selective perception and use of negative attributes in the decision making.

With respect to response mode, it was argued that the judgment mode (ratings) usually leads to the use of compensatory decision rules, whereas the choice mode (selection) leads to the use of noncompensatory rules.

With respect to information display, it was noted that decision makers tend to use only information that is explicitly displayed in the stimulus object and will use it only in the form displayed. This behavior functions to reduce cognitive strain associated with information processing.

With respect to the similarity of alternatives factor, Shugan (1980) argued that the cost of thinking associated with the use of various decision strategies is based, in part, on the perceptual similarity between alternatives. Specifically, the cost of thinking is inversely related to perceptual similarity. That is, the more similar the alternatives the more likely that a compensatory rule will be used (cited in Payne 1982).

These factors seem to indicate whether the consumer might use a compensatory versus a noncompensatory decision rule. They do not help us much with finding out precisely what rule will be used in a given situation.

Payne (1982) referred to at least three theoretical frameworks that are used to explain (or partially explain) contingent decision behavior. These are: cost/benefit principles, perceptual process, and adaptive production systems.

The cost/benefit explanation (Beach and Mitchell 1978) assumes that any decision rule has certain benefits such as the probability that the rule will lead to a "good" decision outcome, the speed of making the decision, and its justifiability. Costs might include information acquisition and computational effort. In terms of the proposed social cognition theory, we can construe the process of selecting a decision rule as an evaluative congruity process comparing alternative decision rules along benefit and cost-related attributes. The alternative decision rule scoring the highest EA, therefore, would be selected for implementation in a given decision situation.

The perceptual process explanation (Kahneman and Tversky 1979; Tversky and Kahneman 1981), called prospect theory, asserts that all decisions involve two major phases—a perceptual phase and an evaluation phase. The perceptual phase is mostly responsible for the variations in decision making. The evaluation

is assumed to be invariant across situations. This theory comes
very close to the social cognition theory's treatment of noncompensatory decision rules. The reader is reminded of the
fact that most of noncompensatory decision rules were translated
in terms of a series of perceptual categorizations and inferences.
Consequently, it is safe to assert that there is a certain degree
of communality between prospect theory and the social cognition
treatment of the various decision rules.

The adaptive production systems' explanation (Pitz 1977;
Newell and Simon 1972) involves the notion that decision rules
are "subroutines" or production systems stored in long-term
memory. The conditions of a subroutine are tested against data
elements contained in short-term memory (working memory).
Further, there is no conscious consideration of which subroutine
to apply. Subroutines are assumed to be arranged along a
hierarchical dimension. The conditions of each subroutine are
tested starting from the top of the hierarchy down. In social
cognition language, these decision subroutines or production
systems are analogous to cognitive categories, or more broadly
to "scripts" containing one or more decision rules. The activation
of a script is dependent on its degree of accessibility in a given
situation. Abelson (1981) argued that a script containing one
or more decision rules (production system) may be activated by
action rules, such as incentive and effort. Incentive action
rules are beliefs associated with reward/punishment properties
of a perceived situation, whereas effort rules are beliefs associated with individual-directed goals and other internal factors.

Furthermore, it is interesting to note that these decision-
making models applied to brand evaluation have used functional
not personality-related attributes. The distinction between
functional and personality-related attributes has been made
by a number of consumer self-concept researchers (for example,
Holman 1981; Munson and Spivey 1980; Sirgy 1982b). Functional
attributes of a brand are those evaluative criteria that have
direct "utilitarian" value to the consumer (cf. Katz 1960). For
example, a specific brand of toothpaste can be described along
functional dimensions such as, fluoride, teeth whitener, breath
freshener, taste, price, etc. However, personality-related
attributes or evaluative criteria are those characteristics of a
brand which are "value-expressive" (Katz 1960), or those characteristics that associate the brand-user with a specific personality profile. For example a brand of toothpaste may have
symbolic or personality-related attributes such as, young,
sexually interested, active, and so forth.

Now the question is, how are personality attributes used
in brand evaluation? To answer this question, we have to delve

into consumer behavior research investigating the interaction between brand image and consumer self-concept.

Self-Image/Brand-Image Congruity Models

The self-concept literature in consumer behavior is muddled with ambiguity and confusion on the precise conceptualization of self-concept. A number of investigators have conceptualized self-concept as a single self-construct and treated it to mean the <u>actual self-concept</u>; that is, the image of oneself as he/she perceives himself/herself (Sirgy 1982b). Within the single self-construct tradition, some investigators have restricted self-concept to merely <u>sex-role self-concept</u>, defined as that image of oneself as he/she perceives his/her sex role.

In the multiple self-constructs tradition, self-concept has been conceptualized as having two or more constructs. Some investigators argued that self-concept has to be treated as having two components—the actual self-concept and the <u>ideal self-concept</u> (the ideal self-concept is defined as that image of oneself as he/she would like to be).

Other investigators have gone beyond the duality dimension. They refer to actual self-image, ideal self-image, social self-image, ideal social self-image, expected self-image, and expressive self-image. The <u>social self-concept</u> (sometimes referred to as "looking-glass self" or "presenting self") was defined as that image that one believes others have of him/her. The <u>ideal social self-concept</u> (sometimes referred to as "desired social self") denotes that image that one would like others to have about him/her. The <u>expected self</u> refers to that image somewhere between the actual and the ideal self-concept. And the <u>expressive self</u> pertains to either the ideal self-concept or social self-concept (Sirgy 1982b).

More recently, Sirgy (1980a, 1981c, 1982b, 1982c, 1982d) and associates (Sirgy and Danes 1982; Samli and Sirgy 1981) introduced a <u>self-concept/product-image congruity theory</u>, which is based on this social cognition theory, and advances the notion that every self-image has a value association that determines the degree of positive or negative affect felt when the particular self-image is activated. This value component associated with a particular self-image replaces the traditional constructs of ideal self-image, ideal social self-image, and so on. Correspondingly, every product image also has a value component reflective of the affective intensity associated with that attribute. A specific value-laden self-image interacts with a corresponding value-laden product image and the result occurs in the form of positive self-congruity (comparison between a positive product image and a positive self-image), positive self-incongruity (comparison between a positive product image and a negative self-image), negative self-congruity (comparison between a negative product image and a negative self-image), or negative self-incongruity (comparison between a negative product image and a positive self-image). Based on self-esteem need dynamics, the theory predicts that an individual would experience more approach motivation toward a particular product given a positive self-incongruity than a positive self-congruity condition. In contrast more avoidance motivation would be felt toward the product under negative self-incongruity than negative self-congruity conditions (see Figure 11.1).

However, these predictions are based only on the psychological dynamics of self-esteem needs. Other self-concept motives involving self-consistency needs are also known to play a significant role in goal-directed behavior. Self-consistency motivation is said to drive the individual to behave in ways consistent with his/her perception of himself/herself, since behaviors that are realized to be inconsistent with his/her self-image threaten the organization of his/her "self-theory." As a result, people guard against the threat of conceptual disorganization by attempting to behave consistently with their self-perceptions.

Therefore, it is maintained that self-consistency motivation counteracts self-esteem motivation under incongruity conditions. The resultant motivational tendency, which is shown in Figure 11.1, is the outcome motivational state determined by the conflict resolution of these two self-concept motives.

Initial tests of these ideas provided moderate to strong support of the theory. Further efforts in refining self-concept methodology are underway based on this theory.

The findings of self-image/brand-image congruity studies can be summarized (Sirgy 1982b) and interpreted in light of the proposed social cognition theory.

First, the relationship between actual self-image/product-image congruity (self-congruity) and brand preference has been supported by numerous studies. In light of social cognition theory, this type of congruity involves product image and belief relations involving the self-concept. The consumer imagines himself/herself using this product (product-image perception), which is then compared with how he/she actually sees himself/herself. The resultant affect will be in the form of cognitive consistency or cognitive dissonance (consistency affect). This process can be modelled through the consistency affect model.

Figure 11.1 The Effects of Self-Esteem and Self-Consistency on Purchase Motivation

SELF-IMAGE	PRODUCT IMAGE	SELF-IMAGE/ PRODUCT-IMAGE CONGRUITY	APPROACH/AVOIDANCE SELF-ESTEEM MOTIVATION	APPROACH/AVOIDANCE SELF-CONSISTENCY MOTIVATION	APPROACH/AVOIDANCE PURCHASE MOTIVATION
Positive	Positive	Positive Self-Congruity	Approach Self-Esteem Motivation	Approach Self-Consistency Motivation	Approach Purchase Motivation
Negative	Positive	Positive Self-Incongruity	Approach Self-Esteem Motivation	Avoidance Self-Consistency Motivation	Conflict
Negative	Negative	Negative Self-Congruity	Avoidance Self-Esteem Motivation	Approach Self-Consistency Motivation	Conflict
Positive	Negative	Negative Self-Incongruity	Avoidance Self-Esteem Motivation	Avoidance Self-Consistency Motivation	Avoidance Purchase Motivation

The resultant response might be in the form of product acceptance or rejection. That is, cognitive consistency will induce
the consumer to accept the product because it fits his/her self-
image, whereas cognitive dissonance might lead to product
rejection because of the lack of fit.

Second, the relationship between ideal self-image/product-
image congruity (ideal congruity) and brand preference has
been generally supported. The consumer would anticipate outcomes related to how others might react to him/her using that
product (and/or how he/she might react himself/herself given
the usage of that product). This situation would induce a
congruity process involving expectancy relations and can be
modelled through the enhancement affect model. The resultant
response may be in the form of product evaluation. Ideal congruity will lead to positive product evaluation, whereas ideal
incongruity may be responsible for negative product evaluation.

Third, the relationship between social-image/product-image
congruity (social congruity) and brand preference has not been
strongly supported. As stated previously, the social self-image
is a belief construct, and social congruity is interpreted as the
match between how others see themselves (social self-image)
and how I might present myself using that product (product-
image perception). As with self-congruity, the consumer may
accept the product given high congruity and reject it given low
congruity. This resultant process can be modelled using the
consistency affect model.

Fourth, the relationship between ideal social self-image/
product-image congruity (ideal social congruity) and brand
preference has been moderately supported. The ideal social
self-image plays the role of an expectancy relation. The resultant
cognitive response is expected to be that of product evaluation
as modelled by the enhancement affect function.

Fifth, the moderating role of product conspicuousness on
the relationship between self-concept/product-image congruity
and brand preference has been largely unsupported. That is,
it was expected that the ideal and/or ideal social self-concepts
would be more related to product preference with respect to
highly conspicuous products than the actual and/or social self-
concepts. With respect to inconspicuous products, it was expected that the actual and/or social self-concept would be more
related to product preference than the ideal and/or ideal social
self-components. Based on the proposed social cognition theory,
a more plausible proposition may be that conspicuous products
(situational cue) might activate those social and ideal social
self-images, whereas inconspicuous products might elicit actual

and ideal self-images. Brand preference, with respect to conspicuous products, might involve the combined enhancement affect (resulting from ideal social congruity) and consistency affect (resulting from social congruity). And similarly, the same consumer behavior phenomena under product inconspicuousness conditions, might involve the combined enhancement affect (resulting from ideal congruity) and consistency affect (resulting from self-congruity). Future research may investigate these theoretical propositions.

Sixth, the moderating role of product personalization on the relationship between self-concept/product-image congruity and brand preference has been also only suggestive. That is, the relationship between self-concept/product-image congruity and brand preference seems stronger for high-personalizing products than for low-personalizing products. In social cognition terms highly personalizing or value-expressive products provide stronger perceptual cues to the activation of self-related schemas.

Finally, the moderating role of type of decision on the relationship between self-concept/product-image congruity and brand preference has been suggested by some findings. The results showed that the ideal and ideal social self-concepts were more related to brand preference than purchase intention, whereas the actual and social self-concepts were more related to purchase intention than brand preference. However, this expected finding did not generalize to all products. In light of the proposed theory, these hypotheses seem highly plausible. The actual and social self-images are directly in those situations where the consumer imagines whether the image presented to himself/herself and/or to others will be or will not be consistent with existing self- and social self-perceptions. And therefore these self-schemas may be more inclined to be activated under real purchase circumstances. This should be contrasted with the other situation in which the consumer imagines what he/she would feel using a specific product without considering the extent to which the use or nonuse of this product is consistent or not consistent with his/her self- or social self-image. Here the consumer might not be restricted by the reality of change and therefore might evaluate a brand in direct comparison with his/her ideal or ideal social self-image. It is argued here that in those situations in which the consumer is not "primed" to buy that product, he/she may evaluate that product using the expectancy relations involving the ideal and ideal social self-image. The resultant process can therefore be modelled by the enhancement affect function. However, in those situations in which the consumer is seriously "primed" to purchase that product, the consumer may consider the extent to which the use of that product is consistent or inconsistent with his/her self-image. The resultant cognitive consistency or dissonance is expected to influence his/her purchase intention.

Traditionally, self-congruity, ideal congruity, social congruity, and/or ideal social congruity have been mathematically modelled through a variety of distance models (Sirgy 1982b). These include the absolute difference model, the difference squared model, the simple difference model, and the Euclidean distance model. These can be represented respectively as follows:

$$A_k = f \left[\sum_{i=1}^{I} |PI_{ik} - SI_{ik}| \right]$$

$$A_k = f \left[\sum_{i=1}^{I} (PI_{ik} - SI_{ik})^2 \right]$$

$$A_k = f \left[\sum_{i=1}^{I} (PI_{ik} - SI_{ik}) \right]$$

$$A_k = f \left[\sqrt{\sum_{i=1}^{I} (PI - SI)^2} \right]$$

where A_k = attitude toward product (o) or toward the purchase or ownership of product (o) of individual (k)

PI_{ik} = product image (i) of individual (k)

SI_{ik} = actual self-image (i), ideal self-image (i), social self-image (i), or ideal social self-image (i) of individual (k)

BRAND SATISFACTION

Once the product is purchased, the consumer evaluates its performance. The result of this evaluation is satisfaction or dissatisfaction with the purchased product.

There is a significant amount of psychological literature involving cognitive evaluation process determining emotional reactions such as satisfaction or dissatisfaction. In the consumer behavior literature a number of theories have been used to explain consumer satisfaction/dissatisfaction. The six psychological theories to be briefly discussed are: contrast theory, cognitive dissonance theory, exchange (or comparison level) theory, assimilation-contrast theory, generalized negative theory, and attribution theory (Anderson 1973; LaTour and Peat 1980; Sirgy 1980b, 1982e).

Contrast theory (Hovland, Harvey, and Sherif 1957), applied to brand satisfaction, states that when brand expectations are not matched by the actual brand performance and benefits, a contrast between expectations and outcome will be felt, and, in turn, this contrast will be exaggerated. If the outcome exceeded expectations, the result would be satisfaction, and if it fell short of expectation, dissatisfaction would be experienced. This theory focuses on the contrast effect, which can be viewed in terms of assimilation-contrast theory. However, in this case, since the emphasis is in the latitude of rejection, this may be a high-involvement situation in which the latitude of acceptance is quite narrow and therefore facilitating the contrast effect. A social cognition interpretation of the assimilation-contrast theory has been provided elsewhere.

According to cognitive dissonance theory (Festinger 1957), unconfirmed expectations create a state of dissonance because the outcome is different from the individual's original expectations. When this occurs, the individual attempts to reduce the dissonance by distorting or changing the cognitions to make them more consistent. The stronger the cognitive dissonance the more motivation there is to change the cognitive elements to reduce this dissonance. As with assimilation-contrast theory, cognitive dissonance theory has been treated elsewhere.

Exchange (or comparison level) theory (Thibaut and Kelley 1959) states that the result of any interaction is conceptualized in terms of costs and rewards. A consumer's satisfaction with the outcome of a purchase may be determined by the discrepancy between the outcome and a standard of comparison known as the Comparison Level (CL). Outcomes above the CL are satisfying while those below are dissatisfying. In terms of social cognition theory, those outcomes refer to the perceived performance of a product along a particular attribute, and the comparison level involves referent relations.

Assimilation-contrast theory (Sherif and Hovland 1961) suggests that individuals have ranges of acceptance, rejection, and neutrality. Product performance evaluation, which differs slightly within a person's range of acceptance, will be assimilated so as to be consistent with expectations. Large discrepancies,

outside a person's range of acceptance, are exaggerated. The
direct translation of this theory into social cognition notions
has previously been made.

Generalized negativity theory (Carlsmith and Aronson
1963) states that any disconfirmation of an expected result
(disconfirmation—either positive or negative—means product
performance is different from what is expected) will be perceived
as less pleasant or less satisfying than if expectancy had been
confirmed. In social cognition terms this might be possible under
those conditions where a positive disconfirmation may be associated with a negative object, event, or person and therefore
neutralizing the positivity of this outcome into a negative one.
For example if a consumer expects 20 MPG from his/her new
car and ends up getting 30 MPG, we should expect him/her to
be quite pleased. However, he/she might not be pleased and
in fact be quite dissatisfied if he/she thought that someone could
be playing a trick on him/her.

Attribution theory (Weiner et al. 1972) postulates that
individuals utilize four elements to interpret and to predict
the outcome of an achievement-related event. Two of the four
components in the model—good or bad usage and lucky or unlucky
choice—describe qualities of the consumer, referred to as "external attributions." The two remaining components—good or
bad product and lucky or unlucky product—consider properties
internal to the product, thus "internal attributions." These
elements also exhibit enduring and variable characteristics.
The four elements in the model can be incorporated within two
dimensions: locus of control (internal versus external) and
degree of stability (fixed versus variable). It is felt that the
locus of control type of attribution is responsible for determining
the extent of satisfaction or dissatisfaction, where the stability
dimension might influence the future expectations (Sirgy 1980b).
The explanation of attribution theory notions in terms of social
cognition has previously been made.

The following section will examine some selected consumer
satisfaction/dissatisfaction (CS/D) models that have a direct
bearing to social cognition. These are: Miller (1977), Swan
and Martin (1981), and Sirgy (1980b, 1982e).

Identifying specific types of expectations to satisfaction
or dissatisfaction is necessary to predict consumer satisfaction
levels. In Miller (1977) the expectations a consumer might use
as comparison standards for performance evaluation are specified
as four types: ideal, expected, minimum tolerable, and deserved.
The "ideal" is the wished for performance. The "expected" is
based on past average performance. The "minimum tolerable"

is the least accepted level. The "deserved" reflects what an individual feels performance should be, given the costs or investments in it.

Depending on the relative position of each component to the others, an individual determines the level of satisfaction or dissatisfaction experienced in the situation. For example if performance falls above the expected level but below the deserved level, dissatisfaction results.

The various types of expectations specified by Miller can be viewed as various types of evoked beliefs. Each type of evoked belief enters into an evaluative congruity independent and/or dependent of the other. The overall brand satisfaction is then the net result of these evaluative congruities.

According to Swan and Martin (1981), there are two different types of expectations: predictive and desired expectations. Predictive expectations are an individual's estimate, prior to use, of the performance of a product that would be necessary for that product to satisfy the individual. The addition of performance outcomes to the combinations of predictive and desired expectations was argued to specify the likely occurrence of positive or negative disconfirmation of overall expectations and hence satisfaction or dissatisfaction.

As with Miller's (1977) various types of expectancies, predictive and desired expectancies can also be interpreted as two different types of evoked beliefs entering into two independent types of evaluative congruities. The net brand satisfaction can therefore be construed as the additive combination of the enhancement affect generated by each evaluative congruity.

This author presented a consumer satisfaction/dissatisfaction model that explains the cognitive processes involved in evaluating differences that occur between ideal, expected, deserved, and perceived outcome before and after product purchase and usage (Sirgy 1980, 1982). The model is mostly based on the evaluative congruity principle discussed here.

Once a behavior takes place, the outcome of the behavior is perceived and compared to the evoked cognition or expected behavior, a variety of levels of positive and negative emotions is felt depending on how well behavior does or does not reduce discrepancies between perceived (A) and expected outcome levels (D) after purchase.

$$CS/D_k = (A_k - D_k)$$

where CS/D_k = an individual's (k) satisfaction/
dissatisfaction

$$D_k = \text{expected outcome level of individual}$$
$$(k) \text{ after purchase}$$
$$A_k = \text{perceived outcome level of individual}$$
$$(k) \text{ after purchase}$$

Satisfaction/dissatisfaction depends on the discrepancy between the perceived outcome experienced before the behavior takes place (O) and the perceived outcome experienced after the onset (A).

$$CS/D_k = (A_k - D_k) + (A_k - O_k)$$

where O_k = perceived old outcome level of individual (k) before purchase

Satisfaction/dissatisfaction is further affected by the discrepancy between the ideal outcome level before the onset of behavior (L) and the expected outcome after purchase (D).

$$CS/D_k = (A_k - D_k) + (A_k - O_k) + (D_k - L_k)$$

where L_k = ideal outcome before purchase of individual (k)

The effects of expected and deserved outcome levels (R) as they correspond to the perceived outcome can be accounted for by introducing an additional component comparing the relationship between the deserved outcome and the expected outcome.

$$CS/D_k = (A_k - D_k) + (A_k - O_k) + (D_k - L_k) + (D_k - R_k)$$

where R_k = deserved outcome level after purchase of individual (k)

Each discrepancy component shown in this model can be viewed as an independent evaluative congruity contributing to enhancement affect (EA) toward the brand being evaluated. The net CS/D is therefore the additive combination of each EA stemming from each evaluative congruity component.

This model was experimentally tested and the results were highly supportive of the model and its theoretical propositions (Sirgy 1982e).

In sum brand satisfaction, according to the proposed social cognition theory, can be treated in terms of one or more evaluative congruities and modelled directly through the enhancement affect function.

BRAND LOYALTY

This concept has been defined as a favorable attitude toward, and consistent purchase of, a single brand over time (Assael 1981). Researchers in brand loyalty have been divided into two camps: those who defined and operationalized brand loyalty in behavioral terms and those who viewed this phenomenon in cognitive terms.

Based on the behavioral perspective, Tucker (1964) argued:

> No consideration should be given to what the subject thinks or what goes on in his central nervous system; his behavior is the full statement of what brand loyalty is (p. 32).

Researchers aligned with this camp have measured this construct in terms of sequence of purchases and/or proportion of purchases (for example, Brown 1952; Tucker 1964; Lawrence 1969; Blattberg and Sem 1976).

Based on the cognitive perspective, Jacoby and Kyner (1973) asserted that brand loyalty implies repeat purchasing behavior based on cognitive, affective, and behavioral factors—the classical primary components of an attitude.

Day (1969) found that the predictive power of the model using both attitude and behavior measures was almost twice as good as the model using behavior alone.

At least four theories are found in the literature of brand loyalty to explain brand loyalty. These are: learning theory, risk perception theory, self-concept theory, and attitude theory.

With respect to learning theory, Assael's (1981) model of habitual purchasing behavior argues that brand loyalty is dictated by habit. This loyalty is reflected in the consumer's psychological set by confirmed beliefs about the brand and a strong attitude toward the brand. Need arousal is limited only to product depletion and not to the activation of other psychological needs. Consumer information search is limited.

Dissatisfaction with product use, introduction of a new product in the market, additional incongruent information about maintained product, and boredom with that product may all be factors that may cause the consumer to change from habit to complex decision making.

Assael's model is based on learning theory, and from this perspective a number of stochastic models have been advanced to mathematically predict brand loyalty. (For an excellent overview of stochastic models and their applications to the analysis of brand choice, see Bass [1974].)

Based on social cognition theory, habitual consumer behavior characterizing brand loyalty can be described through the affect referral decision model referred to previously. The affect referral decision model describes consumer decision making based on past experiences. Once that cognitive category characterizing the contemplated brand is evoked, the affect associated with it (as determined by past experience) induces the consumer to either approach or avoid it.

With respect to risk perception theory, Roselius' (1971) risk reduction model asserts that brand loyalty is a form of risk reducer. Buying a well-known brand time and again reduces the risk of product failure and financial loss (cf. Sheth and Venkatesan 1968). This risk reduction model is based on Bauer's (1960) theory of risk perception. From a social cognition perspective brand loyalty can be construed as an alternative of risk reduction and evaluated against other alternative risk reductions or an ideal form of risk reduction. Of course this type of evaluation is dictated by the rules of the enhancement affect function.

With respect to self-concept theory, some consumer investigators (for example, Bellenger, Steinberg, and Stanton 1976; Samli and Sirgy 1981; Stern, Bush, and Hair 1977) argued that store loyalty is highly dependent on the extent to which the store image matches the consumer's actual and ideal self-concepts. This matching between brand (or store) image with the consumer's actual and ideal self-image has been referred to as self-congruity and ideal congruity, and has been directly related to the proposed social cognition theory in an earlier section.

With respect to attitude theory, Oliver (1980) argued that consumer satisfaction is a function of expectation and expectancy disconfirmation. Satisfaction is believed to influence attitude change and brand loyalty. This model is based on the equation from Howard and Sheth (1969):

$$A_{t+2} = f(S_{t+1} - A_t) + A_t$$

where At+2 = brand loyalty or revised postpurchase
　　　　　　 attitude
　　 At 　 = prepurchase attitude
　　 St+1 = immediate postpurchase satisfaction

The difference, (St+1 - At), is a comparison between anticipated satisfaction and received satisfaction. The equation can be reinterpreted to include the components of attitude (initial and revised postpurchase), satisfaction, and intention (prior and future).

In sum brand loyalty, in view of the proposed theory, is nothing more than brand preference revised. In other words the same rules applied to modelling of brand preference are directly applicable to brand loyalty. The only exception between the two concepts is that brand preference is viewed usually as a prepurchase phenomenon, whereas brand loyalty develops after purchase and usage.

Based on this conceptual treatment of brand loyalty, it must be noted that brand loyalty is distinguished from "repeat purchase behavior." Brand loyalty is treated as a one-point-in-time (that is, micro) psychological disposition toward a given brand, whereas repeat purchase behavior takes a macro perspective of brand choice. Repeat purchase behavior refers to the choice pattern over time with regard to a specific brand. Accordingly, this author feels that these two concepts are miles apart and should be treated separately from one another.

SUMMARY

Product, brand, store, media, and message evaluations have been mostly described in terms of evaluative congruity, affect, decision making, and labeling. With respect to product need recognition, a distinction was made between problem recognition and opportunity recognition. Evaluative congruity was used to describe both constructs.

The evaluative dynamics involved with media preference were elaborated. Media preference was viewed as an evaluative process directed by the enhancement motive.

Under message evaluation, the distinction was made between message interest and message persuasion. Message interest was thought of as a process that instigates enhancement affect but was unrelated to the advertised product. Sex and humor appeals were used as illustrative examples. With respect to message persuasion, it was construed as an evaluative process directly related to the advertised product. Various theories traditionally associated with these marketing communication concepts were interpreted in light of the proposed theory.

With respect to brand (and store) preference, unitary, compensatory, noncompensatory, and self-image/brand-image congruity models were all discussed and interpreted in light of the principles of the proposed theory. Brand satisfaction was also described in terms of evaluative congruity and affect and related to traditional consumer satisfaction/dissatisfaction theories and models. Brand loyalty was also conceptualized as a construct similar to brand preference, however occurring after purchase and usage. Traditional conceptualizations of this construct were also treated in light of the proposed theory.

CHAPTER 12
Consumer Behavior

In this chapter the psychological processes related to brand, store, and media choice are treated.

MEDIA AND STORE CHOICE

Media and store choice phenomena have not been treated in any depth compared to brand choice. There seems to be an implicit consensus among consumer behavior researchers that the principles applied to brand choice behavior generalize to store and media choice behaviors. As a result, the literature covering store choice and media choice is very limited.

Engel et al. (1978) argued that store choice is determined by a comparison process between the perceived characteristics of stores and a set of evaluative criteria. The perceived characteristics of stores (store image) include location, assortment, price, advertising, store personnel, and service. These perceived characteristics are compared with their evaluative criteria counterparts for a given store. The result of this comparison process determines store choice.

As stated in the previous chapter, this model is highly consistent with the principle of evaluative congruity described by this theory.

In addition to the Engel et al. (1978) model of store choice, Monroe and Guiltinian (1975) also produced a model employing constructs compatible with the principles described here. The model shows that store choice follows the attitude toward stores (or store preference) that is determined by perceptions of store attributes and the importance of these store attributes. This

is, of course, the essence of the beliefs/importance model described earlier. All of these constructs have been discussed
previously and interpreted in light of the proposed theory.

BRAND CHOICE

Brand choice, in the consumer behavior literature, has
been treated as:

- an attitude toward purchase
- a self-concept effect
- a stochastic process.

The Attitude Toward Purchase Model

Most researchers argue that brand choice is a manifestation
of brand preference, and, accordingly, brand choice and brand
preference have been used interchangeably. Fishbein and Ajzen
(1975) were the first to argue that an attitude toward an object
is not necessarily the same as an attitude toward an act pertaining
to the same object. Based on this notion, the traditional beliefs/
evaluation model was differentiated from what is called Fishbein's
extended model. Based on this pioneering idea, a paradigm of
research in consumer behavior was formed and is still running
strong. This extended beliefs/evaluation model has been applied
extensively in recent years and has been found to predict purchase intentions and brand choice better than the beliefs/
evaluation model. The precise mathematical formulation of this
model was previously discussed.

Ryan and Bonfield (1975), in a literature review article,
concluded that attitudes toward purchasing a brand were more
highly related to brand choice than were attitudes toward the
brand itself. Also, Wilson, Mathews, and Harvey (1975), in a
major study directly involved with the extended beliefs/evaluation
model, found that attitudes toward the purchase of a brand of
toothpaste were more closely related to behavior than were attitudes toward the brand.

Translating the extended beliefs/evaluation model in terms
of the evaluative congruity principle proposed here, it can be
easily shown that the normative component can be decomposed
into attributes that can be incorporated into the b_{ik} e_{ik} component. Therefore, the only difference between the two models
may lie in the type of evoked frame of reference. That is, the

beliefs/evaluation model evokes a frame of reference involved in the evaluation of the product, whereas the extended model evokes that frame of reference involved with acting toward that product.

The Self-Concept Model

Based on a number of studies involving consumer self-concept, Sirgy (1980a, 1982d) was able to demonstrate that brand preference was more influenced by ideal congruity and ideal social congruity than self-congruity and social congruity. Purchase intention, on the other hand, was found to be more influenced by self-congruity and social congruity than ideal congruity and ideal social congruity.

These findings are consistent with the proposed social cognition theory. It was previously argued that choice-related behaviors are influenced by one or more of the cognitive motives. Applied in this context, purchase intention seems to be more influenced by self-congruity and social congruity due to the operation of the consistency motive. The consumer considers the extent to which the purchase behavior is consistent or inconsistent with his/her image of himself/herself (consistency motive). Since brand preference does not entail behavior, the consumer does not consider the consistency or inconsistency of his/her choice with his/her self-image; instead, he/she considers the extent to which the brand image meets his/her ideal image of himself/herself. This would entail the evocation of the enhancement motive.

In other words the attitude-behavior relationship is explained by invoking the operation of the consistency motive. That is, attitude can be mostly explained by the enhancement motive; however, behavior is explained by both enhancement plus consistency motives. Therefore, attempts to predict purchase behavior should incorporate both enhancement and consistency affect models to maximize the predicted variance.

The Stochastic Model

Stochastic models of brand choice deal mainly with the transition from brand preference to brand choice probabilities. Most applications of stochastic brand choice models have been based mostly on Luce's (1959) choice axiom and probabilistic choice models (for example, LOGIT analysis, McFadden 1974;

PROBIT analysis, Finney 1971; see also Currim 1982 for an overview of the literature in this area). No attempt will be made here to cover this area in any systematic or comprehensive manner. The basic principle of Luce's axiom underlying most of the stochastic models will be briefly discussed and related to the proposed theory.

A basic assumption of most of the stochastic models is that choice is a probabilistic phenomenon. A decision to adopt a specific brand (x) over another brand y entails that there is a probability $P(x, y)$ and that the choice will be x over y. Luce's axiom is usually expressed as:

$$P_{ij} = V_{ij} / \sum_{i=1}^{I} V_{ij}$$

where P_{ij} = probability of individual (j) selecting brand (i)

V_{ij} = value or utility associated with brand (i) of individual (j)

The Luce model has been criticized for assuming that choice is a function of mean scale values and is not dependent on the similarity of the alternatives (Currim 1982). McFadden (1974) developed a model that estimates a beta coefficient to improve the fit of Luce's model. The resultant Luce-McFadden model has been expressed as:

$$P_{ij} = (V_{ij})^{\beta} / \sum_{i=1}^{I} (V_{ij})^{\beta}$$

Other models, such as the independent PROBIT, perceptual interdependence, negative exponential, extreme value, and generalized PROBIT, were developed and applied to brand choice as alternative improved versions to Luce's model (Currim 1982).

In light of the proposed theory, the attractiveness value or utility weight (V_{ij}) for each brand can be represented as an enhancement affect score (EA_k) associated with each brand. In doing this, it is simply argued that there seems not to be an incompatibility between the stochastic model and the principles of evaluation as proposed by this theory. The stochastic model can be used in conjunction with evaluative congruity, affect, and decision making.

SUMMARY

Brand choice has been treated in the consumer behavior literature in terms of an attitude toward purchase, a self-concept effect, and as a stochastic process. Each of these models was overviewed and interpreted in light of the principles of the proposed theory. Store choice determinants were found to have been treated in the literature in terms of the traditional expectancy-value model, and reinterpreted accordingly. No discussion was undertaken on media choice, since it was assumed that the brand choice models were also applicable to media choice.

CHAPTER 13
Consumer Information Need Recognition

In this chapter reference is made to two key behavioral phenomena related to the differentiation motive. These are:

●product familiarity
●information need recognition

PRODUCT FAMILIARITY

The product familiarity construct has been mostly treated atheoretically in the consumer behavior literature (Sirgy 1981c). In other words consumer researchers have not been hesitant to measure product familiarity without justifying the theoretical underpinnings of each measure. For example Park (1976) measured product familiarity in terms of subjects' agreement with statements about the product. Woodruff (1972) used a free-recall method of purchase situations. Raju and Reilly (1979) employed self-reported "frequency of use, overall familiarity, and knowledge of how to select best brand" as measures of product familiarity. Anderson, Engledow, and Becker (1979) and Jacoby, Chestnut, and Fisher (1978) used a frequency of purchase as an indicator of product familiarity. Johnston and Russo (1981) used a global self-report rating measure—subjects were asked to rate their previous knowledge of the product compared to the rest of the population. Tan and Dolich (1981) measured product familiarity by the proportion of brands in the product class that one knew something about.

The main problem with these unidimensional measures is that they are atheoretical. In contrast the multidimensional measurement of product familiarity as established by Olson and his associates (for example, Marks and Olson 1981; Kanwar, Olson, and Sims 1981; Olson and Muderrisoglu 1979) is based on cognitive theory. Three basic dimensions of product familiarity were discussed:

(1) dimensionality, defined as the number of activatable concepts associated with a particular domain

(2) articulation, defined as the number of category representations or levels for each salient dimension in memory

(3) abstraction, defined as the degree to which salient dimensions are abstract versus concrete.

These cognitive dimensions can be translated in light of the discussion of the structural anatomy and arrangement of the cognitive system introduced by the proposed theory. A frame of reference can contain a highly differentiated set of beliefs when it is central. This differentiation is analogous to the concept of dimensionality referred to above. The articulation concept used by Olson was represented by the proposed theory through the discussion on category width. Abstraction was also referred to in terms of belief centrality. Central beliefs are mostly abstract beliefs with a network of related beliefs that can be decomposed into concrete or peripheral beliefs.

Sirgy (1981c), based on the ideas presented in this theory, formally proposed that product familiarity can be characterized along (1) a content dimension, (2) a directionality dimension, (3) a certainty dimension, (4) a centrality dimension, and (5) an articulation dimension, among others. The content refers to the specific content of the association between two concepts. Directionality refers to the specific flow of activation from one concept to another. Certainty denotes the strength of the linkage of the two concepts. Centrality refers to the degree of salience, importance, or abstractness of a given belief. Articulation also refers to the extent to which a given belief is semantically encoded or encoded at a more affective-sensory level. All of the above concepts are consistent with the previous discussion of the structural aspects of the cognitive system.

INFORMATION NEED RECOGNITION

Information need recognition is another term for information acquisition or the affect associated with the deviation state of the need for cognitive differentiation. It occurs when the consumer enters into a perceptual or evaluative congruity with weak evoked beliefs. The resultant affect will be highly indicative of an information acquisition affective state. Given a perceptual or evaluative congruity with strong evoked beliefs, information assimilation will result.

The reader should note that information affect is an affective state that is not induced independent of perceptual or evaluative affect but in conjunction with one or the other. In other words both perceptual and information affects can be experienced simultaneously and similarly with both evaluative and information affects.

Accordingly, the information affect function described earlier can be used here to model the construct of information need recognition.

$$INR_k = IA_k = \sum_{i=1}^{I} [(1 - EB_{ik}) |PV_{ik} \, EV_{ik}| (PB_{ik})]$$

or

$$INR_k = IA_k = \sum_{i=1}^{I} \frac{1}{m} [(1 - EB_{ik}) |PV_{ik} \, EV_{ik}| (PB_{ik})]$$

where INR_k = information need recognition of individual (k)

IA_k = information affect of individual (k)

An example is in order. Suppose that a consumer recognizes that he/she needs to buy a home computer (product need recognition). He/She then is exposed to an advertisement providing information about a brand of computer, information related to "baude rate," "memory capabilities," "portability," and so forth. He/She tries to evaluate the advertised computer with his/her neighbor's computer (reference point). However, he/she feels uncertain about these evaluative criteria concerning the "baude rate," "memory capabilities," and "portability." This uncertainty would automatically be reflected in the sum of the $(1 - EB_{ik})$ component producing a high (IA) uncertainty score. The $(|PV_{ik} \, EV_{ik}|)$ and (PB_{ik}) components serve to underscore the valence of the situation. Therefore, important situations will directly contribute to the uncertainty score through increasing the value of the PV_{ik}, EV_{ik}, and PB_{ik} and vice versa.

The construct of information need recognition has been treated in the consumer behavior literature as information search.

Information search has been surmised to be determined by the extent to which the consumer perceives value to be gained from the information relative to the cost of obtaining and using that information (Engel, Blackwell, and Kollat 1978; Bennett and Mandell 1969). Perceived value is viewed to be function of (1) the quantity and quality of existing information, (2) ability to recall information, (3) perceived risk, and (4) confidence in decision-making ability. With respect to the quantity and quality of existing information, the more the consumer knows, the lower his/her propensity to search for consumer information and vice versa.

With respect to the ability to recall information, the less the ability to recall information, the greater the likelihood that the consumer will seek out external information sources. Also, perceived risk is argued to be reduced through information search. That is, the greater the perceived risk, the greater the tendency to search for information.

In relation to confidence in decision-making ability, the lower the consumer's confidence, the greater the likelihood that he/she will seek information.

The costs of search are usually presented in terms of decision delay, expenditure of time and money, psychological considerations, and information overload. Of course, the greater the costs of search, the less the propensity to seek information.

In applying the proposed social cognition theory to explain these traditional information-related constructs, one important distinction has to be noted immediately. This is the difference between information need recognition and media preference. The former denotes a motivational state to seek information to strengthen those weak evoked beliefs, whereas the latter indicates a motivational state with regard to specific information sources. This latter media phenomenon will be treated in the following sections. This distinction is made to point out the fact that information search as traditionally treated in the consumer behavior literature fails to discriminate between consumer motivation to seek information (information need recognition) and consumer motivation to seek information from a specific information source (media preference).

SUMMARY

Information need recognition was described in terms of the information acquisition affect discussed previously. The traditional treatment of information search was reinterpreted in light of the information acquisition proposition. Also, product familiarity was related to the discussion on the structural anatomy and arrangement of beliefs in the cognitive system.

CHAPTER 14
A Comparative Analysis Of Consumer-Behavior Theories

There are numerous models that are concerned with consumer behavior in general. These models can be categorized according to their orientations: reductive-functional versus holistic. Reductive-functional and holistic theories are distinguished in their basic assumptions about some important characteristics of sociopsychological phenomena and therefore about consumer behavior. Reductive-functional models assume that phenomena can be reducible to a set of small molecular, discrete, and isolatable variables and that the unique relationships existing among these variables can thus be discernible. Holistic models assume, contrariwise, that these characteristics are organized, conceptual, and nonreducible in nature and therefore must be examined as a complete, phenomenalistic, holistic totality.

In the literature of consumer behavior, several reductive models exist that are geared to explaining general consumer behavior. These models include Howard and Sheth's (1969) model, Andreasen's (1968) model, and Engel, Blackwell, and Kollat's (1978) multimediation model. Some holistic models include Clawson's (1950) model, Nicosia's (1966) model, and Markin's (1974) holocentric model.

It should be noted that the utility of the models mentioned previously has apparently been minimal. In a literature review Engel, Blackwell, and Kollat (1978) conceded that the available consumer behavior models have had little influence on consumer research. Until today it is rare to find a published study that has utilized, been based upon, or been greatly influenced by any of these models.

At a more micro level, Hansen (1972) distinguished among the many consumer behavior models by using the following criteria:

(1) exposure versus deliberation versus communication versus consumption versus purchase situations
(2) level-of-analysis
(3) type of choice processes assumed
(4) the unidimensionality versus multidimensionality of the product and/or consumer attributes.

The models which were assessed are:

perceived risk models, utility models, dissonance models, attitude models, interest and value models, image models, perceptual preference models, Lewin-field models, hierarchy-of-effects models, situational-learning models, personality and motivational models, media exposure models, decision processes models, satisficing models, innovation models, fashion models, household budgeting models, plans and inventions models, simple probability models, brand share models, segmentation models, life cycle models, social class models, income hypotheses models, demand function models, and cultural-anthropological models.

All of the above are consumer behavior models that describe consumer behavior phenomena within one or more theoretical frameworks.

The ideas presented in this book make up a theory not a model. A number of predictive models were also addressed, namely the enhancement, consistency, and information affect models as rooted in the overall theory proposed here. This is a social cognition theory unique in its form and can be distinguished from other types of theories (other social cognition theories, learning theory, social learning theory, gestalt theory, and so on).

Consequently, it may not seem proper to undertake a comparative analysis involving this social cognition theory with other consumer behavior models. Only two other consumer behavior theories seem to be directly competing with the theory proposed here. These are Bettman's (1979) information processing theory of consumer choice and Fennell's (1980) motivational theory of consumer behavior.

Before we make any attempt to compare and contrast these three theories of consumer behavior, we will present an overview of Bettman's information processing and Fennell's motivational theories. These were selected because both possess extensive explanatory power.

BETTMAN'S INFORMATION PROCESSING THEORY OF CONSUMER CHOICE

The basic components of the choice process considered by Bettman are processing capacity, motivation, attention and perception, information acquisition and evaluation, memory, decision processes, and learning. All these elements are interrelated through the construct of choice. That is, a consumer becomes motivated, pays attention, perceives, acquires and evaluates information, learns, compares among alternatives for the purpose of making a goal-directed choice or a choice to accomplish one or more goals.

Therefore, it is the author's contention that Bettman's description and explanation of psychological consumer behavior phenomena through a choice perspective is a unique type of information processing theory and should be treated as such (see Figure 14.1).

The various stages in the choice process involving, for example, motivation, attention, and information search and retrieval are subject to the constraints of consumer's limited processing capacity. Processing capacity is allocated by a conscious decision or automatically determined by learned rules. Since most choices require a great amount of processing capacity, the consumer uses simplifying heuristics to avoid overload and minimize processing effort.

Motivation affects the direction and intensity of consumer's choice processes. Thus, choices are directed by consumer goals and arrived at through the intense allocation of processing capacity (high motivational intensity) or through the negligible allocation of processing capacity (low motivational intensity). A goal is defined as a specific state, which, when attained, is instrumental in reaching the desired end state. To attain a goal, the consumer may have to attain one or more subgoals. The set of goals leading to the desired end state is referred to as a goal hierarchy.

Since consumers do not methodically carry out goal after goal in completing a goal hierarchy, they need some mechanism that allows interruption. This is the scanner and interrupt

Figure 14.1 Bettman's Information Processing Theory of
Consumer Choice

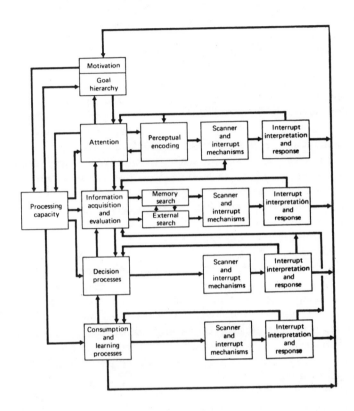

Source: James R. Bettman, <u>An Information Processing Theory</u>
of <u>Consumer Choice</u>, © 1979. Addison-Wesley, Reading, MA.
Figure 2.1. Reprinted with permission.

mechanism. The scanner serves to continually monitor events
in the environment, noticing when conditions require changes
in current activities, and the interrupt mechanism functions to
actually carry out the interruption.

  <u>Attention</u> is distinguished between its voluntary and involuntary components. <u>Voluntary attention</u> refers to the conscious
allocation of processing capacity to those stimuli related to the
consumer's goals or goal hierarchy. <u>Involuntary attention</u> refers
to the allocation of processing capacity to those stimuli <u>not</u>
directly related to the consumer's goals. It is an automatic
mechanism that leads to interrupts.

Perceptual encoding refers to the process by which the individual, having attended to some stimulus, interprets that stimulus. The process requires an analysis utilizing information stored in memory. The results of perceptual encoding influences the subsequent direction of attention.

Two types of interrupting events are relevant to attention and perceptual encoding: conflicts and learning about the environment. Conflict during perceptual encoding and attention can arise from parts of the environment that are competing for attention, disagreement between what was perceived and what was expected, and so on. Responses to conflict may vary depending on the situation. For conflicts arising from attention and perception, the response may be more automatic and less dependent on response strategies. However, in other cases when attention is not automatic, the consumer reacts by selecting a response that would ignore the stimulus, change the emphasis on certain criteria, search for new information, reanalyze and record goals in the goal hierarchy, and so on.

Learning is another type of interrupt event. Learning about the environment can arise from interrupts when something happens to attract the consumer's attention.

In making a choice the consumer may retrieve information from memory, and in cases when the internal information is not sufficient, information may be sought externally. In acquiring external information, the perceived cost of obtaining the information and the value of the information in helping to make a choice are all considered.

Information intake from an environment when the consumer is not actively searching for information is dictated by learning. The scanner and interrupt mechanisms may also impact information search and retrieval. One major cause of an interrupt could be conflicting information, whether from differing external sources, between an external source and what is stored in memory, or between expectations and an external source. The conflict is assessed and a decision is made about how to handle the conflict.

A decision is construed in terms of conflict resolution occurring in any of the previous components. The major focus of the decision processes component is on comparison and selection of alternatives. Consumers use heuristics, or rules of thumb, to accomplish these comparisons. Consumers may also use various methods for implementing choice heuristics depending upon the choice situation and their degree of knowledge. The methods are classified as constructive versus learned stored rules. Constructive methods are used in complex decision making, whereas learned store rules methods are used in simple decision making.

Effects of consumption can be that of learning, causal attributions about causes of product effects, and changes in choice heuristics.

A SOCIAL COGNITION INTERPRETATION
OF BETTMAN'S THEORY

In the language of the proposed social cognition theory, the processing capacity as directly related to attention is translated in terms of the belief-centrality involved with the evoked frame of reference. Peripheral evoked structures to be compared with the incoming stimuli require less cognitive effort or less processing capacity and therefore less attention. Central frames of references, on the other hand, require a greater amount of cognitive effort or more processing capacity and therefore more attention.

The scanner is that mechanism that allows the incoming stimulus to scan through the cognitive structures to find its match as represented by a specific frame of reference. The interrupt mechanism, although not addressed in any explicit way in the proposed social cognition theory, can be described as a mechanism that clears the perceptual platform for an incoming stimulus to be processed through scanning and categorization.

Voluntary and involuntary attention are not distinguished in the proposed social cognition theory. The proposed theory construes a network of frames of references in the form of a script activated by a situational cue involving those cognitive categories that become highly accessible to the scanning of incoming stimuli. This is voluntary perception. Involuntary perception involves the activation of those cognitive categories not involved in that evoked script.

Perceptual encoding is the mechanism that projects value or meaning to those features of the stimulus object. This process was described by social cognition theory in terms of belief change, evaluative decision making, and cognitive labeling of values.

Conflict in Bettman's information processing theory is translated into those cognitive responses involving negative emotion, cognitive dissonance, and information acquisition. These specific responses induce an arousal state discrepant from homeostasis, which can only be brought back to its ranges of stability through conflict resolution responses. With respect to negative emotion as deviation from its homeostatic level, that level is positive emotion. The homeostatic level involving the deviation state of cognitive dissonance is cognitive consistency. And, similarly, the homeostatic level involving the deviation state of information acquisition is information assimilation. Based on the proposed social cognition theory, those conflict resolution responses are represented in terms of approach/avoidance motivations toward specific alternative objects, persons, or situations.

With respect to conflict resolution responses, approach/avoidance motivation directs the consumer to approach or avoid a specific product for the purpose of attaining a goal state that is instrumental in reducing the conflict in question to its homeostatic level, be it positive emotion, cognitive consistency, or information assimilation.

FENNELL'S MOTIVATIONAL THEORY OF CONSUMER BEHAVIOR

Fennell (1975a, 1975b, 1978, 1979, 1980) distinguished three components of a situation—namely, the activating condition, the behavior mode, and the terminating condition. The activating condition selectively affects perception, initiates a behavior mode, and specifies the essential characteristics of the terminating condition.

Seven different activating conditions and their corresponding behavior modes were distinguished. These are:

(1) unavoidable aversiveness as an activating condition initiating escape as a behavior mode
(2) avoidable aversiveness leading to avoidance
(3) deprivation leading to maintenance
(4) exploratory incentive leading to exploration
(5) signaled intrinsic incentive leading to facilitation
(6) at least one of the above five conditions plus termination aversiveness leading to conflict resolution
(7) at least one of the above six conditions plus termination failure leading to the restructuring of the situation

Unavoidable aversiveness is an activating condition in which escape is mostly selected to terminate the condition. For example, taking a vacation in the countryside to escape the noxious stimuli of the big city may be viewed as a behavior mode designed to terminate unavoidable aversiveness of a big city.

Avoidable aversiveness leads to avoidance behavior. An example would be using a mouthwash to avoid the social disapproval arising from having bad breath.

Deprivation is an activating condition that drives the individual to act to restore the deprived state to normal levels. This is characterized as the maintenance behavior mode. An example would be when one runs out of toothpaste (deprivation) one purchases another.

Exploratory incentive is an activating condition that induces exploratory behavior. An example would be reading a book to satisfy one's curiosity.

Signaled intrinsic incentive is a situation in which the stimulus provides an opportunity for reward, and therefore induces a behavior that facilitates the attainment of the reward. A woman using perfume can be viewed as a behavior that may facilitate dating (reward).

Approach-avoidance conflict can also be an activating condition that leads to behavior designed to resolve this conflict. For example, in a situation where a consumer is motivated to purchase a sports car (e.g., signaled intrinsic incentive) but the purchase of this sports car would place him in debt (aversive situation), the individual may attempt to resolve the conflict by purchasing an affordable economy car that is styled like a sports car.

Finally, frustration is an activating condition that arises when a behavior used to terminate an activating condition (one of the aforementioned activating conditions) is perceived to be unsuccessful in terminating the condition, inducing the individual to restructure the situation and attempt an alternative behavior.

The entire process involved in the activation, behavior, and terminating conditions of each of the seven motivating situations (what Fennell calls the vertical dimension), is more thoroughly described along a horizontal dimension using constructs such as motivation, search, judgment, and evaluation (see Figure 14.2).

Motivation is aroused from an activating condition leading to a specified behavior mode through a disparity of a present state and a desired state, the securing of which terminates that situation. Search refers to the tendency to look for internal and/or external information relating to the outcomes of alternative behaviors. Judgment occurs when two or more behaviors are rated along a preference dimension, the result of which ranks the alternative behavior considered. The highest ranking behavior is then subjected to a cost/benefit analysis, which signals the individual whether the contemplated behavior would product benefits that outweigh its costs. Evaluation occurs following performance. The person experiences and evaluates the external and internal outcomes relative to the desired states.

Figure 14.2 Fennell's Motivational Theory of Consumer Behavior

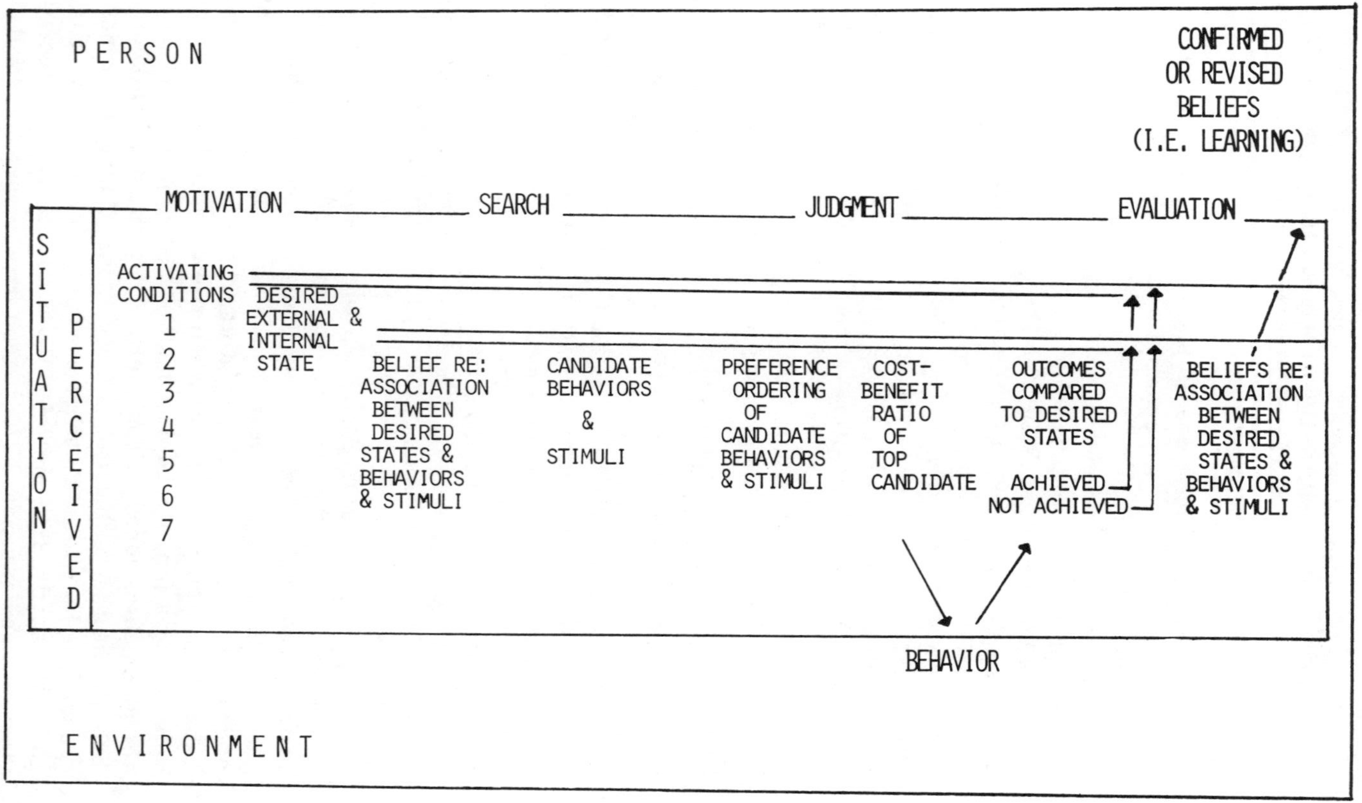

PERSON

——— MOTIVATION ——— SEARCH ——— JUDGMENT ——— EVALUATION

ACTIVATING
CONDITIONS

DESIRED
EXTERNAL &
INTERNAL
STATE

1
2
3
4
5
6
7

S
T
R
U
C
T
I
V
E
D

P
E
R
C
E
I
V
E
D

BELIEF RE:
ASSOCIATION
BETWEEN
DESIRED
STATES &
BEHAVIORS
& STIMULI

CANDIDATE
BEHAVIORS
&
STIMULI

PREFERENCE
ORDERING
OF
CANDIDATE
BEHAVIORS
& STIMULI

COST-
BENEFIT
RATIO
OF
TOP
CANDIDATE

OUTCOMES
COMPARED
TO DESIRED
STATES

ACHIEVED
NOT ACHIEVED

CONFIRMED
OR REVISED
BELIEFS
(I.E. LEARNING)

BELIEFS RE:
ASSOCIATION
BETWEEN
DESIRED
STATES &
BEHAVIORS
& STIMULI

BEHAVIOR

ENVIRONMENT

196

Depending on the extent to which the desired state has been attained, the terminating condition will take effect and <u>learning</u> will occur in terms of expectancy confirmation or disconfirmation.

A SOCIAL COGNITION INTERPRETATION OF FENNELL'S THEORY

Fennell's concept of motivation is very much akin to Bettman's notion of conflict and the social cognition concept of cognitive responses involving negative emotion, cognitive dissonance, and information acquisition. However, Fennell did not limit the motivation concept to conflict conditions or responses involving negative emotion, cognitive dissonance, and information assimilation, but also extended it to those opportunities for conflict resolution or what has been referred to by the proposed social cognition theory as approach/avoidance behavior. In doing so, she specified seven activating conditions resulting in seven different behavior modes.

The unavoidable aversiveness activating condition seems to fit our concept of <u>avoidance</u> motivation, using social cognition theory. Similar are the avoidable aversiveness and the deprivation conditions. The exploratory incentive and signaled intrinsic incentive conditions seem to involve <u>approach</u> motivation.

An <u>activating condition</u> is a situation in which perception of the situation is counteracted by a number of alternative referent relations representing alternative behaviors (behavior mode) designed to approach a desired state (terminating condition) or avoid an undesired state (terminating condition). This congruity process involving alternative evaluation has been treated extensively by the proposed social cognition theory.

<u>Search</u> in the proposed social cognition theory has been treated as a congruity involving weak belief relations instigating information acquisition affect, which, in turn, prompts the individual to engage in evaluating alternative information sources and therefore inducing behavior. This has been discussed in the consumer need recognition chapter.

With respect to the judgment construct, Fennell argues that alternative behaviors will be compared and the behavior that is found to be most instrumental in terminating the activated condition will be selected. Subsequently, a cost/benefit analysis will be performed to determine whether the selected behavior is worth it. In terms of social cognition, the process that identifies the behavior most instrumental in terminating the activated condition can be described in terms of evaluative congruity and affect types of processes between or among two or more alternative behaviors. The final decision to select the most instrumental behavior can be described in terms of a perceptual inference in which that behavior becomes linked with a conceptual attribute of "acceptance or selection decision."

With respect to the cost/benefit type of analysis following the selection of optimal behavior, this can be described in social cognition language as follows: The costs of the selected alternative are evaluated in comparison with some referent using evaluative congruity and affect mechanisms. The negative EA affect associated with this alternative is then cognitively labeled. Also, the benefits associated with the selected alternative are evaluated in comparison with some referent through evaluative congruity and affect dynamics. Subsequently, the alternative and its positive and negative EA scores (perceptual attributes) are identified as whether the difference between EA benefits and EA costs is negative or positive. Consequently, this situation is categorized into a decision-rule cognitive category that links the negative outcome with an "avoidance decision" and the positive outcome with an "approach decision." This is done through perceptual inference mechanisms.

Evaluation in Fennell's theory seems to be comparable to evaluative congruity occurring following purchase and usage. A major treatment of this concept was undertaken under the topic of brand satisfaction. Fennell addresses the concept of learning as a process leading to confirmation or revision of existing beliefs resulting from evaluation. Learning has been treated similarly by the proposed social cognition theory as belief change and described as brand image revision in a consumer context.

SUMMARY

The proposed theory as directly applied to consumer behavior explains the mechanisms involved in consumer motivation, emotion, perception, decision making, learning, and so on. These psychological processes are mainly invoked in goal-directed and outcome-related behaviors in the marketplace. The dynamics involved in consumer behavior are described in terms of congruity processes and effects. Congruity processes and effects are theorized to be directed by the needs for cognitive enhancement, consistency, and differentiation. The theory is construed to be effective in integrating research constructs in consumer psychology. It provides the discipline with a unifying framework from which consumer researchers can explain consumer behavior and model its constructs. The theory is argued to be a "good" theory because of

(1) its parsimony in its use of a few constructs

(2) its extensiveness in its breadth of explanation (that is, it is not designed to narrowly describe the operations of one or two behavioral constructs, but a wider range of constructs)

(3) its testability (that is, specific mathematical models can be analytically derived and tested through empirical means).

Bibliography

Aaker, David A., and John G. Myers. 1982. _Advertising Management_, 2nd ed. Englewood Cliffs, N.J.: Prentice-Hall.

Abelson, R. P. 1981. "Psychological Status of the Script Concept." _American Psychologist_ 36:715-729.

_____. 1976. "A Script Theory of Understanding, Attitude, and Behavior." In _Cognition and Social Behavior_, edited by J. S. Carroll and J. W. Payne. Hillsdale, N.J.: Lawrence Erlbanm Associates.

Ajzen, Icek and Martin Fishbein. 1977. "Attitude-Behavior Relations: A Theoretical Analysis and Review of Empirical Research." _Psychological Bulletin_ 84:888-918.

Allport, Gordon W. 1935. "Attitudes." In _Handbook of Social Psychology_, edited by C. Murchison, pp. 798-884. Worcester, Mass.: Clark University.

Anderson John R. 1980. _Cognitive Psychology and its Implications_. San Francisco: W. H. Freeman.

Anderson, John R., and G. H. Bower. 1974. _Human Associative Memory_. Washington, D.C.: Winston.

Anderson, Norman H. 1974. "Cognitive Algebra: Integration Theory Applied to Social Attribution." In _Advances in Experimental Social Psychology_, vol. 7, edited by Leon Berkowitz, pp. 1-102. New York: Academic Press.

_____. 1968. "A Simple Model for Information Integration." In _Theories of Cognitive Consistency: A Source Book_, edited by R. P. Abelson, Eliot Aronson, W. J. McGuire, T. M. Newcomb, M. J. Rosenberg, and P. H. Tannenbaum, pp. 731-43. Chicago: Rand McNally.

_____. 1967. "Averaging Model Analysis of Set Size Effect in Impression Formation." _Journal of Experimental Psychology_ 75:159-65.

_____. 1965. "Averaging Versus Adding as a Stimulus-Combination Rule in Impression Formation." Journal of Experimental Psychology 70:394-400.

_____, and A. A. Barrios. 1961. "Primacy Effects in Personality Impression Formation." Journal of Abnormal and Social Psychology 63:346-50.

Anderson, Rolph E. 1973. "Consumer Satisfaction: The Effect of Disconfirmed Expectancy as Perceived Product Performance." Journal of Marketing Research 10 (Feb.):38-44.

Anderson, Ronald D., Jack L. Engledow, and Herbert Becker. 1979. "Evaluating the Relationships Among Attitude Toward Business, Product Satisfaction, Experience, and Search Effort." Journal of Marketing Research 16:394-400.

Andreasen, A. R. 1968. "Attitudes and Consumer Behavior: A Decision Model." In Perspectives in Consumer Behavior, edited by Harold H. Kassarjian and Thomas S. Robertson. Glenview, Ill.: Scott, Foresman.

Aronson, E. 1969. "The Theory of Cognitive Dissonance: A Current Perspective." In Advances in Experimental Social Psychology, vol. 4, edited by Leon Berkowitz, pp. 2-35. New York: Academic Press.

Asch, S. E. 1946. "Forming Impressions of Personality." Journal of Abnormal and Social Psychology 41:258-90.

Assael, Henry. 1981. Consumer Behavior and Marketing Action. Boston, Mass.: Kent Publishing.

Atkinson, John W. 1957. "Motivational Determinants of Risk Taking Behavior." Psychological Review 64:359-72.

Axelrod, Joel N. 1963. "Induced Moods and Attitudes Toward Products." Journal of Advertising Research 3 (June):19-24.

Bagozzi, Richard P. 1975. "Marketing as Exchange." Journal of Marketing 39:32-39.

_____, and Robert E. Burnkrant. 1979. "Attitude Organization and the Attitude-Behavior Relationship." Journal of Personality and Social Psychology 37:913-29.

Baker, Michael J., and Gilbert A. Churchill, Jr. 1977. "The Impact of Physically Attractive Models on Advertising Evaluations." Journal of Marketing Research 14 (Nov.):538-55.

Bass, Frank M. 1974. "The Theory of Stochastic Preference and Brand Switching." Journal of Marketing Research 11 (Feb.):1-20.

_____, and W. Wayne Talarzyk. 1972. "An Attitude Model for the Study of Brand Preference." Journal of Marketing Research 9 (Feb.):93-96.

Bauer, Raymond A. 1960. "Consumer Behaviors Risk Taking." In Dynamic Marketing for a Changing World, edited by Robert Hancock, pp. 389-98. Chicago: American Marketing Association.

Beach, L. R., and T. R. Mitchell. 1978. "A Contingency Model for the Selection of Decision Strategies." Academy of Management Review 3:439-449.

Belk, Russell. 1981. "Determinants of Consumption Cue Utilization in Impression Formation: An Association Derivation and an Experimental Verification." In Advances in Consumer Research, vol. 8, edited by Kent B. Monroe, pp. 170-75. Ann Arbor, Mich.: Association for Consumer Research.

Bellenger, Danny N., Earle Steinberg, and Wilbur W. Stanton. 1976. "The Congruence of Store Image and Self Image." Journal of Retailing 52 (Spring):17-32.

Bem, Daryl J. 1972. "Self-Perception Theory." In Advances in Experimental Social Psychology, vol. 6, edited by Leon Berkowitz, pp. 2-62. New York: Academic Press.

_____. 1970. Beliefs, Attitudes, and Human Affairs. Belmont, Calif.: Brooks/Cole.

_____. 1967. "Self-Perception: An Alternative Interpretation of Cognitive Dissonance Phenomena." Psychological Review 74:183-200.

Bennett, Peter D., and Robert M. Mandell. 1969. "Prepurchase Information Seeking Behavior of New Car Purchasers—The Learning Hypothesis." Journal of Marketing Research 6 (Nov.):430-33.

Berrien, Kenneth. 1968. General and Social System. New Brunswick, N.J.: Rutgers University Press.

Bettman, James R. 1979. An Information Processing Theory of Consumer Choice. Reading, Mass.: Addison-Wesley.

____. 1973. "Perceived Risk and Its Components: A Model and Empirical Test." Journal of Marketing Research 10:184-90.

Birdwell, A. 1968. "A Study of Influence of Image Congruence on Consumer Choice." Journal of Business 41:76-88.

Blattberg, Robert C., and Subrata K. Sem. 1976. "Market Segments and Stochastic Brand Choice Models." Journal of Marketing Research 14 (Feb.):34-45.

Block, Carl E., and Kenneth J. Roering. 1979. Essentials of Consumer Behavior. Hinsdale, Ill.: Dryden Press.

Boulding, Kenneth E. 1981. Ecodynamics: A New Theory of Societal Evolution. Beverly Hills: Sage Publications.

Boyd, Harper W., W. Michale L. Ray, and Edward S. Strong. 1972. "An Attitudinal Framework for Advertising Strategy." Journal of Marketing 36 (April):27-33.

Brehm, J. W., and A. R. Cohen. 1962. Explorations in Cognitive Dissonance. New York: Wiley.

Britt, Stewart H. 1960. The Spenders. New York: McGraw-Hill.

Broadbent, D. E. 1958. Perception and Communication. London: Pergamon.

Brown, George. 1952. "Brand Loyalty-Fact or Fiction?" Advertising Age, June 19, pp. 53-55; June 30, pp. 45-47; July 14, pp. 46-48; August 11, pp. 56-58; September 1, pp. 80-82; October 6, pp. 82-86; December 11, pp. 76-79.

Brown, Roger. 1965. Social Psychology. New York: The Free Press.

Brown, W. 1979. "The Family and Consumer Decision Making." Journal of the Academy of Marketing Science 7:333-45.

Bruner, Jerome S. 1957. "Going Beyond the Information Given." In Contemporary Approaches to Cognition, edited by J. S. Bruner, E. Brunswik, L. Festinger, F. Heider, K. F. Muenzinger, C. E. Osgood, and D. Rapaport. Cambridge, Mass.: Harvard University Press.

_____, D. Shapiro, and R. Taguiri. 1958. "The Meaning of Traits in Isolation and in Combination." In Person Perception and Interpersonal Behavior, edited by R. Taguiri and L. Pertullo, pp. 277-88. Stanford, Calif.: Stanford University Press.

_____, and R. Taguiri. 1954. "The Perception of People." In Handbook of Social Psychology, vol. 2, edited by G. Lindzey, pp. 634-54. Reading, Mass.: Wesley.

_____, and L. Postman. 1948. "Symbolic Value as an Organizing Factor in Perception." Journal of Social Psychology 27:103-208.

_____, and C. D. Goodman. 1947. "Value and Need as Organizing Factors in Perception." Journal of Abnormal and Social Psychology 42:33-44.

Brunswik, E. 1956. Perception and the Representative Design of Psychological Experiments. Berkeley: University of California Press.

Busch, Paul, and David T. Wilson. 1976. "An Experimental Analysis of a Salesman's Expert and Referent Bases of Social Power in the Buyer-Seller Dyad." Journal of Marketing Research 13 (Feb.):3-11.

Cantor, N., and W. Mischell. 1979. "Prototypes in Person Perception." In Advances in Experimental Social Psychology, vol. 12, edited by Leon Berkowitz, pp. 3-52. New York: Academic Press.

Capon, Noel, and Richard J. Lutz. 1979. "A Model and Methodology for the Development of Consumer Information." Journal of Marketing 43:58-67.

Carlsmith, J. Merrill, and Elliot Aronson. 1963. "Some Hedonic Consequences of the Confirmation and Disconfirmation of Expectancies." Journal of Abnormal and Social Psychology 66 (Feb.):151-56.

Carroll, J. S., and J. W. Payne, eds. 1976. Cognition and Social Behavior. Hillsdale, N.J.: Erlbaum.

Cavusgil, S. Tamer, and John R. Nevin. 1981. "State-of-the-Art in International Marketing: An Assessment." In Review in Marketing 1981, edited by Ben M. Enis and Kenneth J. Roering, pp. 195-216. Chicago, Ill.: American Marketing Association.

Clawson, J. 1950. "Lewin's Psychology and Motives in Marketing." In Theory in Marketing, edited by R. Cox and Wroe Alderson. New York: Richard D. Irwin.

Cohen, Claudia E. 1981. "Person Categories and Social Perception: Testing Some Boundaries of Processing Effects of Prior Knowledge." Journal of Personality and Social Psychology 40: 441-52.

Coombs, C. H., and R. L. Kao. 1955. Nonmetric Factor Analysis (Research Bulletin No. 38). Ann Arbor: University of Michigan, Engineering Research Institute.

Cooper, Philip D., William J. Kehoe, and Patrick E. Murphy, eds. 1978. Marketing and Preventative Health Care: Interdisciplinary and Interorganizational Perspectives. Chicago: American Marketing Association.

Cox, D. 1967. Risk Taking and Information Handling in Consumer Behavior. Boston: Division of Research, Graduate School of Business, Harvard University.

Currim, Imran S. 1982. "Predictive Testing of Consumer Choice Models Not Subject to Independence of Irrelevant Alternatives." Journal of Marketing Research 19 (May):208-22.

Danes, Jeffery, and John E. Hunter. 1980. "Designing Persuasive Communication Campaigns: A Multimessage Communication Model." Journal of Consumer Research 7 (June):67-77.

Davis, H. 1976. "Decision Making Within the Household." Journal of Consumer Research 2:241-59.

Dawes, R. M. 1964. Toward A General Framework for Evaluation. Ann Arbor: University of Michigan, Department of Psychology.

Day, George. 1969. "A Dimensional Concept of Brand Loyalty." Journal of Advertising Research 9 (Sept.):29-35.

Dholakia, Ruby R., and Brian Sternthal. 1977. "Highly Credible Sources: Persuasive Facilitators or Persuasive Liabilities?" Journal of Consumer Research 3 (Mar.):223-32.

Dixon, N. F. 1971. Subliminal Perception: The Nature of a Controversy. London: McGraw-Hill.

Driver, M. J., and S. Streufert. 1969. "Integrative Complexity: An Approach to Individuals and Groups as Information-Processing Systems." Administratives Science Quarterly 14:272-85.

Dulany, Don E. 1967. "Awareness, Rules, and Propositional Control: A Confrontation With S-R Behavior Theory." In Verbal Behavior and S-R Theory, edited by D. Horton and T. Dixon. Englewood Cliffs, N.J.: Prentice-Hall.

Duncan, C. P. 1980. "Humor in Advertising: A Behavioral Perspective." Journal of The Academy of Marketing Science 7:285-306.

Duncan, J. 1980. "The Locus of Interference in the Perception of Simultaneous Stimuli." Psychological Review 87:272-300.

Eagly, Alice. 1967. "Involvement as a Determinant of Response to Favorable and Unfavorable Information." Journal of Personality and Social Psychology 7: Whole No. 643.

Ebbesen, Ebbe B., and Robert B. Allen. 1979. "Cognitive Processes in Implicit Personality Trait Inferences." Journal of Personality and Social Psychology 37:471-87.

Edwards, W. 1954. "The Theory of Decision Making." Psychological Bulletin 51:380-417.

Ehrlich, H. J. 1969. "Attitudes, Behavior, and Intervening Variables." American Sociologist 4:29-34.

Einhorn, H. J. 1971. "Use of Nonlinear, Noncompensatory Models as a Function of Task and Amount of Information." Organizational Behavior and Human Performance 6:1-27.

Engel, James F., Roger D. Blackwell, and David T. Kollat. 1978. Consumer Behavior. Hinsdale, Ill.: Dryden Press.

Epstein, Seymour. 1973. "The Self-Concept Revisited, or a Theory of a Theory." American Psychologist 28:404-16.

Fennell, Geraldine. 1980. "The Situation." Motivation and Emotion 4:299-322.

____. 1979. "Attention Engagement." In Current Issues and Research in Advertising, edited by J. Leigh and C. R. Martin. Ann Arbor: University of Michigan.

____. 1978. "Consumers' Perceptions of Product-Use Situation." Journal of Marketing 42:38-47.

____. 1975a. "Motivation Research Revisited." Journal of Advertising Research 15:23-28.

____. 1975b. "What is a Situation? A Motivational Paradigm." Journal of Psychology 91:259-69.

Festinger, Leon. 1966. "Studies in Social Comparison—Introduction and Overview." Journal of Experimental Social Psychology 2 (Supplement 1):1-5.

____. 1957. A Theory of Cognitive Dissonance. Stanford, Calif.: Stanford University Press.

Finney, D. 1971. Probit Analysis. Cambridge, England: Cambridge University Press.

Fishbein, Martin. 1963. "An Investigation of the Relationship Between Beliefs About an Object and the Attitude Toward That Object." Human Relations 16:233-40.

____. 1967. "Attitude and The Prediction of Behavior." In Readings in Attitude Theory and Measurement, edited by M. Fishbein. New York: Wiley & Sons.

____, and Icek Ajzen. 1975. Belief, Attitude, Intention, and Behavior. Reading, Mass.: Addison-Wesley.

____, and Icek Ajzen. 1974. "Attitudes Toward Objects as Predictors of Single and Multiple Behavioral Criteria." Psychological Review 81:59-74.

_____, and James Jaccard. 1973. "Theoretical and Methodological Issues and Behavior." Representative Research in Social Psychology 4:37-52.

Fishburn, P. C. 1974. "Lexicographic Order, Utilities and Decision Rules: A Survey." Management Science 20:1442-471.

Freud, Sigmund. 1933. New Introductory Lectures on Psychoanalysis. New York: Norton.

Frost, W. A. K., and R. L. Briane. 1967. "The Application of the Repertory Grid Technique to Problems in Market Research." Commentary 9 (July):161-75.

Gibson, E. J. 1963. "Perceptual Learning." Annual Review in Psychology 14:29-56.

Grass, Robert C., and Wallace H. Wallace. 1974. "Advertising Communication: Print vs. TV." Journal of Advertising Research 14 (Oct.):19-23.

Greenwald, Anthony A. 1968. "Cognitive Learning, Cognitive Response to Persuasion and Attitude Change." In Psychological Foundations of Attitudes, edited by Anthony A. Greenwald, T. C. Brock, and T. W. Ostrom. New York: Academic Press.

Grubb, Edward L., and Harrison L. Grathwhol. 1967. "Consumer Self-Concept, Symbolism, and Market Behavior: A Theoretical Approach." Journal of Marketing 31:22-27.

Hamilton, D. L. 1979. "A Cognitive Attributional Analysis of Stereotyping." In Advances in Experimental Social Psychology, vol. 12, edited by Leon Berkowitz, pp. 53-84. New York: Academic Press.

Hansen, Flemming. 1972. Consumer Choice Behavior: A Cognitive Theory. New York: Free Press.

Hansen, Robert A., and Terry Deutcher. 1977-78. "An Empirical Investigation of Attribute Importance in Retail Store Selection." Journal of Retailing 53 (Winter):59-72.

Hastie, R., and P. A. Kumar. 1979. "Person Memory: Personality Traits as Organizing Principles in Memory for Behavior." Journal of Personality and Social Psychology 37:25-38.

Hawkins, Del I., K. A. Coney, and R. J. Best. 1980. Consumer Behavior. Dallas, Texas: Business Publications.

Hebb, Donald O. 1949. The Organization of Behavior. New York: Wiley.

Heider, Fritz. 1958. The Psychology of Interpersonal Relations. New York: Wiley.

____. 1946. "Attitudes and Cognitive Organization." Journal of Psychology 21:207-12.

Helson, Harry. 1964. Adaptation-Level Theory. New York: Harper and Row.

Holman, Rebecca H. 1981. "Product as Communication: A Fresh Appraisal of a Venerable Topic." In Review of Marketing 1981, edited by Ben M. Enis and Kenneth J. Roering, pp. 106-19. Chicago: American Marketing Association.

Hovland, Carl I., O. J. Harvey, and Muzafer Sherif. 1957. "Assimilation and Contrast Effects in Reactions to Communication and Attitude Change." Journal of Abnormal and Social Psychology 55 (July):244-452.

____, Irving L. Janis, and Harold H. Kelley. 1953. Communication and Persuasion. New Haven, Conn.: Yale University Press.

Howard, John A., and Jadish N. Sheth. 1969. The Theory of Buyer Behavior. New York: Wiley.

Hull, C. L. 1943. Principles of Behavior. New York: Appleton-Century-Crofts.

Hunt, Shelby D., James A. Muncy, and Nina M. Ray. 1981. "Alderson's General Theory of Marketing: A Formalization." In Review in Marketing 1981, edited by Ben M. Enis and Kenneth J. Roering, pp. 267-272. Chicago: American Marketing Association.

Jaccard, James. 1981a. "Toward Theories of Persuasion and Belief Change." Journal of Personality and Social Psychology 40:260-69.

____. 1981b. "Attitudes and Behavior: Implications of Attitudes Toward Behavioral Alternatives." Journal of Experimental Social Psychology 17:286-307.

____, and G. William King. 1977. "The Relation Between Behavioral Intentions and Beliefs: A Probabilistic Model." Human Communication Research 6:326-34.

Jacoby, Jacob, and Carol Kohn Berning. 1974. "Brand Choice Behavior as a Function of Information Load: Replication and Extension." Journal of Marketing Research 10 (Feb.):1-9.

____, Robert W. Chestnut, and William A. Fisher. 1978. "A Behavioral Process Approach to Information Acquisition in Nondurable Purchasing." Journal of Marketing Research 15:539-44.

____, Szybillo, George J., and J. Busato-Schach. 1977. "Information Acquisition Behavior in Brand Choice Situations." Journal of Consumer Research 3 (Mar.):209-16.

____, Donald E. Speller, and Carol Kohn. 1974. "Brand Choice Behavior as a Function of Information Load." Journal of Marketing Research 11:63-69.

____, and David B. Kyner. 1973. "Brand Loyalty Versus Repeat Purchasing Behavior." Journal of Marketing Research 10 (Feb.):1-9.

____, and L. B. Kaplan. 1972. "The Components of Perceived Risk." In Proceedings of The Third Annual Conference of the Association for Consumer Research, edited by M. Vankatesan, pp. 382-93. Ann Arbor, Mich.: Association of Consumer Research.

James, Don L., Richard M. Durand, and Robert A. Dreves. 1976. "The Use of a Multi-Attribute Attitude Model in Store Image Study." Journal of Retailing 52 (Summer):23-32.

Johnson, Wesley J. 1981. "Industrial Buying Behavior: A State of the Art Review." In Review in Marketing 1981, edited by Ben M. Enis and Kenneth J. Roering. Chicago: American Marketing Association.

Johnston, Eric J., and J. Edward Russo. 1981. "Product Familiarity and Learning New Information." In Advances in

Consumer Research, vol. 8, edited by Kent B. Monroe, pp. 151-55. Ann Arbor: Association for Consumer Research.

Jones, E. E., and K. E. Davis. 1965. "From Acts to Dispositions: The Attribution Process in Person Perception." In Advances in Experimental Social Psychology, edited by Leon Berkowitz. New York: Academic Press.

____, and H. B. Gerard. 1967. Foundations of Social Psychology. New York: Wiley.

Jourard, S. 1971. Self-Disclosure: An Experimental Analysis of the Transparent Self. New York: Wiley.

____. 1964. The Transparent Self: Self-Disclosure and Well-Being. Princeton, N.J.: Van Nostrand.

Kahneman, D. 1974. Attention and Effort. Englewood Cliffs, N.J.: Prentice-Hall.

Kahneman, D. and A. Tversky. 1979. "Prospect Theory: An Analysis of Decisions Under Risk." Econometrica 47:263-291.

____. 1973. "On the Psychology of Prediction." Psychological Review 80:237-51.

____. 1972. "Subjective Probability: A Judgment of Representativeness." Cognitive Psychology 3:430-54.

Kanwar, Rajesh, Jerry C. Olson, and Laura S. Sims. 1981. "Toward Conceptualizing and Measuring Cognitive Structures." In Advances in Consumer Research, vol. 8, edited by Kent B. Monroe, pp. 122-27. Ann Arbor, Mich.: Association for Consumer Research.

Kaplan, M. F. 1975. "Information Integration in Social Judgment: Interaction of Judge and Informational Components." In Human Judgment and Decision Processes, edited by M. F. Kaplan and S. Schwartz. New York: Academic Press.

____, and Norman H. Anderson. 1973. "Information Integration Theory and Reinforcement Theory as Approaches to Interpersonal Attraction." Journal of Personality and Social Psychology 28:301-12.

Kassarjian, Harold H., and Waltrud M. Kassarjian. 1979. "Attitudes Under Low Commitment Conditions." In Attitude Research Plays for High Stakes, edited by John C. Maloney, p. 8. Chicago: American Marketing Association.

Katz, Daniel. 1960. "The Functional Approach to the Study of Attitudes." Public Opinion Quarterly 24:163-204.

_____, and E. Stotland. 1959. "A Preliminary Statement of a Theory of Attitude Structure and Change." In Psychology: Study of Science, vol. 3, edited by S. Koch, pp. 423-75. New York: McGraw-Hill.

Kelley, Harold H. 1973. "The Process of Causal Attribution." American Psychologist 28:107-28.

_____. 1967. "Attribution Theory in Social Psychology." In Nebraska Symposium on Motivation 1967, edited by D. Levine, pp. 192-238. Lincoln: University of Nebraska Press.

Kelly, George A. 1955. Psychology of Personal Constructs, vols. 1 and 2. New York: W. W. Norton.

Knapp, Mark L. 1972. Nonverbal Communication in Human Interaction. New York: Holt, Rinehart & Winston.

Kosslyn, S. M., and J. R. Pomerantz. 1977. "Imagery, Propositions, and the Form of Internal Representations." Cognitive Psychology 9:52-76.

Kotler, Philip. 1980. Marketing Management. Englewood Cliffs, N.J.: Prentice-Hall.

_____. 1975. Marketing for Nonprofit Organizations. Englewood Cliffs, N.J.: Prentice-Hall.

_____, and Sidney J. Levy. 1969. "Broadening the Concept of Marketing." Journal of Marketing 33:10-15.

Krech, D., R. S. Crutchfield, and E. L. Ballachey. 1962. Individual in Society. New York: McGraw-Hill.

Krugman, Herbert E. 1977. "Memory without Recall, Exposure without Perception." Journal of Advertising Research 17:7-12.

____. 1965. "The Impact of Television Advertising: Learning Without Involvement." Public Opinion Quarterly 30 (Winter): 584-85.

Kuhn, Alfred. 1975. Unified Social Science: A System Based Introduction. Homewood, Ill.: The Dorsey Press.

Langer, Ellen J., Shelly E. Taylor, S. T. Fiske, and B. Chanowitz. 1972. "Stigma, Staring, and Discomfort: A Novel-Stimulus Hypothesis." Journal of Experimental and Social Psychology 21:228-33.

Lastovika, John L., and David M. Gardner. 1978. "Low Involvement Versus High Involvement Cognitive Structures." In Advances in Consumer Research, vol. 5, edited H. Keith Hunt, pp. 87-92. Ann Arbor, Mich.: Association for Consumer Research.

Laszlo, Ervin, ed. 1972. The Relevance of General Systems Theory. New York: George Braziller.

Latane', B. 1966. "Studies in Social Comparison-Introduction and Overview." Journal of Experimental Social Psychology 2 (Supplement 1):1-5.

LaTour, Stephen A., and Nancy Peat. 1980. "The Role of Situationally Produced Expectations, Others' Experiences, and Prior Experience in Determining Consumer Satisfaction." In Advances in Consumer Research, vol. 7, edited by Jerry Olson, pp. 588-92. Ann Arbor, Mich.: Association for Consumer Research.

Lavidge, R. C., and G. A. Steiner. 1961. "A Model of Predictive Measurements of Advertising Effectiveness." Journal of Marketing 25:59-62.

Lawrence, Raymond J. 1969. "Patterns of Buyer Behaviors: Time for a New Approach?" Journal of Marketing Research 6 (May):137-44.

Lazer, William, and Eugene J. Kelley. eds. 1973. Social Marketing: Perspectives and View Points. Homewood, Ill.: Richard D. Irwin.

Leavitt, C. 1970. "A 1970 Multidimensional Set of Rating Scales for Television Commercials." Journal of Applied Psychology 54 (Aug.):427-29.

Lecky, P. 1969. Self-Consistency: A Theory of Personality. New York: Doubleday.

Lee, W. L. 1971. Decision Theory and Human Behavior. New York: Wiley.

Lehman, Donald R. 1971. "Television Show Preference: Application of a Choice Model." Journal of Marketing Research 8 (Feb.):47-55.

Levy, Sidney J. 1959. "Symbols for Sale." Harvard Business Review 37:117-24.

Lewin, Kurt. 1951. Theory in Social Science. New York: Harper and Brothers.

Lewin, Kurt, T. Dembo, Leon Festinger, and P. S. Sears. 1944. "Level of Aspiration." In Personality and the Behavior Disorders, vol. 1, edited by J. McV. Hunt, pp. 333-78. New York: Ronald Press.

Lindquist, Jay D. 1974-75. "Meaning of Image." Journal of Retailing 50 (Winter):29-38.

Loudon, David L., and Albert Della Bitta. 1978. Consumer Behavior: Concepts and Strategies. New York: McGraw-Hill.

Luce, R. D. 1959. Individual Choice Behavior: A Theoretical Analysis. New York: Wiley.

____, and H. Raiffa. 1957. Games and Decisions. New York: Wiley.

Lutz, Richard J. 1981. "The Role of Attitude Theory in Marketing." In Perspectives in Consumer Behavior, 3rd ed., edited by Harold H. Kassarjian and Thomas S. Robertson, pp. 233-50. Glenview, Ill.: Scott, Foresman.

Maloney, John C., and Bernard Silverman, eds. 1979. Attitude Research for High Stakes. Chicago: American Marketing Association.

March, J. G., and Herbert A. Simon. 1958. Organizations. New York: Wiley.

Markin, Rom J. 1974. Consumer Behavior: A Cognitive Orientation. New York: Macmillan.

Marks, Larry J., and Jerry L. Olson. 1981. "Toward a Cognitive Structure Conceptualization of Product Familiarity." In Advances in Consumer Research, vol. 8, edited by Kent B. Monore, pp. 145-50. Ann Arbor, Mich.: Association for Consumer Research.

Martineau, Pierre. 1958. "The Personality of The Retail Store." Harvard Business Review 36 (Jan.):47.

May, K. O. 1954. "Intransitivity, Utility, and the Aggregation in Preference Patterns." Econometrica 22:1-13.

Mehrabian, Albert. 1972. Nonverbal Communication. Chicago: Aldine.

_____. 1971. Silent Messages. Belmont. Calif.: Wadsworth.

_____. 1968. "Communication Without Words." Psychology Today, February 1, pp. 52-55.

Miller, James G. 1978. Living Systems. New York: McGraw-Hill.

Miller, John. 1977. "Studying Satisfaction: Modifying Models, Eliciting Expectations, Posing Problems, and Making Meaningful Measurements." In The Conceptualization of Consumer Satisfaction and Dissatisfaction, edited by H. Keith Hunt. Cambridge, Mass.: Marketing Science Institute.

Mizerski, Richard W., Linda L. Golden, and Jerome P. Kernan. 1979. "The Attribution Process in Consumer Decision Making." Journal of Consumer Research 6 (Summer):123-40.

Monroe, Kent B. 1973. "Buyers' Subjective Perceptions of Price." Journal of Marketing Research 10 (Feb.):70-80.

_____, and Joseph P. Guiltinian. 1975. "A Path Analytic Exploration of Retail Patronage Influences." Journal of Consumer Research 2 (June):19-28.

____, and Sue M. Petroshius. 1981. "Buyers' Perception of Price: An Update of the Evidence." In Perspectives in Consumer Behavior, 3rd ed., edited by Harold H. Kassarjian and Thomas S. Robertson, pp. 43-54. Glenview, Ill.: Scott, Foresman.

Montgomery, Henry, and Ola Svenson. 1976. "On Decision Rules and Information Processing Strategies for Choice Among Multi-Attribute Alternatives." Scandinavian Journal of Psychology 17:283-91.

Moschis, George P. 1981. "Socialization Perspectives and Consumer Behavior." In Review in Marketing 1981, edited by Ben N. Enis and Kenneth Roering, pp. 43-56. Chicago, Ill.: American Marketing Association.

Munson, J. Michael, and W. Austin Spivey. 1980. "Assessing Self-Concept." In Advances in Consumer Research, vol. 71, edited by Jerry Olson. Ann Arbor, Mich.: Association for Consumer Research.

Myers, James H. 1970. "Finding Determinant Buying Attitudes." Journal of Advertising Research 10 (Dec.):15.

McFadden, D. 1974. "Conditional Logit Analysis of Qualitative Choice Behavior." In Frontiers in Econometrics, edited by Paul Zarembka, pp. 105-42. New York: Academic Press.

McGuire, W. J. 1969. "The Nature of Attitudes and Attitude Change." In Handbook of Social Psychology, edited by G. Lindzey and E. Aronson. Reading, Mass.: Addison-Wesley.

McLeod, J. 1974. "Simulation: From Art to Science." Simulation Today 20:77-80.

Neisser, Ulric. 1976. Cognition and Reality: Principles and Implications of Cognitive Psychology. San Francisco: Freeman.

____. 1967. Cognitive Psychology. Englewood Cliffs, N.J.: Prentice-Hall.

Newell, A., and Herbert A. Simon. 1972. Human Problem Solving. Englewood Cliffs, N.J.: Prentice-Hall.

Newman, J. W. ed. 1957. Motivational Research and Marketing Management. Boston, Mass.: Harvard University, Graduate School of Business Administration, Division of Research.

Nicosia, Francesco M. 1966. Consumer Decision Processes: Marketing and Advertising Implications. Englewood Cliffs, N.J.: Prentice-Hall.

Nisbett, Richard, and Lee Ross. 1981. Human Inference: Strategies and Shortcomings of Social Judgment. Englewood Cliffs, N.J.: Prentice-Hall.

Oliver, Richard L. 1980. "A Cognitive Model of the Antecedents and Consequences of Satisfaction Decisions." Journal of Marketing Research 17 (Nov.): 460-69.

Olson, Jerry C. 1977. "Price as an Information Cue: Effects on Product Evaluations." In Consumer and Industrial Buying Behavior, edited by Arch G. Woodside, Jagdish N. Sheth, and Peter O. Bennett, pp. 267-86. New York: Elsevier, North Holland.

Olson, Jerry C., and Aydin Muderrisoglu. 1979. "The Stability of Response Obtained by Free Elicitation: Implications for Measuring Attribute Salience and Memory Structure." In Advances in Consumer Research, vol. 6, edited by William L. Wilkie, pp. 269-75. Ann Arbor, Mich.: Association for Consumer Research.

Osgood, C. E. 1953. Method and Theory in Experimental Psychology. New York: Oxford University Press.

____, G. J. Suci, and P. H. Tannenbaum. 1957. The Measurement of Meaning. Urbana: University of Illinois Press.

____, and P. H. Tannenbaum. 1955. "The Principle of Congruity in the Prediction of Attitude Change." Psychological Review 62: 42-55.

Paivio, A. 1971. Imagery and Verbal Processes. New York: Holt.

Park, C. Whan. 1976. "The Effect of Individual and Situational-Related Factors on Consumer Selection of Judgment Models." Journal of Marketing Research 13: 144-51.

Payne, John W. 1982. "Contingent Decision Behavior." Psychological Bulletin 92 (2):382-402.

Pennebaker, James W. 1980. "Self-Perception of Emotion and Internal Sensation." In The Self in Social Psychology, edited by Daniel M. Wegner and Robin R. Vallacher, pp. 80-101. New York: Oxford University Press.

Pettigrew, T. T. 1958. "The Measurement and Correlates of Category Width as a Cognitive Variable." Journal of Personality 26:532-44.

Piaget, Jean. 1954. The Construction of Reality in the Child, M. Cook, trans. New York: Basic Books.

Pitz, G. F. 1977. "Decision Making and Cognition." In Decision Making and Change in Human Affairs, edited by H. Jungerman and b. de Zeeuw. Dordrecht, Holland: Reidel.

Porter, L. W., and E. E. Lawler. 1968. Managerial Attitudes and Performance. Homewood, Ill.: Irwin.

Posner, Michael I. 1982. "Cumulative Development of Attribution Process in Consumer Decision Making." Journal of Consumer Research 6 (Sept.):123-40.

Pylyshyn, Z. W. 1973. "What The Mind Tells The Mind's Brain: A Critique of Mental Imagery." Psychological Bulletin 80:1-24.

Raju, P. S., and Michael D. Reilly. 1979. "Product Familiarity and Information Processing Strategies: An Exploratory Investigation." Journal of Business Research 8:187-212.

Robinson, Patrick J. 1980. "Applications of Conjoint Analysis to Pricing Problems." In Market Measurement and Analysis, edited by David B. Montgomery and Dick R. Wittink, pp. 183-89. Cambridge, Mass.: Marketing Science Institute.

Rogers, Everst M. 1978. "New Product Adoption and Diffusion." Journal of Consumer Research 2 (Mar.):290-301.

Rokeach, Milton. 1972. Beliefs, Attitudes, and Values: A Theory of Organization and Change. San Francisco: Jossey-Bass.

_____. 1960. The Open and Closed Mind. New York: Basic Books.

Roselius, Ted. 1971. "Consumer Rankings to Risk Reduction Methods." Journal of Marketing 35:61-66.

Rosenberg, M. J. 1960. "A Structural Theory of Attitude Dynamics." Public Opinion Quarterly 24:319-40.

____. 1956. "Cognitive Structure and Attitudinal Effect." Journal of Abnormal and Social Psychology 53:367-72.

Ross, Ivan. 1971. "Self-Concept and Brand Preference." Journal of Business of the University of Chicago 44:38-50.

Rothbart, M., M. Evans, and S. Fulero. 1979. "Recall for Confirming Events: Memory Processes and the Maintenance of Social Stereotypes." Journal of Experimental Social Psychology 15:343-54.

Rothchild, Michael L., and Michael J. Houston. 1977. "The Consumer Involvement Matrix: Some Preliminary Findings." In Proceedings of the American Marketing Association Educators' Conference, edited by Barnett A. Greenberg and Danny N. Bellenger, pp. 95-98. Chicago: American Marketing Association.

Rotter, Julian B. 1954. Social Learning and Clinical Psychology. Englewood Cliffs, N.J.: Prentice-Hall.

Ryan, Michael, and E. H. Bonfield. 1975. "The Fishbein Extended Model and Consumer Behavior." Journal of Consumer Research 2 (Sept.):118-36.

Samli, A. Coskun, and M. Joseph Sirgy. 1982. "Social Responsibility in Marketing: An Analysis and Synthesis." In Proceedings of the American Marketing Association, Special Educators' Conference on Marketing Theory. Chicago: American Marketing Association, forthcoming.

____. 1981. "A Multidimensional Approach to Analyzing Store Loyalty. A Predictive Model." In The Changing Marketing Environment: New Theories and Applications, edited by Ken Bernhardt and Bill Kehoe. Chicago: American Marketing Association.

Scammon, Debra L. 1977. "Information Load and Consumers." Journal of Consumer Research 4 (Dec.):148-55.

Schachter, Stanley, and Jerome E. Singer. 1962. "Cognitive, Social, and Physiological Determinants of Emotional State." Psychological Review 69:379-99.

Schank, R., and R. R. Abelson. 1977. Scripts, Plans, Goals and Understanding. Hillsdale, N.J.: Lawrence Erlbaum Associates.

Schiffman, Leon G., and K. Kanuk. 1978. Consumer Behavior. Englewood Cliffs, N.J.: Prentice-Hall.

Schneider, D. J. 1973. "Implicit Personality Theory: A Review." Psychological Bulletin 79:294-309.

Selfridge, O. G. 1959. "Pandemonium: A Paradigm for Learning." In The Mechanisation of Thought Processes. London: H. M. Stationary Office.

Selfridge, O. G., and Ulric Neisser. 1960. "Pattern Recognition by Machine." Scientific American 203:60-68.

Settle, Robert B., and Linda L. Golden. 1974. "Attribution Theory and Advertiser Credibility." Journal of Marketing Research 11 (May):181-85.

Shaver, Kelly G. 1981. Principles of Social Psychology. 2nd ed. Cambridge, Mass.: Winthrop Publishers.

Sherif, Muzafer, and Carl I. Hovland. 1961. Social Judgment: Assimilation and Contrast Effects in Communication and Attitude Change. New Haven, Conn.: Yale University Press.

Sherif, C. W., Muzafer Sherif, and R. E. Nebergall. 1965. Attitude and Attitude Change: The Social Judgment-Involvement Approach. Philadelphia: W. B. Saunders.

Sheth, Jagdish N. and W. Wayne Talarzyk. 1972. "Perceived Instrumentality and Value Importance as Determinants of Attitudes." Journal of Marketing Research 9 (Feb.):6-9.

____, and M. Venkatesan. 1968. "Risk-Reduction Processes in Repetitive Consumer Behavior." Journal of Marketing Research 5 (Aug.):307-10.

Shugan, S. M. 1980. "The Cost of Thinking." Journal of Consumer Research 7:99-111.

Simon, Herbert A., and E. A. Feigenbaum. 1964. "An Information Processing Theory of Some Effects of Similarity, Familiarization, and Meaningfulness in Verbal Learning." Journal of Verbal Behavior 3:385-96.

Simon, Herbert A., and A. Newell. 1972. "Human Problem Solving: The State of the Theory in 1970." American Psychologist 26:145-59.

Singson, Ricardo L. 1975. "Multidimensional Scaling Analysis of Store Image and Shopping Behavior." Journal of Retailing 51 (Summer):38-53.

Sirgy, M. Joseph. 1982a. "Consumer Behavior: Its Scope and Boundary." Resources in Education (June), and reproduced by ERIC Reports, Ed. No. 212 522.

_____. 1982b. "Self-Concept in Consumer Behavior: A Critical Review." Journal of Consumer Research (Dec.), forthcoming.

_____. 1982c. "Self-Image/Product-Image Congruity and Advertising Strategy." In Developments in Marketing Science, vol. 5, edited by Vinay Kothari, pp. 129-33. Nacogdoches, Texas: Academy of Marketing Science.

_____. 1982d. "Self-Image/Product-Image Congruity and Product Preference versus Purchase Intention: A Role Playing Experiment." Proceedings of Division 23 Program, 90th Annual Convention of the American Psychological Association, edited by Michael Mazis, forthcoming.

_____. 1982e. "A Social Cognition Model of Consumer Satisfaction/ Dissatisfaction." Blacksburg, Virginia: Virginia Tech. Mimeographed.

_____. 1981a. "Consumer Behavior: Its Scope and Boundary." In Proceedings of the Division of 23 Program, 89th Annual Convention of the American Psychological Association, edited by Richard Lutz, p. 22. Nashville, Tenn.: American Psychological Association, Division 23 (Consumer), Owen Graduate School of Management, Vanderbilt University.

____. 1981b. "Introducing a 'Self-Theory' to Consumer Personality Research." JSAS, Catalog of Selected Documents in Psychology 11 (May):33, Ms. 2250.

____. 1981c. "Testing a Self-Concept Model Using Tangible Products." In Proceedings of Division 23 Program, 89th Annual Convention of the American Psychological Association, edited by Richard J. Lutz, p. 17. Nashville, Tenn.: American Psychological Association, Division 23 (Consumer), Owen Graduate School of Management, Vanderbilt University.

____. 1981d. "Product Familiarity: Critical Comments on Selected Studies and Theoretical Extensions." In Advances in Consumer Research, vol. 8, edited by Kent B. Monroe, pp. 156-60. Ann Arbor, Mich.: Association for Consumer Research.

____. 1980a. "Self-Concept in Relation to Product Preference and Purchase Intention." In Developments in Marketing Science, vol. 3, edited by V. V. Bellur, pp. 350-54. Marquette, Michigan: Academy of Marketing Science.

____. 1980b. "Toward a Psychological Model of Consumer Satisfaction/Dissatisfaction." In Proceedings of the Fifth Conference on Consumer Satisfaction/Dissatisfaction and Complaining Behavior, edited by Ralph Day and H. Keith Hunt. Bloomington: Division of Research, School of Business, Indiana University.

____, and Jeffery Danes. 1982. "Self-Image/Product-Image Congruence Models: Testing Selected Models." In Advances in Consumer Research, vol. 9, edited by Andrew Mitchell, pp. 556-61. Ann Arbor, Mich.: Association for Consumer Research.

____, and Lisa Kassem. 1982. "A Social Cognition Model of Problem Recognition." Blacksburg, Virginia: Virginia Tech. Mimeographed.

____, A. Coskun Samli, and H. Lee Meadow. 1982. "The Interface Between Marketing and Quality of Life: A Theoretical Perspective." Journal of Marketing and Public Policy 1:69-84.

Slovic, P., and S. Lichtenstein. 1975. "Comparison of Bayesian and Regression Approaches to the Study of Information

Processing Judgment." Organizational Behavior and Human Performance 6:649-744.

Stern, Bruce L., Ronald F. Bush, and Joseph F. Hair, Jr. 1977. "The Self-Image/Store Image Matching Process: An Empirical Test." Journal of Business 50 (Jan.):63-69.

Sternthal, Brian, and S. Samuel Craig. 1973. "Humor in Advertising." Journal of Marketing 37 (Oct.):12-18.

Sutherland, John W. 1973. A General Systems Philosophy of the Social and Behavioral Sciences. New York: George Braziller.

Sutherland, N. S. 1959. "Stimulus Analyzing Mechanisms." In The Mechanisation of Thought Processes. London: H. M. Stationary Office.

Swan, John E., and Warren S. Martin. 1981. "Testing Comparison Level and Predictive Expectations Models of Satisfaction." In Advances in Consumer Research, vol. 8, edited by Kent B. Monroe, pp. 77-82. Ann Arbor, Mich.: Association for Consumer Research.

Tan, Chin Tiong, and Ira J. Dolich. 1981. "The Moderation Effects of Cognitive Complexity and Prior Product Familiarity of the Predictive Ability of Selected Multi-Attribute Models." In Advances in Consumer Research, vol. 8, edited by Kent B. Monroe, pp. 140-44. Ann Arbor, Mich.: Association for Consumer Research.

Taylor, Shelly E., S. T. Fiske, N. L. Ectoff, and A. J. Ruderman. 1978. "Categorical and Contextual Bases of Person Memory and Stereotyping." Journal of Personality and Social Psychology 36:778-93.

Thibaut, J. W., and Harold H. Kelley. 1959. The Social Psychology of Groups. New York: Wiley.

Tolman, E. C. 1955. "Principles of Performance." Psychological Review 62:315-26.

____. 1932. Purposive Behavior in Animals and Men. New York: Appleton-Century-Crofts.

Tucker, William. 1964. "The Development of Brand Loyalty." Journal of Marketing Research 1 (Aug.):32-35.

Tversky, A. 1972. "Elimination by Aspects: A Theory of Choice." Psychological Review 79 (July):281-99.

Tversky, A., and D. Kahneman. 1981. "The Framing of Decisions and the Psychology of Choice." Science 211:453-58.

____, and D. Kahneman. 1974. "Judgment Under Certainty: Heuristics and Biases." Science 185:1124-1151.

Uhr, L. 1963. "Pattern Recognition Computers as Models for Form Perception." Psychological Bulletin 60:40-73.

Upshaw, H. S. 1969. "The Personal Reference Scale: An Approach to Social Judgment." In Advances in Experimental Social Psychology, vol. 4, edited by Leon Berkowitz, pp. 315-72. New York: Academic Press.

Van Gigch, J. P. 1974. Applied General Systems Theory. New York: Harper.

Von Bertalanffy, Ludwig. 1968. General System Theory. New York: George Braziller.

Vroom, V. H. 1964. Work and Motivation. New York: Wiley.

Walker, J. H. 1975. "Real-World Variability, Reasonableness Judgments, and qemorys Representations for Concepts." Journal of Verbal Learning and Verbal Behavior 14:241-52.

Watson, Paul J., and Robert J. Gatchel. 1979. "Autonomic Measures of Advertising." Journal of Advertising Research 19:15-26.

Weigel, R., and L. Newman. 1976. "Increasing Attitude-Behavior Correspondence by Broadening the Scope of Behavioral Measure." Journal of Personality and Social Psychology 33:793-802.

Weiner, Bernard, Irene Frieze, Andy Kukla, L. Reed, S. Rest, and R. M. Rosenbaum. 1972. "Perceiving the Causes of Success and Failure." In Attribution: Perceiving the Causes of Behavior, edited by E. E. Jones, D. E. Kanouse, H. H.

Kelley, R. E. Nisbett, S. Valins, and B. Weiner, pp. 95-120. Morristown, N.J.: General Learning Press.

Wicker, A. W. 1971. "An Examination of The 'Other Variables' Explanation of Attitude-Behavior Inconsistency." Journal of Personality and Social Issues 19:18-30.

Wicklund, R. A., and J. W. Brehm. 1976. Perspectives on Cognitive Dissonance. Hillsdale, N.J.: Lawrence Erlbanm Associates.

Wilkie, William L., ed. 1979. Advances in Consumer Research, vol. 6. Ann Arbor, Mich.: Association for Consumer Research.

Williams, Terrel G. 1982. Consumer Behavior, Fundamentals and Strategies. St. Paul, Minn.: West Publishing.

Wilson, David T., H. Lee Mathews, and James W. Harvey. 1975. "An Empirical Test of the Fishbein Behavioral Intention Model." Journal of Consumer Research 1 (Mar.):39-48.

Woodruff, Robert B. 1972. "Measurement of Consumer   ice Brand Information." Journal of Marketing 10:53-62.

Woodside, Arch, and James Davenport. 1976. "Effects of Price and Salesman Expertise on Customer Purchasing Behavior." Journal of Business 49:51-59.

Wright, Peter L. 1978. "Cognitive Responses to Mass Media Advocacy and Cognitive Choice Processes." In Cognitive Responses to Persuasion, edited by Richard Petty, Thomas Ostrom, and Timothy Brock. New York: McGraw-Hill.

_____. 1975. "Consumer Choice Strategies: Simplifying Verse Optimizing." Journal of Marketing Research 11 (Feb.):60-67.

_____. 1973. "The Cognitive Processes Mediating Acceptance of Advertising." Journal of Marketing Research 10 (Feb.): 53-62.

Wyer, Robert S. 1975. "Functional Measurement Analysis of a Subjective Probability Model of Cognitive Functioning." Journal of Personality and Social Psychology 31:94-100.

_____. 1974. Cognitive Organization and Change: An Information-Processing Approach. Potomac, Md.: Lawrence Erlbaum Associates.

_____. 1973. "Category Ratings as Subjective Expected Values: Implications for Attitude Formation and Change." Psychological Review 80:446-67.

_____, and Donald E. Carlston. 1979. Social Cognition, Inference, and Attribution. Hillsdale, N.J.: Lawrence Erlbaum Associates.

_____, and L. Goldberg. 1970. "A Probabilistic Analysis of the Relationships Between Beliefs and Attitudes." Psychological Review 77:100-20.

Zaltman, Gerald, and Melodie Wallendorf. 1979. Consumer Behavior: Basic Findings and Management Implications. New York: Wiley.

Author Index

Subject Index

About The Author

M. JOSEPH SIRGY is a consumer/social psychologist and assistant professor of marketing at Virginia Polytechnic Institute State University. He has authored numerous articles in business and psychology, and has presented many technical papers to professional business and psychology groups. He received his Ph.D. in industrial/social/personality from the University of Massachusetts at Amherst, 1979, an M.A. in experimental psychology from the California State University at Long Beach, 1977, and a B.A. in psychology from the University of California Los Angeles, 1974.